MznLnx

Missing Links Exam Preps

Exam Prep for

One and Several Variables: Calculus

Salas, Hille & Hetgen, 9th Edition

The MznLnx Exam Prep is your link from the texbook and lecture to your exams.
The MznLnx Exam Preps are unauthorized and comprehensive reviews of your textbooks.

All material provided by MznLnx and Rico Publications (c) 2010
Textbook publishers and textbook authors do not particpate in or contribute to these reviews.

MznLnx

Rico
Publications

Exam Prep for One and Several Variables: Calculus
9th Edition
Salas, Hille & Hetgen

Publisher: Raymond Houge
Assistant Editor: Michael Rouger
Text and Cover Designer: Lisa Buckner
Marketing Manager: Sara Swagger
Project Manager, Editorial Production: Jerry Emerson
Art Director: Vernon Lowerui

Product Manager: Dave Mason
Editorial Assitant: Rachel Guzmanji
Pedagogy: Debra Long
Cover Image: Jim Reed/Getty Images
Text and Cover Printer: City Printing, Inc.
Compositor: Media Mix, Inc.

(c) 2010 Rico Publications

ALL RIGHTS RESERVED. No part of this work covered by the copyright may be reproduced or used in any form or by an means--graphic, electronic, or mechanical, including photocopying, recording, taping, Web distribution, information storage, and retrieval systems, or in any other manner--without the written permission of the publisher.

Printed in the United States
ISBN:

For more information about our products, contact us at:
Dave.Mason@RicoPublications.com

For permission to use material from this text or product, submit a request online to:
Dave.Mason@RicoPublications.com

Contents

CHAPTER 1
PRECALCULUS REVIEW — 1
CHAPTER 2
LIMITS AND CONTINUITY — 23
CHAPTER 3
DIFFERENTIATION — 34
CHAPTER 4
THE MEAN-VALUE THEOREM AND APPLICATIONS — 55
CHAPTER 5
INTEGRATION — 75
CHAPTER 6
APPLICATIONS OF THE INTEGRAL — 87
CHAPTER 7
THE TRANSCENDENTAL FUNCTIONS — 101
CHAPTER 8
TECHNIQUES OF INTEGRATION — 122
CHAPTER 9
THE CONIC SECTIONS; POLAR COORDINATES; PARAMETRIC EQUATIONS — 140
CHAPTER 10
SEQUENCES: INDETERMINATE FORMS; IMPROPER INTEGRALS — 160
CHAPTER 11
INFINITE SERIES — 163
CHAPTER 12
VECTORS — 165
CHAPTER 13
VECTOR CALCULUS — 167
CHAPTER 14
FUNCTIONS OF SEVERAL VARIABLES — 169
CHAPTER 15
GRADIENTS; EXTREME VALUES; DIFFERENTIALS — 171
CHAPTER 16
DOUBLE AND TRIPLE INTEGRALS — 173
CHAPTER 17
LINE INTEGRALS AND SURFACE INTEGRALS — 176
CHAPTER 18
ELEMENTARY DIFFERENTIAL EQUATIONS — 179
ANSWER KEY — 181

TO THE STUDENT

COMPREHENSIVE

The *MznLnx* Exam Prep series is designed to help you pass your exams. Editors at MznLnx review your textbooks and then prepare these practice exams to help you master the textbook material. Unlike study guides, workbooks, and practice tests provided by the texbook publisher and textbook authors, *MznLnx* gives you **all** of the material in each chapter in exam form, not just samples, so you can be sure to nail your exam.

MECHANICAL

The MznLnx Exam Prep series creates exams that will help you learn the subject matter as well as test you on your understanding. Each question is designed to help you master the concept. Just working through the exams, you gain an understanding of the subject--its a simple mechanical process that produces success.

INTEGRATED STUDY GUIDE AND REVIEW

MznLnx is not just a set of exams designed to test you, its also a comprehensive review of the subject content. Each exam question is also a review of the concept, making sure that you will get the answer correct without having to go to other sources of material. You learn as you go! Its the easiest way to pass an exam.

HUMOR

Studying can be tedious and dry. MznLnx's instructional design includes moderate humor within the exam questions on occassion, to break the tedium and revitalize the brain

Chapter 1. PRECALCULUS REVIEW

1. _____ is a mathematical subject that includes the study of limits, derivatives, integrals, and power series and constitutes a major part of modern university curriculum.
   a. Calculus0
   b. Thing
   c. Undefined
   d. Undefined

2. _____ is the mathematical action of repeatedly adding or subtracting one, usually to find out how many objects there are or to set aside a desired number of objects.
   a. Thing
   b. Counting0
   c. Undefined
   d. Undefined

3. _____ numerals are a numeral system originating in ancient Rome, adapted from Etruscan numerals.
   a. Roman0
   b. Thing
   c. Undefined
   d. Undefined

4. The _____, the average in everyday English, which is also called the arithmetic _____ (and is distinguished from the geometric _____ or harmonic _____). The average is also called the sample _____. The expected value of a random variable, which is also called the population _____.
   a. Thing
   b. Mean0
   c. Undefined
   d. Undefined

5. _____ is a branch of mathematics which deals with triangles, particularly triangles in a plane where one angle of the triangle is 90 degrees, and a variety of other topological relations such as spheres, in other branches, such as spherical _____.
   a. Trigonometry0
   b. Thing
   c. Undefined
   d. Undefined

6. _____ is a branch of mathematics concerning the study of structure, relation and quantity.
   a. Concept
   b. Algebra0
   c. Undefined
   d. Undefined

7. In mathematics, the _____ of a coordinate system is the point where the axes of the system intersect.
   a. Origin0
   b. Thing
   c. Undefined
   d. Undefined

8. In trigonometry, the _____ is a function defined as $\tan x = \sin x / \cos x$. The function is so-named because it can be defined as the length of a certain segment of a _____ (in the geometric sense) to the unit circle. In plane geometry, a line is _____ to a curve, at some point, if both line and curve pass through the point with the same direction.
   a. Thing
   b. Tangent0
   c. Undefined
   d. Undefined

9. _____ is an interpreted dynamic visual programming language based on Squeak, a smalltalk implementation directly derived from Smalltalk-80.
   a. Scratch0
   b. Thing
   c. Undefined
   d. Undefined

10. Mathematical _____ is used to represent ideas.

a. Notation0
b. Thing
c. Undefined
d. Undefined

11. Sir Isaac _____, was an English physicist, mathematician, astronomer, natural philosopher, and alchemist, regarded by many as the greatest figure in the history of science
   a. Person
   b. Newton0
   c. Undefined
   d. Undefined

12. _____ was a German mathematician and philosopher. He invented calculus independently of Newton, and his notation is the one in general use since.
   a. Person
   b. Leibniz0
   c. Undefined
   d. Undefined

13. Sir _____ was an English physicist, mathematician, astronomer, natural philosopher, and alchemist, regarded by many as the greatest figure in the history of science.
   a. Person
   b. Isaac Newton0
   c. Undefined
   d. Undefined

14. A _____ is 360° or 2δ radians.
   a. Turn0
   b. Thing
   c. Undefined
   d. Undefined

15. _____ is electromagnetic radiation with a wavelength that is visible to the eye (visible _____) or, in a technical or scientific context, electromagnetic radiation of any wavelength.
   a. Light0
   b. Thing
   c. Undefined
   d. Undefined

16. In mathematics, a _____ is a countable collection of open covers of a topological space that satisfies certain separation axioms.
   a. Development0
   b. Thing
   c. Undefined
   d. Undefined

17. In mathematics, the word _____ is used informally to refer to certain distinct bodies of knowledge about mathematics.
   a. Thing
   b. Theoretical0
   c. Undefined
   d. Undefined

18. An _____ or member of a set is an object that when collected together make up the set.
   a. Thing
   b. Element0
   c. Undefined
   d. Undefined

19. In mathematics, the _____, or members of a set or more generally a class are all those objects which when collected together make up the set or class.
   a. Elements0
   b. Thing
   c. Undefined
   d. Undefined

Chapter 1. PRECALCULUS REVIEW

20. _____ is a set of numbers, in the broadest sense of the word, together with one or more operations, such as addition or multiplication.
    a. Number system0
    b. Thing
    c. Undefined
    d. Undefined

21. In mathematics, a _____ may be described informally as a number that can be given by an infinite decimal representation.
    a. Real number0
    b. Thing
    c. Undefined
    d. Undefined

22. In mathematics, _____ is an elementary arithmetic operation. When one of the numbers is a whole number, _____ is the repeated sum of the other number.
    a. Thing
    b. Multiplication0
    c. Undefined
    d. Undefined

23. _____ or arithmetics is the oldest and most elementary branch of mathematics, used by almost everyone, for tasks ranging from simple daily counting to advanced science and business calculations.
    a. Thing
    b. Arithmetic0
    c. Undefined
    d. Undefined

24. The traditional _____ are addition, subtraction, multiplication and division, although more advanced operations (such as manipulations of percentages, square root, exponentiation, and logarithmic functions) are also sometimes included in this subject.
    a. Concept
    b. Arithmetic operations0
    c. Undefined
    d. Undefined

25. A _____ is a numeral used to indicate a count. The most common use of the word today is to name the part of a fraction that tells the number or count of equal parts.
    a. Numerator0
    b. Thing
    c. Undefined
    d. Undefined

26. In mathematics, a _____ number is a number which can be expressed as a ratio of two integers. Non-integer _____ numbers (commonly called fractions) are usually written as the vulgar fraction a / b, where b is not zero.
    a. Rational0
    b. Thing
    c. Undefined
    d. Undefined

27. An _____ of a product of sums expresses it as a sum of products by using the fact that multiplication distributes over addition.
    a. Thing
    b. Expansion0
    c. Undefined
    d. Undefined

28. A _____ is the part of a fraction that tells how many equal parts make up a whole, and which is used in the name of the fraction: "halves", "thirds", "fourths" or "quarters", "fifths" and so on.
    a. Denominator0
    b. Concept
    c. Undefined
    d. Undefined

Chapter 1. PRECALCULUS REVIEW

29. In mathematics, an _____ number is any real number that is not a rational number- that is, it is a number which cannot be expressed as a fraction m/n, where m and n are integers.
    a. Irrational0
    b. Thing
    c. Undefined
    d. Undefined

30. In mathematics, an _____ is any real number that is not a rational number ¡ª that is, it is a number which cannot be expressed as m/n, where m and n are integers.
    a. Thing
    b. Irrational number0
    c. Undefined
    d. Undefined

31. A _____ is a number that is less than zero.
    a. Thing
    b. Negative number0
    c. Undefined
    d. Undefined

32. The _____ of measurement are a globally standardized and modernized form of the metric system.
    a. Thing
    b. Units0
    c. Undefined
    d. Undefined

33. A _____ is a set of numbers that designate location in a given reference system, such as x,y in a planar _____ system or an x,y,z in a three-dimensional _____ system.
    a. Thing
    b. Coordinate0
    c. Undefined
    d. Undefined

34. A _____ is a one-dimensional picture in which the integers are shown as specially-marked points evenly spaced on a line.
    a. Thing
    b. Number line0
    c. Undefined
    d. Undefined

35. _____ are objects, characters, or other concrete representations of ideas, concepts, or other abstractions.
    a. Symbols0
    b. Thing
    c. Undefined
    d. Undefined

36. In mathematics, an _____ is a statement about the relative size or order of two objects.
    a. Inequality0
    b. Thing
    c. Undefined
    d. Undefined

37. The _____ of a mathematical object is its size: a property by which it can be larger or smaller than other objects of the same kind; in technical terms, an ordering of the class of objects to which it belongs.
    a. Thing
    b. Magnitude0
    c. Undefined
    d. Undefined

38. In mathematics, the _____ (or modulus) of a real number is its numerical value without regard to its sign.
    a. Absolute value0
    b. Thing
    c. Undefined
    d. Undefined

39. In geometry, an _____ is a point at which a line segment or ray terminates.

Chapter 1. PRECALCULUS REVIEW

a. Endpoint0
b. Thing
c. Undefined
d. Undefined

40. In elementary algebra, an _____ is a set that contains every real number between two indicated numbers and may contain the two numbers themselves.
   a. Thing
   b. Interval0
   c. Undefined
   d. Undefined

41. A _____ is the result of the addition of a set of numbers. The numbers may be natural numbers, complex numbers, matrices, or still more complicated objects. An infinite _____ is a subtle procedure known as a series.
   a. Sum0
   b. Thing
   c. Undefined
   d. Undefined

42. In plane geometry, a _____ is a polygon with four equal sides, four right angles, and parallel opposite sides. In algebra, the _____ of a number is that number multiplied by itself.
   a. Thing
   b. Square0
   c. Undefined
   d. Undefined

43. _____ is the notation in which permitted values for a variable are expressed as ranging over a certain interval; "5 < x < 9" is an example of the application of _____.
   a. Thing
   b. Interval notation0
   c. Undefined
   d. Undefined

44. In mathematics, _____ geometry was the traditional name for the geometry of three-dimensional Euclidean space — for practical purposes the kind of space we live in.
   a. Solid0
   b. Thing
   c. Undefined
   d. Undefined

45. _____ is the state of being greater than any finite number, however large.
   a. Infinity0
   b. Thing
   c. Undefined
   d. Undefined

46. The plus and _____ signs are mathematical symbols used to represent the notions of positive and negative as well as the operations of addition and subtraction.
   a. Thing
   b. Minus0
   c. Undefined
   d. Undefined

47. In mathematics, especially in order theory, an _____ of a subset S of some partially ordered set is an element of P which is greater than or equal to every element of S.
   a. Upper bound0
   b. Thing
   c. Undefined
   d. Undefined

48. The term _____ is defined dually as an element of P which is lesser than or equal to every element of S.
   a. Lower bound0
   b. Thing
   c. Undefined
   d. Undefined

Chapter 1. PRECALCULUS REVIEW

49. In mathematical analysis and related areas of mathematics, a set is called _____, if it is, in a certain sense, of finite size.
    a. Thing
    b. Bounded0
    c. Undefined
    d. Undefined

50. In mathematics, a _____ of a complex-valued function f is a member x of the domain of f such that f(x) vanishes at x, that is, x : f (x) = 0.
    a. Root0
    b. Thing
    c. Undefined
    d. Undefined

51. In mathematics, a _____ is a polynomial equation of the second degree. The general form is $ax^2 + bx + c = 0$.
    a. Thing
    b. Quadratic equation0
    c. Undefined
    d. Undefined

52. A quadratic equation with real solutions, called roots, which may be real or complex, is given by the _____: $x = \frac{-b \pm \sqrt{b^2 - 4ac}}{2a}$.
    a. Thing
    b. Quadratic formula0
    c. Undefined
    d. Undefined

53. In common philosophical language, a proposition or _____, is the content of an assertion, that is, it is true-or-false and defined by the meaning of a particular piece of language.
    a. Statement0
    b. Concept
    c. Undefined
    d. Undefined

54. The _____ are the only integral domain whose positive elements are well-ordered, and in which order is preserved by addition. Like the natural numbers, the _____ form a countably infinite set. The set of all _____ is usually denoted in mathematics by a boldface Z .
    a. Thing
    b. Integers0
    c. Undefined
    d. Undefined

55. An _____ is a combination of numbers, operators, grouping symbols and/or free variables and bound variables arranged in a meaningful way which can be evaluated..
    a. Expression0
    b. Thing
    c. Undefined
    d. Undefined

56. In mathematics, a _____ is the result of multiplying, or an expression that identifies factors to be multiplied.
    a. Thing
    b. Product0
    c. Undefined
    d. Undefined

57. _____ is the largest positive integer that divides both numbers without remainder.
    a. Thing
    b. Common Factor0
    c. Undefined
    d. Undefined

58. In mathematics, factorization (British English: factorisation) or factoring is the decomposition of an object (for example, a number, a polynomial, or a matrix) into a product of other objects, or _____, which when multiplied together give the original.

Chapter 1. PRECALCULUS REVIEW

a. Factors0
c. Undefined
b. Thing
d. Undefined

59. In mathematics, a _____ of an integer n, also called a factor of n, is an integer which evenly divides n without leaving a remainder.
    a. Thing
    b. Divisor0
    c. Undefined
    d. Undefined

60. In geometry, a _____ is defined as a quadrilateral where all four of its angles are right angles.
    a. Thing
    b. Rectangle0
    c. Undefined
    d. Undefined

61. _____ is the distance around a given two-dimensional object. As a general rule, the _____ of a polygon can always be calculated by adding all the length of the sides together. So, the formula for triangles is P = a + b + c, where a, b and c stand for each side of it. For quadrilaterals the equation is P = a + b + c + d. For equilateral polygons, P = na, where n is the number of sides and a is the side length.
    a. Thing
    b. Perimeter0
    c. Undefined
    d. Undefined

62. In Euclidean geometry, a _____ is the set of all points in a plane at a fixed distance, called the radius, from a given point, the center.
    a. Thing
    b. Circle0
    c. Undefined
    d. Undefined

63. In mathematics, a _____ is a mathematical statement which appears likely to be true, but has not been formally proven to be true under the rules of mathematical logic.
    a. Conjecture0
    b. Concept
    c. Undefined
    d. Undefined

64. A _____ decimal is a decimal fraction which ends after a definite number of digits.
    a. Terminating0
    b. Thing
    c. Undefined
    d. Undefined

65. A _____ is a set of possible values that a variable can take on in order to satisfy a given set of conditions, which may include equations and inequalities.
    a. Solution set0
    b. Thing
    c. Undefined
    d. Undefined

66. A _____ decimal is a number whose decimal representation eventually becomes periodic (i.e. the same number sequence _____ indefinitely).
    a. Thing
    b. Repeating0
    c. Undefined
    d. Undefined

67. Recurring or _____ are numbers which when expressed as decimals have a set of "final" digits which repeat an infinite number of times.

Chapter 1. PRECALCULUS REVIEW

    a. Thing
    b. Repeating decimals0
    c. Undefined
    d. Undefined

68. A _____ is one of the basic shapes of geometry: a polygon with three vertices and three sides which are straight line segments.
    a. Thing
    b. Triangle0
    c. Undefined
    d. Undefined

69. _____ is the theorem stating that for any triangle, the measure of a given side must be less than the sum of the other two sides but greater than the difference between the two sides.
    a. Triangle inequality0
    b. Thing
    c. Undefined
    d. Undefined

70. In set theory and other branches of mathematics, the _____ of a collection of sets is the set that contains everything that belongs to any of the sets, but nothing else.
    a. Thing
    b. Union0
    c. Undefined
    d. Undefined

71. _____ is bother the congnitive process of transferring information from a particular subject , and a linguistic expression corresponding to such a process.
    a. Thing
    b. Analogy0
    c. Undefined
    d. Undefined

72. The _____ integers are all the integers from zero on upwards.
    a. Thing
    b. Nonnegative0
    c. Undefined
    d. Undefined

73. _____ of a list of numbers is the sum of all the members of the list divided by the number of items in the list.
    a. Thing
    b. Arithmetic mean0
    c. Undefined
    d. Undefined

74. In mathematics and its applications, a _____ is a system for assigning an n-tuple of numbers or scalars to each point in an n-dimensional space.
    a. Coordinate system0
    b. Concept
    c. Undefined
    d. Undefined

75. _____ is the study of geometry using the principles of algebra. _____ can be explained more simply: it is concerned with defining geometrical shapes in a numerical way and extracting numerical information from that representation.
    a. Analytic geometry0
    b. Thing
    c. Undefined
    d. Undefined

76. In mathematics, a _____ is a two-dimensional manifold or surface that is perfectly flat.
    a. Thing
    b. Plane0
    c. Undefined
    d. Undefined

Chapter 1. PRECALCULUS REVIEW

77. In geometry, two lines or planes if one falls on the other in such a way as to create congruent adjacent angles. The term may be used as a noun or adjective. Thus, referring to Figure 1, the line AB is the _____ to CD through the point B.
    a. Perpendicular0
    b. Thing
    c. Undefined
    d. Undefined

78. An _____ is when two lines intersect somewhere on a plane creating a right angle at intersection
    a. Thing
    b. Axes0
    c. Undefined
    d. Undefined

79. In astronomy, geography, geometry and related sciences and contexts, a plane is said to be _____ at a given point if it is locally perpendicular to the gradient of the gravity field, i.e., with the direction of the gravitational force at that point.
    a. Thing
    b. Horizontal0
    c. Undefined
    d. Undefined

80. An _____ is a straight line around which a geometric figure can be rotated.
    a. Thing
    b. Axis0
    c. Undefined
    d. Undefined

81. A _____ consists of one quarter of the coordinate plane.
    a. Thing
    b. Quadrant0
    c. Undefined
    d. Undefined

82. An _____ is a collection of two not necessarily distinct objects, one of which is distinguished as the first coordinate and the other as the second coordinate.
    a. Ordered pair0
    b. Thing
    c. Undefined
    d. Undefined

83. The _____ is the y- coordinate of a point within a two dimensional coordinate system. It is sometimes used to refer to the axis rather than the distance along the coordinate system.
    a. Ordinate0
    b. Thing
    c. Undefined
    d. Undefined

84. _____ means of or relating to the French philosopher and mathematician René Descartes.
    a. Thing
    b. Cartesian0
    c. Undefined
    d. Undefined

85. In mathematics, the _____ is used to determine each point uniquely in a plane through two numbers, usually called the x-coordinate and the y-coordinate of the point.
    a. Thing
    b. Cartesian coordinate system0
    c. Undefined
    d. Undefined

86. _____ was a highly influential French philosopher, mathematician, scientist, and writer. Dubbed the "Founder of Modern Philosophy", and the "Father of Modern Mathematics". His theories provided the basis for the calculus of Newton and Leibniz, by applying infinitesimal calculus to the tangent line problem, thus permitting the evolution of that branch of modern mathematics

Chapter 1. PRECALCULUS REVIEW

    a. Descartes0
    c. Undefined
    b. Person
    d. Undefined

87. _____ consists of the first element in a coordinate pair. When graphed in the coordinate plane, it is the distance from the y-axis. Frequently called the x coordinate.
    - a. Thing
    - b. Abscissa0
    - c. Undefined
    - d. Undefined

88. _____ is the middle point of a line segment.
    - a. Midpoint0
    - b. Thing
    - c. Undefined
    - d. Undefined

89. In mathematics, defined and _____ are used to explain whether or not expressions have meaningful, sensible, and unambiguous values.
    - a. Undefined0
    - b. Thing
    - c. Undefined
    - d. Undefined

90. _____ is often used to describe the measurement of the steepness, incline, gradient, or grade of a straight line. The _____ is defined as the ratio of the "rise" divided by the "run" between two points on a line, or in other words, the ratio of the altitude change to the horizontal distance between any two points on the line.
    - a. Slope0
    - b. Thing
    - c. Undefined
    - d. Undefined

91. In mathematics, the _____ functions are functions of an angle; they are important when studying triangles and modeling periodic phenomena, among many other applications.
    - a. Thing
    - b. Trigonometric0
    - c. Undefined
    - d. Undefined

92. The _____ are functions of an angle; they are important when studying triangles and modeling periodic phenomena, among many other applications.
    - a. Trigonometric functions0
    - b. Thing
    - c. Undefined
    - d. Undefined

93. A _____ is a symbolic representation denoting a quantity or expression. It often represents an "unknown" quantity that has the potential to change.
    - a. Thing
    - b. Variable0
    - c. Undefined
    - d. Undefined

94. Any point where a graph makes contact with an coordinate axis is called an _____ of the graph
    - a. Thing
    - b. Intercept0
    - c. Undefined
    - d. Undefined

95. The mathematical concept of a _____ expresses the intuitive idea of deterministic dependence between two quantities, one of which is viewed as primary and the other as secondary. A _____ then is a way to associate a unique output for each input of a specified type, for example, a real number or an element of a given set.

Chapter 1. PRECALCULUS REVIEW

a. Thing
c. Undefined
b. Function0
d. Undefined

96. In geometry, _____ lines are two lines that share one or more common points.
a. Thing
c. Undefined
b. Intersecting0
d. Undefined

97. The existence and properties of _____ are the basis of Euclid's parallel postulate. _____ are two lines on the same plane that do not intersect even assuming that lines extend to infinity in either direction.
a. Thing
c. Undefined
b. Parallel lines0
d. Undefined

98. In mathematics, the _____ of two sets A and B is the set that contains all elements of A that also belong to B (or equivalently, all elements of B that also belong to A), but no other elements.
a. Intersection0
c. Undefined
b. Thing
d. Undefined

99. _____ are the basic objects of study in graph theory. Informally speaking, a graph is a set of objects called points, nodes, or vertices connected by links called lines or edges.
a. Graphs0
c. Undefined
b. Thing
d. Undefined

100. In mathematics, a _____ section is a curve that can be formed by intersecting a cone with a plane.
a. Conic0
c. Undefined
b. Thing
d. Undefined

101. In mathematics, an _____ .
a. Thing
c. Undefined
b. Ellipse0
d. Undefined

102. In geometry, a line _____ is a part of a line that is bounded by two end points, and contains every point on the line between its end points.
a. Segment0
c. Undefined
b. Concept
d. Undefined

103. A _____ is a part of a line that is bounded by two end points, and contains every point on the line between its end points.
a. Thing
c. Undefined
b. Line segment0
d. Undefined

104. In geometry, a _____ is a special kind of point, usually a corner of a polygon, polyhedron, or higher dimensional polytope. In the geometry of curves a _____ is a point of where the first derivative of curvature is zero. In graph theory, a _____ is the fundamental unit out of which graphs are formed
a. Thing
c. Undefined
b. Vertex0
d. Undefined

Chapter 1. PRECALCULUS REVIEW

105. In geometry, the _____ of an object is a point in some sense in the middle of the object.
  a. Thing
  b. Center0
  c. Undefined
  d. Undefined

106. In classical geometry, a _____ of a circle or sphere is any line segment from its center to its boundary. By extension, the _____ of a circle or sphere is the length of any such segment. The _____ is half the diameter. In science and engineering the term _____ of curvature is commonly used as a synonym for _____.
  a. Thing
  b. Radius0
  c. Undefined
  d. Undefined

107. In mathematics, the _____ is a conic section generated by the intersection of a right circular conical surface and a plane parallel to a generating straight line of that surface. It can also be defined as locus of points in a plane which are equidistant from a given point.
  a. Thing
  b. Parabola0
  c. Undefined
  d. Undefined

108. In mathematics, a _____ is a type of conic section defined as the intersection between a right circular conical surface and a plane which cuts through both halves of the cone.
  a. Thing
  b. Hyperbola0
  c. Undefined
  d. Undefined

109. _____ has two distinct but etymologically-related meanings: one in geometry and one in trigonometry.
  a. Thing
  b. Tangent line0
  c. Undefined
  d. Undefined

110. _____ has one 90° internal angle a right angle.
  a. Thing
  b. Right triangle0
  c. Undefined
  d. Undefined

111. An _____ triange is a triangle with at least two sides of equal length.
  a. Thing
  b. Isosceles0
  c. Undefined
  d. Undefined

112. In geometry, an _____ polygon is a polygon which has all sides of the same length.
  a. Thing
  b. Equilateral0
  c. Undefined
  d. Undefined

113. An _____ is a triangle in which all sides are of equal length.
  a. Thing
  b. Equilateral triangle0
  c. Undefined
  d. Undefined

114. The _____ of a right triangle is the triangle's longest side; the side opposite the right angle.
  a. Thing
  b. Hypotenuse0
  c. Undefined
  d. Undefined

Chapter 1. PRECALCULUS REVIEW

115. In geometry, the _____ or barycenter of an object X in n-dimensional space is the intersection of all hyperplanes that divide X into two parts of equal moment about the hyperplane
    a. Centroid0
    b. Thing
    c. Undefined
    d. Undefined

116. In probability theory and statistics, a _____ is a number dividing the higher half of a sample, a population, or a probability distribution from the lower half.
    a. Median0
    b. Concept
    c. Undefined
    d. Undefined

117. A _____ is a four-sided plane figure that has two sets of opposite parallel sides.
    a. Parallelogram0
    b. Concept
    c. Undefined
    d. Undefined

118. A _____ is a polygon with four sides and four vertices.
    a. Quadrilateral0
    b. Thing
    c. Undefined
    d. Undefined

119. In geometry, _____ angles are angles that have a common ray coming out of the vertex going between two other rays.
    a. Concept
    b. Adjacent0
    c. Undefined
    d. Undefined

120. _____ is a temperature scale named after the German physicist Daniel Gabriel _____ , who proposed it in 1724.
    a. Thing
    b. Fahrenheit0
    c. Undefined
    d. Undefined

121. The word _____ comes from the Latin word linearis, which means created by lines.
    a. Linear0
    b. Thing
    c. Undefined
    d. Undefined

122. _____ is, or relates to, the _____ temperature scale .
    a. Thing
    b. Celsius0
    c. Undefined
    d. Undefined

123. In mathematics, there are several meanings of _____ depending on the subject.
    a. Degree0
    b. Thing
    c. Undefined
    d. Undefined

124. _____ is a physical property of a system that underlies the common notions of hot and cold; something that is hotter has the greater _____ .
    a. Thing
    b. Temperature0
    c. Undefined
    d. Undefined

125. _____ is a process of combining or accumulating. It may also refer to:

a. Thing
b. Integration0
c. Undefined
d. Undefined

126. _____, a field in mathematics, is the study of how functions change when their inputs change. The primary object of study in _____ is the derivative.
a. Differential calculus0
b. Thing
c. Undefined
d. Undefined

127. In mathematics, the _____ of a function is the set of all "output" values produced by that function. Given a function $f : A \to B$, the _____ of f, is defined to be the set $\{x \in B : x = f(a) \text{ for some } a \in A\}$.
a. Thing
b. Range0
c. Undefined
d. Undefined

128. In mathematics, a _____ of a k-place relation $L \subseteq X_1 \times \ldots \times X_k$ is one of the sets X_j, $1 \le j \le k$. In the special case where $k = 2$ and $L \subseteq X_1 \times X_2$ is a function $L : X_1 \to X_2$, it is conventional to refer to X_1 as the _____ of the function and to refer to X_2 as the codomain of the function.
a. Domain0
b. Thing
c. Undefined
d. Undefined

129. In mathematics, _____ is a part of the set theoretic notion of function.
a. Thing
b. Image0
c. Undefined
d. Undefined

130. In mathematics, an _____ is any of the arguments, i.e. "inputs", to a function. Thus if we have a function f(x), then x is a _____.
a. Independent variable0
b. Thing
c. Undefined
d. Undefined

131. In a function the _____, is the variable which is the value, i.e. the "output", of the function.
a. Dependent variable0
b. Thing
c. Undefined
d. Undefined

132. In mathematics, the _____ f is the collection of all ordered pairs . In particular, graph means the graphical representation of this collection, in the form of a curve or surface, together with axes, etc. Graphing on a Cartesian plane is sometimes referred to as curve sketching.
a. Graph of a function0
b. Thing
c. Undefined
d. Undefined

133. In mathematics, the concept of a _____ tries to capture the intuitive idea of a geometrical one-dimensional and continuous object. A simple example is the circle.
a. Curve0
b. Thing
c. Undefined
d. Undefined

134. _____ means "constancy", i.e. if something retains a certain feature even after we change a way of looking at it, then it is symmetric.

Chapter 1. PRECALCULUS REVIEW

    a. Thing
    c. Undefined
    b. Symmetry0
    d. Undefined

135. _____ are functions which satisfy particular symmetry relations, with respect to taking additive inverses.
    a. Thing
    c. Undefined
    b. Even function0
    d. Undefined

136. In mathematics, the multiplicative inverse of a number x, denoted 1/x or x^{-1}, is the number which, when multiplied by x, yields 1. The multiplicative inverse of x is also called the _____ of x.
    a. Thing
    c. Undefined
    b. Reciprocal0
    d. Undefined

137. In geometry, a _____ is the intersection of a body in 2-dimensional space with a line, or of a body in 3-dimensional space with a plane
    a. Thing
    c. Undefined
    b. Cross section0
    d. Undefined

138. The _____ of a solid object is the three-dimensional concept of how much space it occupies, often quantified numerically.
    a. Thing
    c. Undefined
    b. Volume0
    d. Undefined

139. In mathematics, a _____ is a quadric surface, with the following equation in Cartesian coordinates: $(x/_a)^2 + (y/_b)^2 = 1$.
    a. Cylinder0
    c. Undefined
    b. Thing
    d. Undefined

140. A _____ surface is the surface or face of a solid on its sides. It can also be defined as any face or surface that is not a base.
    a. Thing
    c. Undefined
    b. Lateral0
    d. Undefined

141. A _____ is a three-dimensional solid object bounded by six square faces, facets, or sides, with three meeting at each vertex.
    a. Cube0
    c. Undefined
    b. Thing
    d. Undefined

142. A _____ can refer to a line joining two nonadjacent vertices of a polygon or polyhedron, or in some contexts any upward or downward sloping line. .
    a. Diagonal0
    c. Undefined
    b. Thing
    d. Undefined

143. In a right triangle, the _____ of the triangle are the two sides that are perpendicular to each other, as opposed to the hypotenuse.

a. Legs0
b. Thing
c. Undefined
d. Undefined

144. A _____ is a three-dimensional geometric shape formed by straight lines through a fixed point (vertex) to the points of a fixed curve (directrix)
   a. Concept
   b. Cone0
   c. Undefined
   d. Undefined

145. In geographic information systems, a _____ comprises an entity with a geographic location, typically determined by points, arcs, or polygons. Carriageways and cadastres exemplify _____ data.
   a. Thing
   b. Feature0
   c. Undefined
   d. Undefined

146. The _____ is the distance around a closed curve. _____ is a kind of perimeter.
   a. Thing
   b. Circumference0
   c. Undefined
   d. Undefined

147. In mathematics, a _____ is the set of all points in three-dimensional space (R^3) which are at distance r from a fixed point of that space, where r is a positive real number called the radius of the _____. The fixed point is called the center or centre, and is not part of the _____ itself.
   a. Sphere0
   b. Thing
   c. Undefined
   d. Undefined

148. In mathematics, a _____ is any function which can be written as the ratio of two polynomial functions.
   a. Thing
   b. Rational function0
   c. Undefined
   d. Undefined

149. In mathematics, _____ growth occurs when the growth rate of a function is always proportional to the function's current size.
   a. Thing
   b. Exponential0
   c. Undefined
   d. Undefined

150. _____ is one of the most important functions in mathematics. A function commonly used to study growth and decay
   a. Thing
   b. Exponential function0
   c. Undefined
   d. Undefined

151. In mathematics, a _____ of a number x is the exponent y of the power by such that $x = b^y$. The value used for the base b must be neither 0 nor 1, nor a root of 1 in the case of the extension to complex numbers, and is typically 10, e, or 2.
   a. Logarithm0
   b. Thing
   c. Undefined
   d. Undefined

152. In mathematics, a _____ is an expression that is constructed from one or more variables and constants, using only the operations of addition, subtraction, multiplication, and constant positive whole number exponents. is a _____. Note in particular that division by an expression containing a variable is not in general allowed in polynomials. [1]

Chapter 1. PRECALCULUS REVIEW

a. Polynomial0
b. Thing
c. Undefined
d. Undefined

153. In mathematics, a _____ is a constant multiplicative factor of a certain object. The object can be such things as a variable, a vector, a function, etc. For example, the _____ of $9x^2$ is 9.
   a. Thing
   b. Coefficient0
   c. Undefined
   d. Undefined

154. In mathematics and the mathematical sciences, a _____ is a fixed, but possibly unspecified, value. This is in contrast to a variable, which is not fixed.
   a. Thing
   b. Constant0
   c. Undefined
   d. Undefined

155. _____ is a function whose values do not vary and thus are constant.
   a. Thing
   b. Constant function0
   c. Undefined
   d. Undefined

156. The _____ is a theorem for finding out the factors of a polynomial.
   a. Thing
   b. Factor theorem0
   c. Undefined
   d. Undefined

157. In mathematics, a _____ is a statement that can be proved on the basis of explicitly stated or previously agreed assumptions.
   a. Theorem0
   b. Thing
   c. Undefined
   d. Undefined

158. A _____ is a first degree polynomial mathematical function of the form: $f(x) = mx + b$ where m and b are real constants and x is a real variable.
   a. Linear function0
   b. Thing
   c. Undefined
   d. Undefined

159. A _____ is a polynomial function of the form $f(x) = ax^2 + bx + c$, where a, b, c are real numbers and a , 0.
   a. Quadratic function0
   b. Event
   c. Undefined
   d. Undefined

160. _____ are external two-dimensional outlines, with the appearance or configuration of some thing - in contrast to the matter or content or substance of which it is composed.
   a. Shapes0
   b. Thing
   c. Undefined
   d. Undefined

161. _____ is a straight line or curve A to which another curve B the one being studied approaches closer and closer as one moves along it.
   a. Vertical asymptote0
   b. Thing
   c. Undefined
   d. Undefined

Chapter 1. PRECALCULUS REVIEW

162. An _____ is a straight line or curve A to which another curve B approaches closer and closer as one moves along it. As one moves along B, the space between it and the _____ A becomes smaller and smaller, and can in fact be made as small as one could wish by going far enough along. A curve may or may not touch or cross its _____. In fact, the curve may intersect the _____ an infinite number of times.
   a. Asymptote0
   b. Thing
   c. Undefined
   d. Undefined

163. A _____ given two distinct points A and B on the _____, is the set of points C on the line containing points A and B such that A is not strictly between C and B.
   a. Ray0
   b. Thing
   c. Undefined
   d. Undefined

164. Initial objects are also called _____, and terminal objects are also called final.
   a. Coterminal0
   b. Thing
   c. Undefined
   d. Undefined

165. A _____ is a function that assigns a number to subsets of a given set.
   a. Measure0
   b. Thing
   c. Undefined
   d. Undefined

166. A _____ is a movement of an object in a circular motion. A two-dimensional object rotates around a center (or point) of _____. A three-dimensional object rotates around a line called an axis. If the axis of _____ is within the body, the body is said to rotate upon itself, or spin—which implies relative speed and perhaps free-movement with angular momentum. A circular motion about an external point, e.g. the Earth about the Sun, is called an orbit or more properly an orbital revolution.
   a. Rotation0
   b. Thing
   c. Undefined
   d. Undefined

167. The _____ is a unit of plane angle. It is represented by the symbol "rad" or, more rarely, by the superscript c (for "circular measure"). For example, an angle of 1.2 radians would be written "1.2 rad" or "1.2c" (second symbol can produce confusion with centigrads).
   a. Thing
   b. Radian0
   c. Undefined
   d. Undefined

168. _____ is a unit of plane angle, equal to 180/δ degrees, or about 57.2958 degrees
   a. Thing
   b. Radian measure0
   c. Undefined
   d. Undefined

169. _____ is a term in Trigonometry used to describe the secant of the complement of a cirlce.
   a. Thing
   b. Cosecant0
   c. Undefined
   d. Undefined

170. _____ is the ratio of the adjacent to the opposite side of a right-angled triangle
   a. Cotangent0
   b. Thing
   c. Undefined
   d. Undefined

Chapter 1. PRECALCULUS REVIEW

171. _____ is a trigonemtric function that is important when studying triangles and modeling periodic phenomena, among other applications.
   a. Sine0
   b. Thing
   c. Undefined
   d. Undefined

172. The _____ of an angle is the ratio of the length of the adjacent side to the length of the hypotenuse.
   a. Cosine0
   b. Concept
   c. Undefined
   d. Undefined

173. _____ is a trigonometric function that is the reciprocal of cosine.
   a. Secant0
   b. Thing
   c. Undefined
   d. Undefined

174. In business, particularly accounting, a _____ is the time intervals that the accounts, statement, payments, or other calculations cover.
   a. Period0
   b. Thing
   c. Undefined
   d. Undefined

175. A _____ is a quantity that denotes the proportional amount or magnitude of one quantity relative to another.
   a. Thing
   b. Ratio0
   c. Undefined
   d. Undefined

176. In mathematics, the additive inverse, or _____ of a number n is the number that, when added to n, yields zero. The additive inverse of n is denoted −n. For example, 7 is −7, because 7 + (−7) = 0, and the additive inverse of −0.3 is 0.3, because −0.3 + 0.3 = 0.
   a. Thing
   b. Opposite0
   c. Undefined
   d. Undefined

177. In mathematics, the _____ of a number n is the number that, when added to n, yields zero. The _____ of n is denoted −n. For example, 7 is −7, because 7 + (−7) = 0, and the _____ of −0.3 is 0.3, because −0.3 + 0.3 = 0.
   a. Thing
   b. Additive inverse0
   c. Undefined
   d. Undefined

178. The _____ is a statement about a general triangle which relates the lengths of its sides to the cosine of one of its angles.
   a. Thing
   b. Law of cosines0
   c. Undefined
   d. Undefined

179. In linear algebra, the _____ of an n-by-n square matrix A is defined to be the sum of the elements on the main diagonal of A,
   a. Trace0
   b. Thing
   c. Undefined
   d. Undefined

180. In geometry and trigonometry, a _____ is defined as an angle between two straight intersecting lines of ninety degrees, or one-quarter of a circle.

Chapter 1. PRECALCULUS REVIEW

a. Right angle0
b. Thing
c. Undefined
d. Undefined

181. _____ is a circle with a unit radius, i.e., a circle whose radius is 1.
   a. Unit circle0
   b. Thing
   c. Undefined
   d. Undefined

182. Equivalence is the condition of being _____ or essentially equal.
   a. Thing
   b. Equivalent0
   c. Undefined
   d. Undefined

183. If the sides of the triangle are a, b and c and the angles opposite those sides are A, B and C, then the _____ states: a/sin A=b/sin B=c/sin C=2R where R is the radius of the triangle's circumcircle.
   a. Law of sines0
   b. Thing
   c. Undefined
   d. Undefined

184. In mathematics, an inequality is a statement about the relative size or order of two objects. For example 14 > 10, or 14 is _____ 10.
   a. Thing
   b. Greater than0
   c. Undefined
   d. Undefined

185. In mathematics and elsewhere, the adjective _____ means fourth order, such as the function x4. A _____ number is a number which equals the fourth power of an integer.
   a. Thing
   b. Quartic0
   c. Undefined
   d. Undefined

186. In mathematics, a _____ is the end result of a division problem. It can also be expressed as the number of times the divisor divides into the dividend.
   a. Thing
   b. Quotient0
   c. Undefined
   d. Undefined

187. In combinatorial mathematics, a _____ is an un-ordered collection of unique elements.
   a. Combination0
   b. Concept
   c. Undefined
   d. Undefined

188. In mathematics, a _____ of a positive integer n is a way of writing n as a sum of positive integers.
   a. Composition0
   b. Thing
   c. Undefined
   d. Undefined

189. _____ has many meanings, most of which simply .
   a. Thing
   b. Power0
   c. Undefined
   d. Undefined

190. In mathematics, a _____ is a demonstration that, assuming certain axioms, some statement is necessarily true.

Chapter 1. PRECALCULUS REVIEW

a. Proof0
c. Undefined
b. Thing
d. Undefined

191. _____ is a method of mathematical proof typically used to establish that a given statement is true of all natural numbers
   a. Thing
   b. Mathematical induction0
   c. Undefined
   d. Undefined

192. In mathematics, a matrix can be thought of as each row or _____ being a vector. Hence, a space formed by row vectors or _____ vectors are said to be a row space or a _____ space.
   a. Column0
   b. Concept
   c. Undefined
   d. Undefined

193. _____, also known as _____ of Alexandria, was a Greek mathematician. His Elements is the most successful textbook in the history of mathematics. In it, the principles of geometry are deduced from a small set of axioms. His method of proving mathematical theorems by logical reasoning from accepted first principles remains the backbone of mathematics and is responsible for the field's characteristic rigor
   a. Person
   b. Euclid0
   c. Undefined
   d. Undefined

194. _____ was a Greek philosopher, a student of Plato and teacher of Alexander the Great. He wrote on diverse subjects, including physics, metaphysics, poetry, biology and zoology, logic, rhetoric, politics, government, and ethics.
   a. Aristotle0
   b. Person
   c. Undefined
   d. Undefined

195. A _____ consists either of a suggested explanation for a phenomenon or of a reasoned proposal suggesting a possible correlation between multiple phenomena.
   a. Thing
   b. Hypothesis0
   c. Undefined
   d. Undefined

196. In a mathematical proof or a syllogism, a _____ is a statement that is the logical consequence of preceding statements.
   a. Conclusion0
   b. Concept
   c. Undefined
   d. Undefined

197. _____ Logic is a concept in traditional logic referring to a "type of immediate inference in which from a given proposition another proposition is inferred which has as its subject the predicate of the original proposition and as its predicate the subject of the original proposition (the quality of the proposition being retained)."
   a. Concept
   b. Converse0
   c. Undefined
   d. Undefined

198. An _____ is any starting assumption from which other statements are logically derived
   a. Thing
   b. Axiom0
   c. Undefined
   d. Undefined

199. In mathematics, _____ is the decomposition of an object into a product of other objects, or factors, which when multiplied together give the original.
   a. Factoring0
   b. Thing
   c. Undefined
   d. Undefined

200. A _____ function curves downwards. The graph of a _____ function of one variable remains above its tangents and below its cords.
   a. Convex0
   b. Thing
   c. Undefined
   d. Undefined

201. In geometry, a _____ is a simple polygon whose interior is a convex set.
   a. Thing
   b. Convex polygon0
   c. Undefined
   d. Undefined

202. A _____ is a set whose members are members of another set or a set contained within another set.
   a. Subset0
   b. Thing
   c. Undefined
   d. Undefined

203. _____ are groups whose members are members of another set or a set contained within another set.
   a. Subsets0
   b. Thing
   c. Undefined
   d. Undefined

204. In geometry a _____ is a plane figure that is bounded by a closed path or circuit, composed of a finite number of sequential line segments.
   a. Polygon0
   b. Thing
   c. Undefined
   d. Undefined

205. An _____ is an angle formed by two sides of a simple polygon that share an endpoint, namely, the angle on the inner side of the polygon.
   a. Interior angle0
   b. Thing
   c. Undefined
   d. Undefined

206. In mathematics and more specifically set theory, the _____ set is the unique set which contains no elements.
   a. Empty0
   b. Thing
   c. Undefined
   d. Undefined

Chapter 2. LIMITS AND CONTINUITY

1. _____ is a mathematical subject that includes the study of limits, derivatives, integrals, and power series and constitutes a major part of modern university curriculum.
   a. Thing
   b. Calculus0
   c. Undefined
   d. Undefined

2. In geometry, a _____ is defined as a quadrilateral where all four of its angles are right angles.
   a. Thing
   b. Rectangle0
   c. Undefined
   d. Undefined

3. A _____ is the result of the addition of a set of numbers. The numbers may be natural numbers, complex numbers, matrices, or still more complicated objects. An infinite _____ is a subtle procedure known as a series.
   a. Sum0
   b. Thing
   c. Undefined
   d. Undefined

4. The _____, the average in everyday English, which is also called the arithmetic _____ (and is distinguished from the geometric _____ or harmonic _____). The average is also called the sample _____. The expected value of a random variable, which is also called the population _____.
   a. Thing
   b. Mean0
   c. Undefined
   d. Undefined

5. The mathematical concept of a _____ expresses the intuitive idea of deterministic dependence between two quantities, one of which is viewed as primary and the other as secondary. A _____ then is a way to associate a unique output for each input of a specified type, for example, a real number or an element of a given set.
   a. Thing
   b. Function0
   c. Undefined
   d. Undefined

6. In mathematics, the _____ f is the collection of all ordered pairs . In particular, graph means the graphical representation of this collection, in the form of a curve or surface, together with axes, etc. Graphing on a Cartesian plane is sometimes referred to as curve sketching.
   a. Graph of a function0
   b. Thing
   c. Undefined
   d. Undefined

7. In mathematics, the concept of a _____ tries to capture the intuitive idea of a geometrical one-dimensional and continuous object. A simple example is the circle.
   a. Curve0
   b. Thing
   c. Undefined
   d. Undefined

8. The _____ is a fundamental concept in analysis. Informally, a function f can be made as close to L as desired, by making x close enough to p.
   a. Limit of a function0
   b. Thing
   c. Undefined
   d. Undefined

9. In mathematics, a _____ may be described informally as a number that can be given by an infinite decimal representation.
   a. Real number0
   b. Thing
   c. Undefined
   d. Undefined

Chapter 2. LIMITS AND CONTINUITY

10. A _____ is a number that is less than zero.
    a. Thing
    b. Negative number0
    c. Undefined
    d. Undefined

11. In mathematics, an inequality is a statement about the relative size or order of two objects. For example 14 > 10, or 14 is _____ 10.
    a. Thing
    b. Greater than0
    c. Undefined
    d. Undefined

12. In mathematics, a _____ number is a number which can be expressed as a ratio of two integers. Non-integer _____ numbers (commonly called fractions) are usually written as the vulgar fraction a / b, where b is not zero.
    a. Rational0
    b. Thing
    c. Undefined
    d. Undefined

13. In mathematics, an _____ number is any real number that is not a rational number- that is, it is a number which cannot be expressed as a fraction m/n, where m and n are integers.
    a. Irrational0
    b. Thing
    c. Undefined
    d. Undefined

14. In mathematics, an _____ is any real number that is not a rational number ¡ª that is, it is a number which cannot be expressed as m/n, where m and n are integers.
    a. Irrational number0
    b. Thing
    c. Undefined
    d. Undefined

15. In mathematics, _____ are any real number that is not a rational number ¡ª that is, it is a number which cannot be expressed as m/n, where m and n are integers.
    a. Irrational numbers0
    b. Thing
    c. Undefined
    d. Undefined

16. A _____ is a quantity that denotes the proportional amount or magnitude of one quantity relative to another.
    a. Ratio0
    b. Thing
    c. Undefined
    d. Undefined

17. In mathematics, a _____ is the end result of a division problem. It can also be expressed as the number of times the divisor divides into the dividend.
    a. Thing
    b. Quotient0
    c. Undefined
    d. Undefined

18. The _____ is a unit of plane angle. It is represented by the symbol "rad" or, more rarely, by the superscript c (for "circular measure"). For example, an angle of 1.2 radians would be written "1.2 rad" or "1.2c" (second symbol can produce confusion with centigrads).
    a. Radian0
    b. Thing
    c. Undefined
    d. Undefined

19. _____ is a unit of plane angle, equal to 180/ð degrees, or about 57.2958 degrees

Chapter 2. LIMITS AND CONTINUITY

a. Thing
b. Radian measure0
c. Undefined
d. Undefined

20. A _____ is a function that assigns a number to subsets of a given set.
a. Thing
b. Measure0
c. Undefined
d. Undefined

21. _____ is often used to describe the measurement of the steepness, incline, gradient, or grade of a straight line. The _____ is defined as the ratio of the "rise" divided by the "run" between two points on a line, or in other words, the ratio of the altitude change to the horizontal distance between any two points on the line.
a. Thing
b. Slope0
c. Undefined
d. Undefined

22. _____ Any process by which a specified characteristic usually amplitude of the output of a device is prevented from exceeding a predetermined value.
a. Limiting0
b. Thing
c. Undefined
d. Undefined

23. _____ is a trigonometric function that is the reciprocal of cosine.
a. Thing
b. Secant0
c. Undefined
d. Undefined

24. _____ of a curve is a line that intersects two or more points on the curve.
a. Secant line0
b. Thing
c. Undefined
d. Undefined

25. In trigonometry, the _____ is a function defined as $\tan x = \sin x / \cos x$. The function is so-named because it can be defined as the length of a certain segment of a _____ (in the geometric sense) to the unit circle. In plane geometry, a line is _____ to a curve, at some point, if both line and curve pass through the point with the same direction.
a. Tangent0
b. Thing
c. Undefined
d. Undefined

26. _____ has two distinct but etymologically-related meanings: one in geometry and one in trigonometry.
a. Thing
b. Tangent line0
c. Undefined
d. Undefined

27. In the scientific method, an _____ (Latin: ex-+-periri, "of (or from) trying"), is a set of actions and observations, performed in the context of solving a particular problem or question, in order to support or falsify a hypothesis or research concerning phenomena.
a. Experiment0
b. Thing
c. Undefined
d. Undefined

28. In elementary algebra, an _____ is a set that contains every real number between two indicated numbers and may contain the two numbers themselves.

a. Thing
b. Interval0
c. Undefined
d. Undefined

29. In mathematics and the mathematical sciences, a _____ is a fixed, but possibly unspecified, value. This is in contrast to a variable, which is not fixed.
   a. Constant0
   b. Thing
   c. Undefined
   d. Undefined

30. In mathematics, science including computer science, linguistics and engineering, an _____ is, generally speaking, an independent variable or input to a function.
   a. Argument0
   b. Thing
   c. Undefined
   d. Undefined

31. In mathematics, an _____ is a statement about the relative size or order of two objects.
   a. Inequality0
   b. Thing
   c. Undefined
   d. Undefined

32. In mathematics, the _____ (or modulus) of a real number is its numerical value without regard to its sign.
   a. Absolute value0
   b. Thing
   c. Undefined
   d. Undefined

33. In mathematics, a _____ is a demonstration that, assuming certain axioms, some statement is necessarily true.
   a. Proof0
   b. Thing
   c. Undefined
   d. Undefined

34. _____ the expected value of a random variable displays the average or central value of the variable. It is a summary value of the distribution of the variable.
   a. Thing
   b. Determining0
   c. Undefined
   d. Undefined

35. In a mathematical proof or a syllogism, a _____ is a statement that is the logical consequence of preceding statements.
   a. Concept
   b. Conclusion0
   c. Undefined
   d. Undefined

36. _____ are the basic objects of study in graph theory. Informally speaking, a graph is a set of objects called points, nodes, or vertices connected by links called lines or edges.
   a. Thing
   b. Graphs0
   c. Undefined
   d. Undefined

37. In astronomy, geography, geometry and related sciences and contexts, a plane is said to be _____ at a given point if it is locally perpendicular to the gradient of the gravity field, i.e., with the direction of the gravitational force at that point.
   a. Thing
   b. Horizontal0
   c. Undefined
   d. Undefined

Chapter 2. LIMITS AND CONTINUITY

38. _____ Logic is a concept in traditional logic referring to a "type of immediate inference in which from a given proposition another proposition is inferred which has as its subject the predicate of the original proposition and as its predicate the subject of the original proposition (the quality of the proposition being retained)."
   a. Converse0
   b. Concept
   c. Undefined
   d. Undefined

39. In mathematics, a _____ is a statement that can be proved on the basis of explicitly stated or previously agreed assumptions.
   a. Thing
   b. Theorem0
   c. Undefined
   d. Undefined

40. _____ is a method of mathematical proof typically used to establish that a given statement is true of all natural numbers
   a. Thing
   b. Mathematical induction0
   c. Undefined
   d. Undefined

41. In mathematics, a set is called _____ if there is a bijection between the set and some set of the form {1, 2, ..., n} where n is a natural number.
   a. Thing
   b. Finite0
   c. Undefined
   d. Undefined

42. In mathematics, a _____ is an expression that is constructed from one or more variables and constants, using only the operations of addition, subtraction, multiplication, and constant positive whole number exponents. is a _____. Note in particular that division by an expression containing a variable is not in general allowed in polynomials. [1]
   a. Polynomial0
   b. Thing
   c. Undefined
   d. Undefined

43. A _____ function is a function for which, intuitively, small changes in the input result in small changes in the output.
   a. Continuous0
   b. Event
   c. Undefined
   d. Undefined

44. A _____ is a numeral used to indicate a count. The most common use of the word today is to name the part of a fraction that tells the number or count of equal parts.
   a. Thing
   b. Numerator0
   c. Undefined
   d. Undefined

45. In mathematics, a _____ is the result of multiplying, or an expression that identifies factors to be multiplied.
   a. Thing
   b. Product0
   c. Undefined
   d. Undefined

46. An _____ is a combination of numbers, operators, grouping symbols and/or free variables and bound variables arranged in a meaningful way which can be evaluated..
   a. Thing
   b. Expression0
   c. Undefined
   d. Undefined

Chapter 2. LIMITS AND CONTINUITY

47. _____ is an adjective usually refering to being in the centre.
    a. Central0
    b. Thing
    c. Undefined
    d. Undefined

48. The function difference divided by the point difference is known as the _____
    a. Thing
    b. Difference quotient0
    c. Undefined
    d. Undefined

49. Continuous functions are of utmost importance in mathematics and applications. However, not all functions are continuous. If a function is not continuous at a point in its domain, one says that it has a _____ there. The set of all points of _____ of a function may be a discrete set, a dense set, or even the entire domain of the function.
    a. Discontinuity0
    b. Thing
    c. Undefined
    d. Undefined

50. In mathematics, a _____ of a k-place relation $L \subseteq X_1 \times ... \times X_k$ is one of the sets X_j, $1 \leq j \leq k$. In the special case where k = 2 and $L \subseteq X_1 \times X_2$ is a function $L : X_1 \to X_2$, it is conventional to refer to X_1 as the _____ of the function and to refer to X_2 as the codomain of the function.
    a. Domain0
    b. Thing
    c. Undefined
    d. Undefined

51. _____ is the state of being greater than any finite real or natural number, however large.
    a. Infinite0
    b. Thing
    c. Undefined
    d. Undefined

52. In Euclidean geometry, a _____ is moving every point a constant distance in a specified direction.
    a. Concept
    b. Translation0
    c. Undefined
    d. Undefined

53. In mathematics and logic, a _____ proof is a way of showing the truth or falsehood of a given statement by a straightforward combination of established facts, usually existing lemmas and theorems, without making any further assumptions.
    a. Direct0
    b. Thing
    c. Undefined
    d. Undefined

54. A _____ number is a positive integer which has a positive divisor other than one or itself.
    a. Thing
    b. Composite0
    c. Undefined
    d. Undefined

55. A _____, formed by the composition of one function on another, represents the application of the former to the result of the application of the latter to the argument of the composite.
    a. Composite function0
    b. Thing
    c. Undefined
    d. Undefined

56. A _____, is a symbolized depiction of space which highlights relations between components of that space. Most usually a _____ is a two-dimensional, geometrically accurate representation of a three-dimensional space.

Chapter 2. LIMITS AND CONTINUITY

a. Map0
b. Thing
c. Undefined
d. Undefined

57. In mathematics, a _____ occurs if there is a bijection between the set and some set of the form 1, 2, ..., n where n is a natural number.
   a. Finite set0
   b. Concept
   c. Undefined
   d. Undefined

58. In calculus, the _____ is a theorem regarding the limit of a function. The theorem asserts that if two functions approach the same limit at a point, and if a third function is "squeezed" between those functions, then the third function also approaches that limit at that point.
   a. Squeeze Theorem0
   b. Thing
   c. Undefined
   d. Undefined

59. In mathematics, the _____ functions are functions of an angle; they are important when studying triangles and modeling periodic phenomena, among many other applications.
   a. Thing
   b. Trigonometric0
   c. Undefined
   d. Undefined

60. The _____ are functions of an angle; they are important when studying triangles and modeling periodic phenomena, among many other applications.
   a. Thing
   b. Trigonometric functions0
   c. Undefined
   d. Undefined

61. _____ is a trigonemtric function that is important when studying triangles and modeling periodic phenomena, among other applications.
   a. Sine0
   b. Thing
   c. Undefined
   d. Undefined

62. A _____ is a function for which, intuitively, small changes in the input result in small changes in the output.
   a. Event
   b. Continuous function0
   c. Undefined
   d. Undefined

63. In mathematics, a _____ of a complex-valued function f is a member x of the domain of f such that f(x) vanishes at x, that is, $x : f(x) = 0$.
   a. Thing
   b. Root0
   c. Undefined
   d. Undefined

64. A _____ is a set of possible values that a variable can take on in order to satisfy a given set of conditions, which may include equations and inequalities.
   a. Thing
   b. Solution set0
   c. Undefined
   d. Undefined

65. In geometry, an _____ is a point at which a line segment or ray terminates.

a. Thing
b. Endpoint0
c. Undefined
d. Undefined

66. In mathematics, a _____ is any function which can be written as the ratio of two polynomial functions.
   a. Rational function0
   b. Thing
   c. Undefined
   d. Undefined

67. In mathematical analysis and related areas of mathematics, a set is called _____, if it is, in a certain sense, of finite size.
   a. Bounded0
   b. Thing
   c. Undefined
   d. Undefined

68. A _____ consists either of a suggested explanation for a phenomenon or of a reasoned proposal suggesting a possible correlation between multiple phenomena.
   a. Thing
   b. Hypothesis0
   c. Undefined
   d. Undefined

69. An _____ is an equality that remains true regardless of the values of any variables that appear within it, to distinguish it from an equality which is true under more particular conditions.
   a. Thing
   b. Identity0
   c. Undefined
   d. Undefined

70. An _____ is a function that does not have any effect: it always returns the same value that was used as its argument.
   a. Identity function0
   b. Thing
   c. Undefined
   d. Undefined

71. The _____ are the only integral domain whose positive elements are well-ordered, and in which order is preserved by addition. Like the natural numbers, the _____ form a countably infinite set. The set of all _____ is usually denoted in mathematics by a boldface Z.
   a. Thing
   b. Integers0
   c. Undefined
   d. Undefined

72. _____ means in succession or back-to-back
   a. Consecutive0
   b. Thing
   c. Undefined
   d. Undefined

73. In mathematics, the _____ of a function is the set of all "output" values produced by that function. Given a function $f : A \to B$, the _____ of f, is defined to be the set $\{x \in B : x = f(a) \text{ for some } a \in A\}$.
   a. Range0
   b. Thing
   c. Undefined
   d. Undefined

74. A _____ is a three-dimensional solid object bounded by six square faces, facets, or sides, with three meeting at each vertex.

a. Thing
b. Cube0
c. Undefined
d. Undefined

75. A _____ of a number is a number a such that $a^3 = x$.
   a. Cube root0
   b. Thing
   c. Undefined
   d. Undefined

76. In mathematics, there are several meanings of _____ depending on the subject.
   a. Degree0
   b. Thing
   c. Undefined
   d. Undefined

77. In mathematics, a _____ is a polynomial equation of the third degree.
   a. Cubic equation0
   b. Thing
   c. Undefined
   d. Undefined

78. The _____ of a geographic location is its height above a fixed reference point, often the mean sea level.
   a. Elevation0
   b. Thing
   c. Undefined
   d. Undefined

79. The _____ integers are all the integers from zero on upwards.
   a. Thing
   b. Nonnegative0
   c. Undefined
   d. Undefined

80. An _____ of a number a is a number b such that $b^n = a$.
   a. Thing
   b. Nth root0
   c. Undefined
   d. Undefined

81. _____ is a physical property of a system that underlies the common notions of hot and cold; something that is hotter has the greater _____.
   a. Thing
   b. Temperature0
   c. Undefined
   d. Undefined

82. The metre (or _____, see spelling differences) is a measure of length. It is the basic unit of length in the metric system and in the International System of Units (SI), used around the world for general and scientific purposes.
   a. Meter0
   b. Concept
   c. Undefined
   d. Undefined

83. The _____ is an imaginary line on the Earth's surface equidistant from the North Pole and South Pole.
   a. Equator0
   b. Thing
   c. Undefined
   d. Undefined

84. In mathematics, the additive inverse, or _____ of a number n is the number that, when added to n, yields zero. The additive inverse of n is denoted −n. For example, 7 is −7, because 7 + (−7) = 0, and the additive inverse of −0.3 is 0.3, because −0.3 + 0.3 = 0.

Chapter 2. LIMITS AND CONTINUITY

a. Opposite0
b. Thing
c. Undefined
d. Undefined

85. In mathematics, the _____ of a number n is the number that, when added to n, yields zero. The _____ of n is denoted −n. For example, 7 is −7, because 7 + (−7) = 0, and the _____ of −0.3 is 0.3, because −0.3 + 0.3 = 0.
   a. Thing
   b. Additive inverse0
   c. Undefined
   d. Undefined

86. In Euclidean geometry, a _____ is the set of all points in a plane at a fixed distance, called the radius, from a given point, the center.
   a. Thing
   b. Circle0
   c. Undefined
   d. Undefined

87. In classical geometry, a _____ of a circle or sphere is any line segment from its center to its boundary. By extension, the _____ of a circle or sphere is the length of any such segment. The _____ is half the diameter. In science and engineering the term _____ of curvature is commonly used as a synonym for _____.
   a. Thing
   b. Radius0
   c. Undefined
   d. Undefined

88. In plane geometry, a _____ is a polygon with four equal sides, four right angles, and parallel opposite sides. In algebra, the _____ of a number is that number multiplied by itself.
   a. Thing
   b. Square0
   c. Undefined
   d. Undefined

89. _____ is the distance around a given two-dimensional object. As a general rule, the _____ of a polygon can always be calculated by adding all the length of the sides together. So, the formula for triangles is P = a + b + c, where a, b and c stand for each side of it. For quadrilaterals the equation is P = a + b + c + d. For equilateral polygons, P = na, where n is the number of sides and a is the side length.
   a. Thing
   b. Perimeter0
   c. Undefined
   d. Undefined

90. An _____ or member of a set is an object that when collected together make up the set.
   a. Thing
   b. Element0
   c. Undefined
   d. Undefined

91. The _____ is a root-finding algorithm which works by repeatedly dividing an interval in half and then selecting the subinterval in which the root exists.
   a. Thing
   b. Bisection method0
   c. Undefined
   d. Undefined

92. In mathematics, the _____ , or members of a set or more generally a class are all those objects which when collected together make up the set or class.
   a. Elements0
   b. Thing
   c. Undefined
   d. Undefined

Chapter 2. LIMITS AND CONTINUITY

93. A _____ is a number, figure, or indicator that appears below the normal line of type, typically used in a formula, mathematical expression, or description of a chemical compound.
   a. Subscript0
   b. Thing
   c. Undefined
   d. Undefined

94. _____ is the middle point of a line segment.
   a. Midpoint0
   b. Thing
   c. Undefined
   d. Undefined

95. A _____ is a special kind of ratio, indicating a relationship between two measurements with different units, such as miles to gallons or cents to pounds.
   a. Rate0
   b. Thing
   c. Undefined
   d. Undefined

96. In common philosophical language, a proposition or _____, is the content of an assertion, that is, it is true-or-false and defined by the meaning of a particular piece of language.
   a. Concept
   b. Statement0
   c. Undefined
   d. Undefined

97. _____ or arithmetics is the oldest and most elementary branch of mathematics, used by almost everyone, for tasks ranging from simple daily counting to advanced science and business calculations.
   a. Arithmetic0
   b. Thing
   c. Undefined
   d. Undefined

98. In mathematics, a _____ of a positive integer n is a way of writing n as a sum of positive integers.
   a. Composition0
   b. Thing
   c. Undefined
   d. Undefined

Chapter 3. DIFFERENTIATION

1. _____ is a trigonometric function that is the reciprocal of cosine.
   a. Secant0
   b. Thing
   c. Undefined
   d. Undefined

2. _____ of a curve is a line that intersects two or more points on the curve.
   a. Thing
   b. Secant line0
   c. Undefined
   d. Undefined

3. In trigonometry, the _____ is a function defined as $\tan x = \sin x / \cos x$. The function is so-named because it can be defined as the length of a certain segment of a _____ (in the geometric sense) to the unit circle. In plane geometry, a line is _____ to a curve, at some point, if both line and curve pass through the point with the same direction.
   a. Thing
   b. Tangent0
   c. Undefined
   d. Undefined

4. _____ Any process by which a specified characteristic usually amplitude of the output of a device is prevented from exceeding a predetermined value.
   a. Limiting0
   b. Thing
   c. Undefined
   d. Undefined

5. _____ is often used to describe the measurement of the steepness, incline, gradient, or grade of a straight line. The _____ is defined as the ratio of the "rise" divided by the "run" between two points on a line, or in other words, the ratio of the altitude change to the horizontal distance between any two points on the line.
   a. Thing
   b. Slope0
   c. Undefined
   d. Undefined

6. _____ has two distinct but etymologically-related meanings: one in geometry and one in trigonometry.
   a. Thing
   b. Tangent line0
   c. Undefined
   d. Undefined

7. A _____ is a function that assigns a number to subsets of a given set.
   a. Measure0
   b. Thing
   c. Undefined
   d. Undefined

8. The _____ is a measurement of how a function changes when the values of its inputs change.
   a. Derivative0
   b. Thing
   c. Undefined
   d. Undefined

9. _____, a field in mathematics, is the study of how functions change when their inputs change. The primary object of study in _____ is the derivative.
   a. Thing
   b. Differential calculus0
   c. Undefined
   d. Undefined

10. The mathematical concept of a _____ expresses the intuitive idea of deterministic dependence between two quantities, one of which is viewed as primary and the other as secondary. A _____ then is a way to associate a unique output for each input of a specified type, for example, a real number or an element of a given set.

Chapter 3. DIFFERENTIATION

    a. Function0
    c. Undefined
    b. Thing
    d. Undefined

11. Mathematical _____ is used to represent ideas.
    a. Notation0
    c. Undefined
    b. Thing
    d. Undefined

12. In mathematics, a _____ number (or a _____) is a natural number that has exactly two (distinct) natural number divisors, which are 1 and the _____ number itself.
    a. Thing
    c. Undefined
    b. Prime0
    d. Undefined

13. In mathematics, a _____ of a k-place relation $L \subseteq X_1 \times ... \times X_k$ is one of the sets X_j, $1 \leq j \leq k$. In the special case where k = 2 and $L \subseteq X_1 \times X_2$ is a function $L : X_1 \rightarrow X_2$, it is conventional to refer to X_1 as the _____ of the function and to refer to X_2 as the codomain of the function.
    a. Thing
    c. Undefined
    b. Domain0
    d. Undefined

14. In elementary algebra, an _____ is a set that contains every real number between two indicated numbers and may contain the two numbers themselves.
    a. Interval0
    c. Undefined
    b. Thing
    d. Undefined

15. In mathematics, a _____ is the end result of a division problem. It can also be expressed as the number of times the divisor divides into the dividend.
    a. Thing
    c. Undefined
    b. Quotient0
    d. Undefined

16. The word _____ comes from the Latin word linearis, which means created by lines.
    a. Thing
    c. Undefined
    b. Linear0
    d. Undefined

17. A _____ is a first degree polynomial mathematical function of the form: f(x) = mx + b where m and b are real constants and x is a real variable.
    a. Thing
    c. Undefined
    b. Linear function0
    d. Undefined

18. The function difference divided by the point difference is known as the _____
    a. Difference quotient0
    c. Undefined
    b. Thing
    d. Undefined

19. A _____ is a set whose members are members of another set or a set contained within another set.
    a. Subset0
    c. Undefined
    b. Thing
    d. Undefined

Chapter 3. DIFFERENTIATION

20. A _____ is a numeral used to indicate a count. The most common use of the word today is to name the part of a fraction that tells the number or count of equal parts.
    a. Numerator0
    b. Thing
    c. Undefined
    d. Undefined

21. In plane geometry, a _____ is a polygon with four equal sides, four right angles, and parallel opposite sides. In algebra, the _____ of a number is that number multiplied by itself.
    a. Thing
    b. Square0
    c. Undefined
    d. Undefined

22. An _____ is a combination of numbers, operators, grouping symbols and/or free variables and bound variables arranged in a meaningful way which can be evaluated..
    a. Thing
    b. Expression0
    c. Undefined
    d. Undefined

23. A _____ is the part of a fraction that tells how many equal parts make up a whole, and which is used in the name of the fraction: "halves", "thirds", "fourths" or "quarters", "fifths" and so on.
    a. Denominator0
    b. Concept
    c. Undefined
    d. Undefined

24. In geometry, two lines or planes if one falls on the other in such a way as to create congruent adjacent angles. The term may be used as a noun or adjective. Thus, referring to Figure 1, the line AB is the _____ to CD through the point B.
    a. Perpendicular0
    b. Thing
    c. Undefined
    d. Undefined

25. In astronomy, geography, geometry and related sciences and contexts, a plane is said to be _____ at a given point if it is locally perpendicular to the gradient of the gravity field, i.e., with the direction of the gravitational force at that point.
    a. Thing
    b. Horizontal0
    c. Undefined
    d. Undefined

26. In mathematics, the _____ of a coordinate system is the point where the axes of the system intersect.
    a. Thing
    b. Origin0
    c. Undefined
    d. Undefined

27. In geometry, an _____ is a point at which a line segment or ray terminates.
    a. Endpoint0
    b. Thing
    c. Undefined
    d. Undefined

28. A _____ function is a function for which, intuitively, small changes in the input result in small changes in the output.
    a. Continuous0
    b. Event
    c. Undefined
    d. Undefined

29. In mathematics, a _____ is a demonstration that, assuming certain axioms, some statement is necessarily true.

Chapter 3. DIFFERENTIATION

    a. Proof0
    c. Undefined
    b. Thing
    d. Undefined

30. In mathematics, a _____ is a statement that can be proved on the basis of explicitly stated or previously agreed assumptions.
    a. Thing
    c. Undefined
    b. Theorem0
    d. Undefined

31. In mathematics, the _____ f is the collection of all ordered pairs . In particular, graph means the graphical representation of this collection, in the form of a curve or surface, together with axes, etc. Graphing on a Cartesian plane is sometimes referred to as curve sketching.
    a. Graph of a function0
    c. Undefined
    b. Thing
    d. Undefined

32. In mathematics, a _____ may be described informally as a number that can be given by an infinite decimal representation.
    a. Thing
    c. Undefined
    b. Real number0
    d. Undefined

33. In mathematics, a _____ number is a number which can be expressed as a ratio of two integers. Non-integer _____ numbers (commonly called fractions) are usually written as the vulgar fraction a / b, where b is not zero.
    a. Rational0
    c. Undefined
    b. Thing
    d. Undefined

34. In mathematics, an _____ number is any real number that is not a rational number- that is, it is a number which cannot be expressed as a fraction m/n, where m and n are integers.
    a. Thing
    c. Undefined
    b. Irrational0
    d. Undefined

35. _____ are the basic objects of study in graph theory. Informally speaking, a graph is a set of objects called points, nodes, or vertices connected by links called lines or edges.
    a. Graphs0
    c. Undefined
    b. Thing
    d. Undefined

36. In linear algebra, the _____ of an n-by-n square matrix A is defined to be the sum of the elements on the main diagonal of A,
    a. Trace0
    c. Undefined
    b. Thing
    d. Undefined

37. In mathematics and the mathematical sciences, a _____ is a fixed, but possibly unspecified, value. This is in contrast to a variable, which is not fixed.
    a. Thing
    c. Undefined
    b. Constant0
    d. Undefined

38. _____ is a function whose values do not vary and thus are constant.

a. Thing
c. Undefined
b. Constant function0
d. Undefined

39. A _____ of a number is the product of that number with any integer.
    a. Multiple0
    c. Undefined
    b. Thing
    d. Undefined

40. A _____ is the result of the addition of a set of numbers. The numbers may be natural numbers, complex numbers, matrices, or still more complicated objects. An infinite _____ is a subtle procedure known as a series.
    a. Sum0
    c. Undefined
    b. Thing
    d. Undefined

41. An _____ is an equality that remains true regardless of the values of any variables that appear within it, to distinguish it from an equality which is true under more particular conditions.
    a. Identity0
    c. Undefined
    b. Thing
    d. Undefined

42. An _____ is a function that does not have any effect: it always returns the same value that was used as its argument.
    a. Thing
    c. Undefined
    b. Identity function0
    d. Undefined

43. In linear algebra, real numbers are called scalars and relate to vectors in a vector space through the operation of _____ multiplication, in which a vector can be multiplied by a number to produce another vector.
    a. Scalar0
    c. Undefined
    b. Thing
    d. Undefined

44. In mathematics, a _____ is the result of multiplying, or an expression that identifies factors to be multiplied.
    a. Product0
    c. Undefined
    b. Thing
    d. Undefined

45. The _____ governs the differentiation of products of differentiable functions.
    a. Product rule0
    c. Undefined
    b. Thing
    d. Undefined

46. A _____ consists either of a suggested explanation for a phenomenon or of a reasoned proposal suggesting a possible correlation between multiple phenomena.
    a. Hypothesis0
    c. Undefined
    b. Thing
    d. Undefined

47. In mathematics, a _____ is an expression that is constructed from one or more variables and constants, using only the operations of addition, subtraction, multiplication, and constant positive whole number exponents. is a _____. Note in particular that division by an expression containing a variable is not in general allowed in polynomials. [1]
    a. Polynomial0
    c. Undefined
    b. Thing
    d. Undefined

Chapter 3. DIFFERENTIATION

48. In mathematics, _____ is an elementary arithmetic operation. When one of the numbers is a whole number, _____ is the repeated sum of the other number.
    a. Thing
    b. Multiplication0
    c. Undefined
    d. Undefined

49. In mathematics, the multiplicative inverse of a number x, denoted 1/x or x^{-1}, is the number which, when multiplied by x, yields 1. The multiplicative inverse of x is also called the _____ of x.
    a. Thing
    b. Reciprocal0
    c. Undefined
    d. Undefined

50. In calculus and other branches of mathematical analysis, an _____ is an algebraic expression obtained in the context of limits.
    a. Indeterminate form0
    b. Thing
    c. Undefined
    d. Undefined

51. The _____ is a method of finding the derivative of a function that is the quotient of two other functions for which derivatives exist.
    a. Quotient rule0
    b. Thing
    c. Undefined
    d. Undefined

52. The plus and _____ signs are mathematical symbols used to represent the notions of positive and negative as well as the operations of addition and subtraction.
    a. Thing
    b. Minus0
    c. Undefined
    d. Undefined

53. In mathematics, a _____ is any function which can be written as the ratio of two polynomial functions.
    a. Rational function0
    b. Thing
    c. Undefined
    d. Undefined

54. A _____ is one of the basic shapes of geometry: a polygon with three vertices and three sides which are straight line segments.
    a. Triangle0
    b. Thing
    c. Undefined
    d. Undefined

55. A _____ is a polynomial function of the form $f(x) = ax^2 + bx + c$, where a, b, c are real numbers and a , 0.
    a. Quadratic function0
    b. Event
    c. Undefined
    d. Undefined

56. In mathematics, a _____ is a constant multiplicative factor of a certain object. The object can be such things as a variable, a vector, a function, etc. For example, the _____ of $9x^2$ is 9.
    a. Thing
    b. Coefficient0
    c. Undefined
    d. Undefined

57. In mathematics, the concept of a _____ tries to capture the intuitive idea of a geometrical one-dimensional and continuous object. A simple example is the circle.

Chapter 3. DIFFERENTIATION

a. Curve0
b. Thing
c. Undefined
d. Undefined

58. The _____ of measurement are a globally standardized and modernized form of the metric system.
   a. Thing
   b. Units0
   c. Undefined
   d. Undefined

59. A _____ is a set of numbers that designate location in a given reference system, such as x,y in a planar _____ system or an x,y,z in a three-dimensional _____ system.
   a. Coordinate0
   b. Thing
   c. Undefined
   d. Undefined

60. An _____ is when two lines intersect somewhere on a plane creating a right angle at intersection
   a. Axes0
   b. Thing
   c. Undefined
   d. Undefined

61. In mathematics, the _____ of two sets A and B is the set that contains all elements of A that also belong to B (or equivalently, all elements of B that also belong to A), but no other elements.
   a. Thing
   b. Intersection0
   c. Undefined
   d. Undefined

62. In mathematics, for a statement to be mathematically _____, such a statement must be true of all natural numbers.
   a. Thing
   b. Inductive0
   c. Undefined
   d. Undefined

63. _____ is a trigonemtric function that is important when studying triangles and modeling periodic phenomena, among other applications.
   a. Thing
   b. Sine0
   c. Undefined
   d. Undefined

64. The _____ of an angle is the ratio of the length of the adjacent side to the length of the hypotenuse.
   a. Cosine0
   b. Concept
   c. Undefined
   d. Undefined

65. A _____ is a quantity that denotes the proportional amount or magnitude of one quantity relative to another.
   a. Thing
   b. Ratio0
   c. Undefined
   d. Undefined

66. _____ is the design, analysis, and/or construction of works for practical purposes.
   a. Thing
   b. Engineering0
   c. Undefined
   d. Undefined

67. An _____ or member of a set is an object that when collected together make up the set.

Chapter 3. DIFFERENTIATION

    a. Thing
    c. Undefined
    b. Element0
    d. Undefined

68. In mathematics, the _____ , or members of a set or more generally a class are all those objects which when collected together make up the set or class.
    - a. Elements0
    - b. Thing
    - c. Undefined
    - d. Undefined

69. _____ was a German mathematician and philosopher. He invented calculus independently of Newton, and his notation is the one in general use since.
    - a. Leibniz0
    - b. Person
    - c. Undefined
    - d. Undefined

70. _____ named in honor of the 17th century German philosopher and mathematician Gottfried Wilhelm Leibniz, was originally the use of expressions such as dx and dy and to represent "infinitely small" or infinitesimal increments of quantities x and y, just as Äx and Äy represent finite increments of x and y respectively.
    - a. Leibniz notation0
    - b. Thing
    - c. Undefined
    - d. Undefined

71. A _____ is 360° or 2δ radians.
    - a. Thing
    - b. Turn0
    - c. Undefined
    - d. Undefined

72. In mathematics, an inequality is a statement about the relative size or order of two objects. For example 14 > 10, or 14 is _____ 10.
    - a. Thing
    - b. Greater than0
    - c. Undefined
    - d. Undefined

73. In mathematics, there are several meanings of _____ depending on the subject.
    - a. Degree0
    - b. Thing
    - c. Undefined
    - d. Undefined

74. _____ is a method of mathematical proof typically used to establish that a given statement is true of all natural numbers
    - a. Thing
    - b. Mathematical induction0
    - c. Undefined
    - d. Undefined

75. In mathematics, a _____ is a mathematical statement which appears likely to be true, but has not been formally proven to be true under the rules of mathematical logic.
    - a. Conjecture0
    - b. Concept
    - c. Undefined
    - d. Undefined

76. A _____ is a special kind of ratio, indicating a relationship between two measurements with different units, such as miles to gallons or cents to pounds.

a. Rate0
b. Thing
c. Undefined
d. Undefined

77. _____ has many meanings, most of which simply .
a. Power0
b. Thing
c. Undefined
d. Undefined

78. In mathematics, the _____ is an important formula giving the expansion of powers of sums.
a. Thing
b. Binomial Theorem0
c. Undefined
d. Undefined

79. An _____ of a product of sums expresses it as a sum of products by using the fact that multiplication distributes over addition.
a. Expansion0
b. Thing
c. Undefined
d. Undefined

80. In elementary algebra, a _____ is a polynomial with two terms: the sum of two monomials. It is the simplest kind of polynomial except for a monomial.
a. Binomial0
b. Thing
c. Undefined
d. Undefined

81. In mathematics, an _____, mean, or central tendency of a data set refers to a measure of the "middle" or "expected" value of the data set.
a. Concept
b. Average0
c. Undefined
d. Undefined

82. _____ of an object is its speed in a particular direction.
a. Velocity0
b. Thing
c. Undefined
d. Undefined

83. In business, particularly accounting, a _____ is the time intervals that the accounts, statement, payments, or other calculations cover.
a. Period0
b. Thing
c. Undefined
d. Undefined

84. A _____ is a simplified and structured visual representation of concepts, ideas, constructions, relations, statistical data, anatomy etc used in all aspects of human activities to visualize and clarify the topic.
a. Thing
b. Diagram0
c. Undefined
d. Undefined

85. _____ is defined as the rate of change or derivative with respect to time of velocity.
a. Acceleration0
b. Thing
c. Undefined
d. Undefined

86. The metre (or _____, see spelling differences) is a measure of length. It is the basic unit of length in the metric system and in the International System of Units (SI), used around the world for general and scientific purposes.

Chapter 3. DIFFERENTIATION

a. Concept
b. Meter0
c. Undefined
d. Undefined

87. A _____ is a unit of length, usually used to measure distance, in a number of different systems, including Imperial units, United States customary units and Norwegian/Swedish mil. Its size can vary from system to system, but in each is between 1 and 10 kilometers. In contemporary English contexts _____ refers to either:
a. Thing
b. Mile0
c. Undefined
d. Undefined

88. _____ is a unit of speed, expressing the number of international miles covered per hour.
a. Thing
b. Miles per hour0
c. Undefined
d. Undefined

89. _____ was an Italian physicist, mathematician, astronomer, and philosopher who is closely associated with the scientific revolution.
a. Galileo Galilei0
b. Person
c. Undefined
d. Undefined

90. In geometry, an _____ of a triangle is a straight line through a vertex and perpendicular to (i.e. forming a right angle with) the opposite side or an extension of the opposite side.
a. Concept
b. Altitude0
c. Undefined
d. Undefined

91. Initial objects are also called _____, and terminal objects are also called final.
a. Coterminal0
b. Thing
c. Undefined
d. Undefined

92. A _____ is a deliberate process for transforming one or more inputs into one or more results.
a. Thing
b. Calculation0
c. Undefined
d. Undefined

93. The _____ of a geographic location is its height above a fixed reference point, often the mean sea level.
a. Thing
b. Elevation0
c. Undefined
d. Undefined

94. The _____ is an imaginary line on the Earth's surface equidistant from the North Pole and South Pole.
a. Equator0
b. Thing
c. Undefined
d. Undefined

95. _____, from Latin meaning "to make progress", is defined in two different ways. Pure economic _____ is the increase in wealth that an investor has from making an investment, taking into consideration all costs associated with that investment including the opportunity cost of capital.
a. Thing
b. Profit0
c. Undefined
d. Undefined

Chapter 3. DIFFERENTIATION

96. A _____ is a symbolic representation denoting a quantity or expression. It often represents an "unknown" quantity that has the potential to change.
   a. Thing
   b. Variable0
   c. Undefined
   d. Undefined

97. _____ is a business term for the amount of money that a company receives from its activities in a given period, mostly from sales of products and/or services to customers
   a. Revenue0
   b. Thing
   c. Undefined
   d. Undefined

98. The _____ integers are all the integers from zero on upwards.
   a. Nonnegative0
   b. Thing
   c. Undefined
   d. Undefined

99. _____ is the change in total cost that arises when the quantity produced changes by one unit.
   a. Thing
   b. Marginal cost0
   c. Undefined
   d. Undefined

100. _____ is the extra revenue that an additional unit of product will bring a firm. It can also be described as the change in total revenue/change in number of units sold.
   a. Marginal revenue0
   b. Thing
   c. Undefined
   d. Undefined

101. In mathematics, in the field of group theory, a _____ of a group is a quasisimple subnormal subgroup.
   a. Component0
   b. Concept
   c. Undefined
   d. Undefined

102. In Euclidean geometry, a _____ is the set of all points in a plane at a fixed distance, called the radius, from a given point, the center.
   a. Thing
   b. Circle0
   c. Undefined
   d. Undefined

103. In classical geometry, a _____ of a circle or sphere is any line segment from its center to its boundary. By extension, the _____ of a circle or sphere is the length of any such segment. The _____ is half the diameter. In science and engineering the term _____ of curvature is commonly used as a synonym for _____.
   a. Thing
   b. Radius0
   c. Undefined
   d. Undefined

104. The _____ of a solid object is the three-dimensional concept of how much space it occupies, often quantified numerically.
   a. Volume0
   b. Thing
   c. Undefined
   d. Undefined

105. A _____ is a three-dimensional solid object bounded by six square faces, facets, or sides, with three meeting at each vertex.

Chapter 3. DIFFERENTIATION

a. Cube0
b. Thing
c. Undefined
d. Undefined

106. A _____ can refer to a line joining two nonadjacent vertices of a polygon or polyhedron, or in some contexts any upward or downward sloping line. .
   a. Diagonal0
   b. Thing
   c. Undefined
   d. Undefined

107. In mathematics, a _____ is the set of all points in three-dimensional space (R^3) which are at distance r from a fixed point of that space, where r is a positive real number called the radius of the _____. The fixed point is called the center or centre, and is not part of the _____ itself.
   a. Thing
   b. Sphere0
   c. Undefined
   d. Undefined

108. In geometry, a _____ (Greek words diairo = divide and metro = measure) of a circle is any straight line segment that passes through the centre and whose endpoints are on the circular boundary, or, in more modern usage, the length of such a line segment. When using the word in the more modern sense, one speaks of the _____ rather than a _____, because all diameters of a circle have the same length. This length is twice the radius. The _____ of a circle is also the longest chord that the circle has.
   a. Diameter0
   b. Thing
   c. Undefined
   d. Undefined

109. The _____ is the distance around a closed curve. _____ is a kind of perimeter.
   a. Circumference0
   b. Thing
   c. Undefined
   d. Undefined

110. In geometry, a _____ is defined as a quadrilateral where all four of its angles are right angles.
   a. Thing
   b. Rectangle0
   c. Undefined
   d. Undefined

111. A circular _____ or circle _____ also known as a pie piece is the portion of a circle enclosed by two radii and an arc.
   a. Thing
   b. Sector0
   c. Undefined
   d. Undefined

112. _____ is an adjective usually refering to being in the centre.
   a. Central0
   b. Thing
   c. Undefined
   d. Undefined

113. The _____ is a unit of plane angle. It is represented by the symbol "rad" or, more rarely, by the superscript c (for "circular measure"). For example, an angle of 1.2 radians would be written "1.2 rad" or "1.2c" (second symbol can produce confusion with centigrads).
   a. Thing
   b. Radian0
   c. Undefined
   d. Undefined

Chapter 3. DIFFERENTIATION

114. In mathematics, a _____ is a quadric surface, with the following equation in Cartesian coordinates: $(x/a)^2 + (y/b)^2 = 1$.
   a. Thing
   b. Cylinder0
   c. Undefined
   d. Undefined

115. _____, in economics and political economy, are the distributions or payments awarded to the various suppliers of the factors of production.
   a. Returns0
   b. Thing
   c. Undefined
   d. Undefined

116. _____ is a kind of property which exists as magnitude or multitude. It is among the basic classes of things along with quality, substance, change, and relation.
   a. Amount0
   b. Thing
   c. Undefined
   d. Undefined

117. In calculus, the _____ is a formula for the derivative of the composite of two functions.
   a. Chain rule0
   b. Concept
   c. Undefined
   d. Undefined

118. In mathematics and its applications, a _____ is a system for assigning an n-tuple of numbers or scalars to each point in an n-dimensional space.
   a. Concept
   b. Coordinate system0
   c. Undefined
   d. Undefined

119. Mathematical _____ are demonstrations that, assuming certain axioms, some statement is necessarily true.
   a. Thing
   b. Proofs0
   c. Undefined
   d. Undefined

120. _____, either of the curved-bracket punctuation marks that together make a set of _____
   a. Parentheses0
   b. Thing
   c. Undefined
   d. Undefined

121. A _____ is a negotiable instrument instructing a financial institution to pay a specific amount of a specific currency from a specific demand account held in the maker/depositor's name with that institution. Both the maker and payee may be natural persons or legal entities.
   a. Check0
   b. Thing
   c. Undefined
   d. Undefined

122. In mathematics, a _____ of a positive integer n is a way of writing n as a sum of positive integers.
   a. Thing
   b. Composition0
   c. Undefined
   d. Undefined

123. In mathematics, science including computer science, linguistics and engineering, an _____ is, generally speaking, an independent variable or input to a function.

Chapter 3. DIFFERENTIATION

    a. Thing
    c. Undefined
    b. Argument0
    d. Undefined

124. In physics, _____ is an influence that may cause an object to accelerate. It may be experienced as a lift, a push, or a pull. The actual acceleration of the body is determined by the vector sum of all forces acting on it, known as net _____ or resultant _____.
    a. Force0
    c. Undefined
    b. Thing
    d. Undefined

125. _____ is a three-dimensional geometric shape formed by straight lines through a fixed point vertex to the points of a fixed curve directrix.
    a. Right circular cone0
    c. Undefined
    b. Thing
    d. Undefined

126. A _____ is a three-dimensional geometric shape formed by straight lines through a fixed point (vertex) to the points of a fixed curve (directrix)
    a. Concept
    c. Undefined
    b. Cone0
    d. Undefined

127. In mathematics, a _____ is an n-tuple with n being 3.
    a. Triple0
    c. Undefined
    b. Thing
    d. Undefined

128. The _____ of a member of a multiset is how many memberships in the multiset it has.
    a. Multiplicity0
    c. Undefined
    b. Thing
    d. Undefined

129. The _____ is a theorem for finding out the factors of a polynomial.
    a. Factor theorem0
    c. Undefined
    b. Thing
    d. Undefined

130. In geometry, an _____ polygon is a polygon which has all sides of the same length.
    a. Equilateral0
    c. Undefined
    b. Thing
    d. Undefined

131. An _____ is a triangle in which all sides are of equal length.
    a. Thing
    c. Undefined
    b. Equilateral triangle0
    d. Undefined

132. Sir Isaac _____, was an English physicist, mathematician, astronomer, natural philosopher, and alchemist, regarded by many as the greatest figure in the history of science
    a. Newton0
    c. Undefined
    b. Person
    d. Undefined

133. In mathematics, the _____ functions are functions of an angle; they are important when studying triangles and modeling periodic phenomena, among many other applications.

a. Trigonometric0
b. Thing
c. Undefined
d. Undefined

134. The _____ are functions of an angle; they are important when studying triangles and modeling periodic phenomena, among many other applications.
- a. Thing
- b. Trigonometric functions0
- c. Undefined
- d. Undefined

135. _____ is a unit of plane angle, equal to 180/δ degrees, or about 57.2958 degrees
- a. Thing
- b. Radian measure0
- c. Undefined
- d. Undefined

136. A _____ is an object that is attached to a pivot point so that it can swing freely.
- a. Thing
- b. Pendulum0
- c. Undefined
- d. Undefined

137. In physics, the _____ momentum of an object rotating about some reference point is the measure of the extent to which the object will continue to rotate about that point unless acted upon by an external torque.
- a. Thing
- b. Angular0
- c. Undefined
- d. Undefined

138. An _____ triange is a triangle with at least two sides of equal length.
- a. Thing
- b. Isosceles0
- c. Undefined
- d. Undefined

139. _____ is to give an equation R(x,y) = S(x,y) that at least in part has the same graph as y = f(x).
- a. Implicit differentiation0
- b. Thing
- c. Undefined
- d. Undefined

140. In mathematics, an _____ is any of the arguments, i.e. "inputs", to a function. Thus if we have a function f(x), then x is a _____.
- a. Thing
- b. Independent variable0
- c. Undefined
- d. Undefined

141. In a function the _____, is the variable which is the value, i.e. the "output", of the function.
- a. Dependent variable0
- b. Thing
- c. Undefined
- d. Undefined

142. The _____ are the only integral domain whose positive elements are well-ordered, and in which order is preserved by addition. Like the natural numbers, the _____ form a countably infinite set. The set of all _____ is usually denoted in mathematics by a boldface Z .
- a. Integers0
- b. Thing
- c. Undefined
- d. Undefined

143. In common philosophical language, a proposition or _____, is the content of an assertion, that is, it is true-or-false and defined by the meaning of a particular piece of language.

Chapter 3. DIFFERENTIATION

a. Statement0
b. Concept
c. Undefined
d. Undefined

144. One of the three formats applicable to a quadratic function is the _____ which is defined as $f = ax^2 + bx + c$.
   a. General form0
   b. Thing
   c. Undefined
   d. Undefined

145. In geometry, the _____ of an object is a point in some sense in the middle of the object.
   a. Center0
   b. Thing
   c. Undefined
   d. Undefined

146. In mathematics, the _____ is a conic section generated by the intersection of a right circular conical surface and a plane parallel to a generating straight line of that surface. It can also be defined as locus of points in a plane which are equidistant from a given point.
   a. Parabola0
   b. Thing
   c. Undefined
   d. Undefined

147. In mathematics, _____ are the intuitive idea of a geometrical one-dimensional and continuous object.
   a. Curves0
   b. Thing
   c. Undefined
   d. Undefined

148. In mathematics, _____ is synonymous with perpendicular when used as a simple adjective that is not part of any longer phrase with a standard definition. It means at right angles. It comes from the Greek ἀνά ὀρθός, orthos, meaning "straight", used by Euclid to mean right; and γωνία gonia, meaning angle. Two streets that cross each other at a right angle are _____ to one another.
   a. Thing
   b. Orthogonal0
   c. Undefined
   d. Undefined

149. In geometry and trigonometry, a _____ is defined as an angle between two straight intersecting lines of ninety degrees, or one-quarter of a circle.
   a. Thing
   b. Right angle0
   c. Undefined
   d. Undefined

150. In mathematics, an _____ .
   a. Thing
   b. Ellipse0
   c. Undefined
   d. Undefined

151. In mathematics, a _____ is a family of curves in the plane that intersect a given family of curves at right angles.
   a. Thing
   b. Orthogonal trajectory0
   c. Undefined
   d. Undefined

152. In mathematics, a _____ is a type of conic section defined as the intersection between a right circular conical surface and a plane which cuts through both halves of the cone.
   a. Thing
   b. Hyperbola0
   c. Undefined
   d. Undefined

Chapter 3. DIFFERENTIATION

153. In mathematics, the _____ of Bernoulli is an eight-shaped algebraic curve described by a Cartesian equation
   a. Lemniscate0
   b. Thing
   c. Undefined
   d. Undefined

154. _____ statistics are statistics that estimate population parameters.
   a. Thing
   b. Parametric0
   c. Undefined
   d. Undefined

155. In statistics, _____ means the most frequent value assumed by a random variable, or occurring in a sampling of a random variable.
   a. Concept
   b. Mode0
   c. Undefined
   d. Undefined

156. A _____ is a curve derived from a fixed point O and two other curves á and â. Every line through O cutting á at A and â at B cuts the _____ at the midpoint of AB.
   a. Thing
   b. Cissoid0
   c. Undefined
   d. Undefined

157. _____ is a circle with a unit radius, i.e., a circle whose radius is 1.
   a. Unit circle0
   b. Thing
   c. Undefined
   d. Undefined

158. A _____, sea mile or nautimile is a unit of length. It is accepted for use with the International System of Units (SI), but it is not an SI unit.[1] The _____ is used around the world for maritime and aviation purposes. It is commonly used in international law and treaties, especially regarding the limits of territorial waters. It developed from the geographical mile.
   a. Thing
   b. Nautical mile0
   c. Undefined
   d. Undefined

159. A _____ is a method for fastening or securing linear material such as rope by tying or interweaving. It may consist of a length of one or more segments of rope, string, webbing, twine, strap or even chain interwoven so as to create in the line the ability to bind to itself or to some other object - the "load". Knots have been the subject of interest both for their ancient origins, common use, and the mathematical implications of _____ theory.
   a. Thing
   b. Knot0
   c. Undefined
   d. Undefined

160. In mathematics, the additive inverse, or _____ of a number n is the number that, when added to n, yields zero. The additive inverse of n is denoted −n. For example, 7 is −7, because 7 + (−7) = 0, and the additive inverse of −0.3 is 0.3, because −0.3 + 0.3 = 0.
   a. Thing
   b. Opposite0
   c. Undefined
   d. Undefined

161. In mathematics, the _____ of a number n is the number that, when added to n, yields zero. The _____ of n is denoted −n. For example, 7 is −7, because 7 + (−7) = 0, and the _____ of −0.3 is 0.3, because −0.3 + 0.3 = 0.

Chapter 3. DIFFERENTIATION

a. Additive inverse0
b. Thing
c. Undefined
d. Undefined

162. _____ are flexible, elastic objects used to store mechanical energy.
   a. Thing
   b. Springs0
   c. Undefined
   d. Undefined

163. In physics, an _____ is the path that an object makes around another object while under the influence of a source of centripetal force, such as gravity.
   a. Thing
   b. Orbit0
   c. Undefined
   d. Undefined

164. _____ is the distance around a given two-dimensional object. As a general rule, the _____ of a polygon can always be calculated by adding all the length of the sides together. So, the formula for triangles is P = a + b + c, where a, b and c stand for each side of it. For quadrilaterals the equation is P = a + b + c + d. For equilateral polygons, P = na, where n is the number of sides and a is the side length.
   a. Perimeter0
   b. Thing
   c. Undefined
   d. Undefined

165. _____ are a measure of time.
   a. Thing
   b. Minutes0
   c. Undefined
   d. Undefined

166. _____ is electromagnetic radiation with a wavelength that is visible to the eye (visible _____) or, in a technical or scientific context, electromagnetic radiation of any wavelength.
   a. Thing
   b. Light0
   c. Undefined
   d. Undefined

167. The _____ in a vacuum is an important physical constant denoted by the letter c for constant or the Latin word celeritas meaning "swiftness
   a. Speed of light0
   b. Thing
   c. Undefined
   d. Undefined

168. _____ is the property of a physical object that quantifies the amount of matter and energy it is equivalent to.
   a. Thing
   b. Mass0
   c. Undefined
   d. Undefined

169. In geometry a _____, or deltoid, is a quadrilateral with two pairs of congruent adjacent sides.
   a. Thing
   b. Kite0
   c. Undefined
   d. Undefined

170. In mathematics, a _____ is a two-dimensional manifold or surface that is perfectly flat.
   a. Thing
   b. Plane0
   c. Undefined
   d. Undefined

Chapter 3. DIFFERENTIATION

171. In physics, the _____ is a vector quantity (more precisely, a pseudovector) which specifies the angular speed at which an object is rotating along with the direction in which it is rotating.
   a. Thing
   b. Angular velocity0
   c. Undefined
   d. Undefined

172. A _____ is traditionally an infinitesimally small change in a variable.
   a. Differential0
   b. Thing
   c. Undefined
   d. Undefined

173. In physics, _____ is rotation along a circle: a circular path or a circular orbit. The rotation around a fixed axis of a three-dimensional body involves _____ of its parts. We can talk about _____ of an object if we ignore its size, so that we have the motion of a point mass in a plane.
   a. Circular motion0
   b. Thing
   c. Undefined
   d. Undefined

174. In Euclidean geometry, an _____ is a closed segment of a differentiable curve in the two-dimensional plane; for example, a circular _____ is a segment of a circle.
   a. Concept
   b. Arc0
   c. Undefined
   d. Undefined

175. The _____ of an object is the extra energy which it possesses due to its motion.
   a. Thing
   b. Kinetic energy0
   c. Undefined
   d. Undefined

176. In mathematics, a _____ is any one of several different types of functions, mappings, operations, or transformations.
   a. Projection0
   b. Thing
   c. Undefined
   d. Undefined

177. An _____ is an increase, either of some fixed amount, for example added regularly, or of a variable amount.
   a. Increment0
   b. Thing
   c. Undefined
   d. Undefined

178. In mathematics, a _____ of a complex-valued function f is a member x of the domain of f such that f(x) vanishes at x, that is, x : f (x) = 0.
   a. Root0
   b. Thing
   c. Undefined
   d. Undefined

179. A _____ fraction is a fraction in which the absolute value of the numerator is less than the denominator--hence, the absolute value of the fraction is less than 1.
   a. Proper0
   b. Thing
   c. Undefined
   d. Undefined

180. In mathematics, a _____ is an ordered list of objects. Like a set, it contains members, also called elements or terms, and the number of terms is called the length of the _____. Unlike a set, order matters, and the exact same elements can appear multiple times at different positions in the _____.

Chapter 3. DIFFERENTIATION

    a. Thing
    b. Sequence0
    c. Undefined
    d. Undefined

181. The word _____ means curving in or hollowed inward.
    a. Concavity0
    b. Thing
    c. Undefined
    d. Undefined

182. In mathematics, a _____ is an algebraic structure in which addition and multiplication are defined and have properties listed below.
    a. Thing
    b. Ring0
    c. Undefined
    d. Undefined

183. U.S. liquid _____ is legally defined as 231 cubic inches, and is equal to 3.785411784 litres or abotu 0.13368 cubic feet. This is the most common definition of a _____. The U.S. fluid ounce is defined as 1/128 of a U.S. _____.
    a. Thing
    b. Gallon0
    c. Undefined
    d. Undefined

184. The _____ is a nonnegative scalar measure of a wave's magnitude of oscillation, that is, the magnitude of the maximum disturbance in the medium during one wave cycle.
    a. Amplitude0
    b. Thing
    c. Undefined
    d. Undefined

185. _____ is a physical property of a system that underlies the common notions of hot and cold; something that is hotter has the greater _____.
    a. Temperature0
    b. Thing
    c. Undefined
    d. Undefined

186. _____ are functions which satisfy particular symmetry relations, with respect to taking additive inverses.
    a. Even function0
    b. Thing
    c. Undefined
    d. Undefined

187. In mathematics, computing, linguistics, and related disciplines, an _____ is a finite list of well-defined instructions for accomplishing some task which, given an initial state, will terminate in a defined end-state.
    a. Algorithm0
    b. Concept
    c. Undefined
    d. Undefined

188. In geographic information systems, a _____ comprises an entity with a geographic location, typically determined by points, arcs, or polygons. Carriageways and cadastres exemplify _____ data.
    a. Thing
    b. Feature0
    c. Undefined
    d. Undefined

189. In mathematics, a _____ is a number which can be expressed as a ratio of two integers. Non-integer rational numbers (commonly called fractions) are usually written as the vulgar fraction a / b, where b is not zero.

a. Concept
b. Rational Number0
c. Undefined
d. Undefined

Chapter 4. THE MEAN-VALUE THEOREM AND APPLICATIONS

1. A _____ function is a function for which, intuitively, small changes in the input result in small changes in the output.
   a. Continuous0
   b. Event
   c. Undefined
   d. Undefined

2. Mathematical _____ is used to represent ideas.
   a. Notation0
   b. Thing
   c. Undefined
   d. Undefined

3. In mathematics, a _____ number (or a _____) is a natural number that has exactly two (distinct) natural number divisors, which are 1 and the _____ number itself.
   a. Prime0
   b. Thing
   c. Undefined
   d. Undefined

4. _____ is often used to describe the measurement of the steepness, incline, gradient, or grade of a straight line. The _____ is defined as the ratio of the "rise" divided by the "run" between two points on a line, or in other words, the ratio of the altitude change to the horizontal distance between any two points on the line.
   a. Slope0
   b. Thing
   c. Undefined
   d. Undefined

5. The _____, the average in everyday English, which is also called the arithmetic _____ (and is distinguished from the geometric _____ or harmonic _____). The average is also called the sample _____. The expected value of a random variable, which is also called the population _____.
   a. Mean0
   b. Thing
   c. Undefined
   d. Undefined

6. In mathematics, a _____ is a statement that can be proved on the basis of explicitly stated or previously agreed assumptions.
   a. Thing
   b. Theorem0
   c. Undefined
   d. Undefined

7. The _____ is a measurement of how a function changes when the values of its inputs change.
   a. Thing
   b. Derivative0
   c. Undefined
   d. Undefined

8. _____, a field in mathematics, is the study of how functions change when their inputs change. The primary object of study in _____ is the derivative.
   a. Thing
   b. Differential calculus0
   c. Undefined
   d. Undefined

9. In elementary algebra, an _____ is a set that contains every real number between two indicated numbers and may contain the two numbers themselves.
   a. Interval0
   b. Thing
   c. Undefined
   d. Undefined

10. _____ of an object is its speed in a particular direction.

Chapter 4. THE MEAN-VALUE THEOREM AND APPLICATIONS

    a. Thing
    b. Velocity0
    c. Undefined
    d. Undefined

11. In astronomy, geography, geometry and related sciences and contexts, a plane is said to be _____ at a given point if it is locally perpendicular to the gradient of the gravity field, i.e., with the direction of the gravitational force at that point.
    a. Thing
    b. Horizontal0
    c. Undefined
    d. Undefined

12. In trigonometry, the _____ is a function defined as $\tan x = \sin x / \cos x$. The function is so-named because it can be defined as the length of a certain segment of a _____ (in the geometric sense) to the unit circle. In plane geometry, a line is _____ to a curve, at some point, if both line and curve pass through the point with the same direction.
    a. Thing
    b. Tangent0
    c. Undefined
    d. Undefined

13. _____ has two distinct but etymologically-related meanings: one in geometry and one in trigonometry.
    a. Tangent line0
    b. Thing
    c. Undefined
    d. Undefined

14. In a mathematical proof or a syllogism, a _____ is a statement that is the logical consequence of preceding statements.
    a. Conclusion0
    b. Concept
    c. Undefined
    d. Undefined

15. In mathematics, a _____ is a demonstration that, assuming certain axioms, some statement is necessarily true.
    a. Proof0
    b. Thing
    c. Undefined
    d. Undefined

16. In mathematics, a _____ is an expression that is constructed from one or more variables and constants, using only the operations of addition, subtraction, multiplication, and constant positive whole number exponents. is a _____. Note in particular that division by an expression containing a variable is not in general allowed in polynomials. [1]
    a. Polynomial0
    b. Thing
    c. Undefined
    d. Undefined

17. The mathematical concept of a _____ expresses the intuitive idea of deterministic dependence between two quantities, one of which is viewed as primary and the other as secondary. A _____ then is a way to associate a unique output for each input of a specified type, for example, a real number or an element of a given set.
    a. Function0
    b. Thing
    c. Undefined
    d. Undefined

18. A _____ is a negotiable instrument instructing a financial institution to pay a specific amount of a specific currency from a specific demand account held in the maker/depositor's name with that institution. Both the maker and payee may be natural persons or legal entities.
    a. Thing
    b. Check0
    c. Undefined
    d. Undefined

Chapter 4. THE MEAN-VALUE THEOREM AND APPLICATIONS

19. In mathematics, a _____ of a complex-valued function f is a member x of the domain of f such that f(x) vanishes at x, that is, x : f (x) = 0.
    a. Thing
    b. Root0
    c. Undefined
    d. Undefined

20. _____ means in succession or back-to-back
    a. Consecutive0
    b. Thing
    c. Undefined
    d. Undefined

21. In mathematics, a _____ may be described informally as a number that can be given by an infinite decimal representation.
    a. Real number0
    b. Thing
    c. Undefined
    d. Undefined

22. In mathematics and the mathematical sciences, a _____ is a fixed, but possibly unspecified, value. This is in contrast to a variable, which is not fixed.
    a. Thing
    b. Constant0
    c. Undefined
    d. Undefined

23. _____ is defined as the rate of change or derivative with respect to time of velocity.
    a. Thing
    b. Acceleration0
    c. Undefined
    d. Undefined

24. A _____ is a unit of length, usually used to measure distance, in a number of different systems, including Imperial units, United States customary units and Norwegian/Swedish mil. Its size can vary from system to system, but in each is between 1 and 10 kilometers. In contemporary English contexts _____ refers to either:
    a. Mile0
    b. Thing
    c. Undefined
    d. Undefined

25. _____ is a unit of speed, expressing the number of international miles covered per hour.
    a. Miles per hour0
    b. Thing
    c. Undefined
    d. Undefined

26. _____ are a measure of time.
    a. Thing
    b. Minutes0
    c. Undefined
    d. Undefined

27. _____ consists either of a suggested explanation for a phenomenon or of a reasoned proposal suggesting a possible correlation between multiple phenomena.
    a. Event
    b. Hypotheses0
    c. Undefined
    d. Undefined

28. _____ are the basic objects of study in graph theory. Informally speaking, a graph is a set of objects called points, nodes, or vertices connected by links called lines or edges.

Chapter 4. THE MEAN-VALUE THEOREM AND APPLICATIONS

    a. Thing
    c. Undefined
    b. Graphs0
    d. Undefined

29. Any point where a graph makes contact with an coordinate axis is called an _____ of the graph
    a. Intercept0
    b. Thing
    c. Undefined
    d. Undefined

30. In mathematics, a _____ number is a number which can be expressed as a ratio of two integers. Non-integer _____ numbers (commonly called fractions) are usually written as the vulgar fraction a / b, where b is not zero.
    a. Rational0
    b. Thing
    c. Undefined
    d. Undefined

31. In mathematics, an _____ number is any real number that is not a rational number- that is, it is a number which cannot be expressed as a fraction m/n, where m and n are integers.
    a. Irrational0
    b. Thing
    c. Undefined
    d. Undefined

32. _____ is the state of being greater than any finite real or natural number, however large.
    a. Thing
    b. Infinite0
    c. Undefined
    d. Undefined

33. In geometry, an _____ is a point at which a line segment or ray terminates.
    a. Thing
    b. Endpoint0
    c. Undefined
    d. Undefined

34. In mathematics, a _____ of a k-place relation $L \subseteq X_1 \times \ldots \times X_k$ is one of the sets X_j, $1 \leq j \leq k$. In the special case where k = 2 and $L \subseteq X_1 \times X_2$ is a function $L : X_1 \to X_2$, it is conventional to refer to X_1 as the _____ of the function and to refer to X_2 as the codomain of the function.
    a. Thing
    b. Domain0
    c. Undefined
    d. Undefined

35. Continuous functions are of utmost importance in mathematics and applications. However, not all functions are continuous. If a function is not continuous at a point in its domain, one says that it has a _____ there. The set of all points of _____ of a function may be a discrete set, a dense set, or even the entire domain of the function.
    a. Thing
    b. Discontinuity0
    c. Undefined
    d. Undefined

36. In mathematics, the concept of a _____ tries to capture the intuitive idea of a geometrical one-dimensional and continuous object. A simple example is the circle.
    a. Curve0
    b. Thing
    c. Undefined
    d. Undefined

37. In mathematics, _____ are the intuitive idea of a geometrical one-dimensional and continuous object.
    a. Curves0
    b. Thing
    c. Undefined
    d. Undefined

Chapter 4. THE MEAN-VALUE THEOREM AND APPLICATIONS

38. A _____ is a function for which, intuitively, small changes in the input result in small changes in the output.
   a. Continuous function0
   b. Event
   c. Undefined
   d. Undefined

39. _____ Logic is a concept in traditional logic referring to a "type of immediate inference in which from a given proposition another proposition is inferred which has as its subject the predicate of the original proposition and as its predicate the subject of the original proposition (the quality of the proposition being retained)."
   a. Converse0
   b. Concept
   c. Undefined
   d. Undefined

40. In logic and mathematics, logical _____ is a logical relation that holds between a set T of formulas and a formula B when every model (or interpretation or valuation) of T is also a model of B.
   a. Implication0
   b. Concept
   c. Undefined
   d. Undefined

41. In physics, a _____ may refer to the scalar _____ or to the vector _____.
   a. Potential0
   b. Thing
   c. Undefined
   d. Undefined

42. _____, Greek for "knowledge of nature," is the branch of science concerned with the discovery and characterization of universal laws which govern matter, energy, space, and time.
   a. Physics0
   b. Thing
   c. Undefined
   d. Undefined

43. The _____ of an object is the extra energy which it possesses due to its motion.
   a. Thing
   b. Kinetic energy0
   c. Undefined
   d. Undefined

44. In physics, the _____ states that the total amount of energy in an isolated system remains constant, although it may change forms, e.g. friction turns kinetic energy into thermal energy.
   a. Law of Conservation of Energy0
   b. Thing
   c. Undefined
   d. Undefined

45. An _____ is a combination of numbers, operators, grouping symbols and/or free variables and bound variables arranged in a meaningful way which can be evaluated..
   a. Expression0
   b. Thing
   c. Undefined
   d. Undefined

46. Equivalence is the condition of being _____ or essentially equal.
   a. Thing
   b. Equivalent0
   c. Undefined
   d. Undefined

47. The metre (or _____, see spelling differences) is a measure of length. It is the basic unit of length in the metric system and in the International System of Units (SI), used around the world for general and scientific purposes.

Chapter 4. THE MEAN-VALUE THEOREM AND APPLICATIONS

a. Concept
b. Meter0
c. Undefined
d. Undefined

48. The easiest _____ prime numbers resides in the use of the Sieve of Eratosthenes, an algorithm that discovers all prime numbers to a specified integer.
   a. Thing
   b. Method for finding0
   c. Undefined
   d. Undefined

49. _____ is the design, analysis, and/or construction of works for practical purposes.
   a. Engineering0
   b. Thing
   c. Undefined
   d. Undefined

50. The term _____ refers to the largest and the smallest element of a set.
   a. Thing
   b. Extreme value0
   c. Undefined
   d. Undefined

51. A real-valued function f defined on the real line is said to have a _____ point at the point x∗, if there exists some ε > 0, such that f when x − x∗ < ε.
   a. Thing
   b. Local maximum0
   c. Undefined
   d. Undefined

52. _____ is a free computer algebra system based on a 1982 version of Macsyma
   a. Thing
   b. Maxima0
   c. Undefined
   d. Undefined

53. _____ are points in the domain of a function at which the function takes a largest value or smallest value, either within a given neighborhood or on the function domain in its entirety.
   a. Thing
   b. Maxima and minima0
   c. Undefined
   d. Undefined

54. In mathematics, maxima and _____, known collectively as extrema, are points in the domain of a function at which the function takes a largest value.
   a. Minima0
   b. Thing
   c. Undefined
   d. Undefined

55. _____ is a point on the domain of a function
   a. Thing
   b. Critical point0
   c. Undefined
   d. Undefined

56. In mathematics, the _____ is a conic section generated by the intersection of a right circular conical surface and a plane parallel to a generating straight line of that surface. It can also be defined as locus of points in a plane which are equidistant from a given point.
   a. Parabola0
   b. Thing
   c. Undefined
   d. Undefined

Chapter 4. THE MEAN-VALUE THEOREM AND APPLICATIONS 61

57. Acid _____ ratio measures the ability of a company to use its near cash or quick assets to immediately extinguish its current liabilities.
   a. Test0
   b. Thing
   c. Undefined
   d. Undefined

58. _____ the expected value of a random variable displays the average or central value of the variable. It is a summary value of the distribution of the variable.
   a. Determining0
   b. Thing
   c. Undefined
   d. Undefined

59. In mathematics and logic, a _____ proof is a way of showing the truth or falsehood of a given statement by a straightforward combination of established facts, usually existing lemmas and theorems, without making any further assumptions.
   a. Thing
   b. Direct0
   c. Undefined
   d. Undefined

60. A _____ consists either of a suggested explanation for a phenomenon or of a reasoned proposal suggesting a possible correlation between multiple phenomena.
   a. Thing
   b. Hypothesis0
   c. Undefined
   d. Undefined

61. _____ is a trigonemtric function that is important when studying triangles and modeling periodic phenomena, among other applications.
   a. Sine0
   b. Thing
   c. Undefined
   d. Undefined

62. _____, from Latin meaning "to make progress", is defined in two different ways. Pure economic _____ is the increase in wealth that an investor has from making an investment, taking into consideration all costs associated with that investment including the opportunity cost of capital.
   a. Thing
   b. Profit0
   c. Undefined
   d. Undefined

63. _____ is the change in total cost that arises when the quantity produced changes by one unit.
   a. Marginal cost0
   b. Thing
   c. Undefined
   d. Undefined

64. _____ is the extra revenue that an additional unit of product will bring a firm. It can also be described as the change in total revenue/change in number of units sold.
   a. Marginal revenue0
   b. Thing
   c. Undefined
   d. Undefined

65. _____ is a business term for the amount of money that a company receives from its activities in a given period, mostly from sales of products and/or services to customers
   a. Thing
   b. Revenue0
   c. Undefined
   d. Undefined

Chapter 4. THE MEAN-VALUE THEOREM AND APPLICATIONS

66. Sir Isaac _____, was an English physicist, mathematician, astronomer, natural philosopher, and alchemist, regarded by many as the greatest figure in the history of science
   a. Newton0
   b. Person
   c. Undefined
   d. Undefined

67. Deductive _____ is the kind of _____ in which the conclusion is necessitated by, or reached from, previously known facts (the premises).
   a. Reasoning0
   b. Thing
   c. Undefined
   d. Undefined

68. In mathematical analysis and related areas of mathematics, a set is called _____, if it is, in a certain sense, of finite size.
   a. Bounded0
   b. Thing
   c. Undefined
   d. Undefined

69. in mathematics, maxima and minima, known collectively as _____, are the largest value maximum or smallest value minimum, that a function takes in a point either within a given neighborhood or on the function domain in its entirety global extremum.
   a. Thing
   b. Extrema0
   c. Undefined
   d. Undefined

70. A _____ is a number that is less than zero.
   a. Negative number0
   b. Thing
   c. Undefined
   d. Undefined

71. _____ is a mathematical operation, written a^n, involving two numbers, the base a and the exponent n.
   a. Thing
   b. Exponentiating0
   c. Undefined
   d. Undefined

72. _____ is a mathematical operation, written a^n, involving two numbers, the base a and the exponent n.
   a. Thing
   b. Exponentiation0
   c. Undefined
   d. Undefined

73. In mathematics, a _____ is a number which can be expressed as a ratio of two integers. Non-integer rational numbers (commonly called fractions) are usually written as the vulgar fraction a / b, where b is not zero.
   a. Concept
   b. Rational Number0
   c. Undefined
   d. Undefined

74. In mathematics, a _____ is a constant multiplicative factor of a certain object. The object can be such things as a variable, a vector, a function, etc. For example, the _____ of $9x^2$ is 9.
   a. Thing
   b. Coefficient0
   c. Undefined
   d. Undefined

75. In acoustics and telecommunication, the _____ of a wave is a component frequency of the signal that is an integer multiple of the fundamental frequency.

Chapter 4. THE MEAN-VALUE THEOREM AND APPLICATIONS

a. Harmonic0
b. Thing
c. Undefined
d. Undefined

76. Simple _____ is the motion of a simple harmonic oscillator, a motion that is neither driven nor damped. Complex _____ is the superposition — linear combination — of several simultaneous simple harmonic motions.
a. Harmonic motion0
b. Thing
c. Undefined
d. Undefined

77. A _____ is a three-dimensional solid object bounded by six square faces, facets, or sides, with three meeting at each vertex.
a. Thing
b. Cube0
c. Undefined
d. Undefined

78. _____ are of a number n in its third power-the result of multiplying it by itself three times.
a. Cubes0
b. Thing
c. Undefined
d. Undefined

79. A _____ is the result of the addition of a set of numbers. The numbers may be natural numbers, complex numbers, matrices, or still more complicated objects. An infinite _____ is a subtle procedure known as a series.
a. Thing
b. Sum0
c. Undefined
d. Undefined

80. A _____ is any object propelled through space by the applicationp of a force.
a. Projectile0
b. Thing
c. Undefined
d. Undefined

81. The _____ of a geographic location is its height above a fixed reference point, often the mean sea level.
a. Thing
b. Elevation0
c. Undefined
d. Undefined

82. In mathematics, the _____ of a function is the set of all "output" values produced by that function. Given a function $f: A \to B$, the _____ of f, is defined to be the set $\{x \in B : x = f(a) \text{ for some } a \in A\}$.
a. Range0
b. Thing
c. Undefined
d. Undefined

83. A _____ is one of the basic shapes of geometry: a polygon with three vertices and three sides which are straight line segments.
a. Triangle0
b. Thing
c. Undefined
d. Undefined

84. In plane geometry, a _____ is a polygon with four equal sides, four right angles, and parallel opposite sides. In algebra, the _____ of a number is that number multiplied by itself.
a. Thing
b. Square0
c. Undefined
d. Undefined

85. In geometry, an _____ polygon is a polygon which has all sides of the same length.

Chapter 4. THE MEAN-VALUE THEOREM AND APPLICATIONS

  a. Thing
  c. Undefined
  b. Equilateral0
  d. Undefined

86. An _____ is a triangle in which all sides are of equal length.
  a. Thing
  b. Equilateral triangle0
  c. Undefined
  d. Undefined

87. In logic and mathematics, logical _____ (usual symbol and) is a two-place logical operation that results in a value of true if both of its operands are true, otherwise a value of false.
  a. Concept
  b. Conjunction0
  c. Undefined
  d. Undefined

88. A _____ is a symbolic representation denoting a quantity or expression. It often represents an "unknown" quantity that has the potential to change.
  a. Variable0
  b. Thing
  c. Undefined
  d. Undefined

89. The _____ of measurement are a globally standardized and modernized form of the metric system.
  a. Units0
  b. Thing
  c. Undefined
  d. Undefined

90. An _____ triange is a triangle with at least two sides of equal length.
  a. Isosceles0
  b. Thing
  c. Undefined
  d. Undefined

91. In geometry, a _____ is defined as a quadrilateral where all four of its angles are right angles.
  a. Rectangle0
  b. Thing
  c. Undefined
  d. Undefined

92. A _____ is a set of numbers that designate location in a given reference system, such as x,y in a planar _____ system or an x,y,z in a three-dimensional _____ system.
  a. Coordinate0
  b. Thing
  c. Undefined
  d. Undefined

93. In mathematics and its applications, a _____ is a system for assigning an n-tuple of numbers or scalars to each point in an n-dimensional space.
  a. Concept
  b. Coordinate system0
  c. Undefined
  d. Undefined

94. In mathematics, a _____ is the result of multiplying, or an expression that identifies factors to be multiplied.
  a. Product0
  b. Thing
  c. Undefined
  d. Undefined

95. The _____ of a solid object is the three-dimensional concept of how much space it occupies, often quantified numerically.

Chapter 4. THE MEAN-VALUE THEOREM AND APPLICATIONS

a. Thing
b. Volume0
c. Undefined
d. Undefined

96. In classical geometry, a _____ of a circle or sphere is any line segment from its center to its boundary. By extension, the _____ of a circle or sphere is the length of any such segment. The _____ is half the diameter. In science and engineering the term _____ of curvature is commonly used as a synonym for _____.
a. Thing
b. Radius0
c. Undefined
d. Undefined

97. In mathematics, a _____ is a quadric surface, with the following equation in Cartesian coordinates: $(x/_a)^2 + (y/_b)^2 = 1$.
a. Thing
b. Cylinder0
c. Undefined
d. Undefined

98. A _____ surface is the surface or face of a solid on its sides. It can also be defined as any face or surface that is not a base.
a. Lateral0
b. Thing
c. Undefined
d. Undefined

99. _____ is a kind of property which exists as magnitude or multitude. It is among the basic classes of things along with quality, substance, change, and relation.
a. Thing
b. Amount0
c. Undefined
d. Undefined

100. _____ is electromagnetic radiation with a wavelength that is visible to the eye (visible _____) or, in a technical or scientific context, electromagnetic radiation of any wavelength.
a. Light0
b. Thing
c. Undefined
d. Undefined

101. _____ is the distance around a given two-dimensional object. As a general rule, the _____ of a polygon can always be calculated by adding all the length of the sides together. So, the formula for triangles is P = a + b + c, where a, b and c stand for each side of it. For quadrilaterals the equation is P = a + b + c + d. For equilateral polygons, P = na, where n is the number of sides and a is the side length.
a. Perimeter0
b. Thing
c. Undefined
d. Undefined

102. A quadratic equation with real solutions, called roots, which may be real or complex, is given by the _____: $x = \frac{-b \pm \sqrt{b^2 - 4ac}}{2a}$.
a. Quadratic formula0
b. Thing
c. Undefined
d. Undefined

103. In mathematics, a _____ (also spelled reflexion) is a map that transforms an object into its mirror image.
a. Reflection0
b. Concept
c. Undefined
d. Undefined

Chapter 4. THE MEAN-VALUE THEOREM AND APPLICATIONS

104. In the scientific method, an _____ (Latin: ex-+-periri, "of (or from) trying"), is a set of actions and observations, performed in the context of solving a particular problem or question, in order to support or falsify a hypothesis or research concerning phenomena.
   a. Thing
   b. Experiment0
   c. Undefined
   d. Undefined

105. In geometry, the relations of _____ are those such as 'lies on' between points and lines (as in 'point P lies on line L'), and 'intersects' (as in 'line L_1 intersects line L_2', in three-dimensional space). That is, they are the binary relations describing how subsets meet.
   a. Thing
   b. Incidence0
   c. Undefined
   d. Undefined

106. _____ is the transport of people on a trip/journey or the process or time involved in a person or object moving from one location to another.
   a. Thing
   b. Travel0
   c. Undefined
   d. Undefined

107. _____ is a mathematical subject that includes the study of limits, derivatives, integrals, and power series and constitutes a major part of modern university curriculum.
   a. Calculus0
   b. Thing
   c. Undefined
   d. Undefined

108. In set theory and other branches of mathematics, the _____ of a collection of sets is the set that contains everything that belongs to any of the sets, but nothing else.
   a. Union0
   b. Thing
   c. Undefined
   d. Undefined

109. The _____ are the only integral domain whose positive elements are well-ordered, and in which order is preserved by addition. Like the natural numbers, the _____ form a countably infinite set. The set of all _____ is usually denoted in mathematics by a boldface Z .
   a. Thing
   b. Integers0
   c. Undefined
   d. Undefined

110. In mathematics, a set is called _____ if there is a bijection between the set and some set of the form {1, 2, ..., n} where n is a natural number.
   a. Thing
   b. Finite0
   c. Undefined
   d. Undefined

111. The word _____ comes from the 15th Century Latin word discretus which means separate.
   a. Thing
   b. Discrete0
   c. Undefined
   d. Undefined

112. _____ is the application of tools and a processing medium to the transformation of raw materials into finished goods for sale.

Chapter 4. THE MEAN-VALUE THEOREM AND APPLICATIONS 67

  a. Thing
  c. Undefined
  b. Manufacturing0
  d. Undefined

113. _____ is the ability to hold, receive or absorb, or a measure thereof, similar to the concept of volume.
  a. Concept
  c. Undefined
  b. Capacity0
  d. Undefined

114. A _____ signifies a point or points of probability on a subject e.g., the _____ of creativity, which allows for the formation of rule or norm or law by interpretation of the phenomena events that can be created.
  a. Thing
  c. Undefined
  b. Principle0
  d. Undefined

115. In economics, supply and _____ describe market relations between prospective sellers and buyers of a good.
  a. Thing
  c. Undefined
  b. Demand0
  d. Undefined

116. A _____ is a deliberate process for transforming one or more inputs into one or more results.
  a. Calculation0
  c. Undefined
  b. Thing
  d. Undefined

117. In geometry, a _____ is a special kind of point, usually a corner of a polygon, polyhedron, or higher dimensional polytope. In the geometry of curves a _____ is a point of where the first derivative of curvature is zero. In graph theory, a _____ is the fundamental unit out of which graphs are formed
  a. Thing
  c. Undefined
  b. Vertex0
  d. Undefined

118. In Euclidean geometry, a _____ is the set of all points in a plane at a fixed distance, called the radius, from a given point, the center.
  a. Thing
  c. Undefined
  b. Circle0
  d. Undefined

119. _____ is a set, with some particular properties and usually some additional structure, such as the operations of addition or multiplication, for instance.
  a. Thing
  c. Undefined
  b. Space0
  d. Undefined

120. The word _____ comes from the Latin word linearis, which means created by lines.
  a. Linear0
  c. Undefined
  b. Thing
  d. Undefined

121. An _____ is when two lines intersect somewhere on a plane creating a right angle at intersection
  a. Thing
  c. Undefined
  b. Axes0
  d. Undefined

122. In geometry, a _____ is any five-sided polygon.

Chapter 4. THE MEAN-VALUE THEOREM AND APPLICATIONS

    a. Thing
    b. Pentagon0
    c. Undefined
    d. Undefined

123. _____ usually refers to the biological _____ of a population level that can be supported for an organism, given the quantity of food, habitat, water and other life infrastructure present.
    a. Thing
    b. Carrying capacity0
    c. Undefined
    d. Undefined

124. In geometry, a line _____ is a part of a line that is bounded by two end points, and contains every point on the line between its end points.
    a. Segment0
    b. Concept
    c. Undefined
    d. Undefined

125. In mathematics, the _____ of a coordinate system is the point where the axes of the system intersect.
    a. Origin0
    b. Thing
    c. Undefined
    d. Undefined

126. A _____ is a part of a line that is bounded by two end points, and contains every point on the line between its end points.
    a. Line segment0
    b. Thing
    c. Undefined
    d. Undefined

127. In geometry and trigonometry, a _____ is defined as an angle between two straight intersecting lines of ninety degrees, or one-quarter of a circle.
    a. Thing
    b. Right angle0
    c. Undefined
    d. Undefined

128. In geometry, the _____ of an object is a point in some sense in the middle of the object.
    a. Thing
    b. Center0
    c. Undefined
    d. Undefined

129. _____ is a three-dimensional geometric shape formed by straight lines through a fixed point vertex to the points of a fixed curve directrix.
    a. Right circular cone0
    b. Thing
    c. Undefined
    d. Undefined

130. A _____ is a three-dimensional geometric shape formed by straight lines through a fixed point (vertex) to the points of a fixed curve (directrix)
    a. Cone0
    b. Concept
    c. Undefined
    d. Undefined

131. In geometry, two sets are called _____ if one can be transformed into the other by an isometry, i.e., a combination of translations, rotations and reflections.
    a. Congruent0
    b. Thing
    c. Undefined
    d. Undefined

Chapter 4. THE MEAN-VALUE THEOREM AND APPLICATIONS

132. In mathematics, a _____ is a two-dimensional manifold or surface that is perfectly flat.
 a. Plane0
 b. Thing
 c. Undefined
 d. Undefined

133. In physics, _____ is an influence that may cause an object to accelerate. It may be experienced as a lift, a push, or a pull. The actual acceleration of the body is determined by the vector sum of all forces acting on it, known as net _____ or resultant _____.
 a. Force0
 b. Thing
 c. Undefined
 d. Undefined

134. The _____ of a mathematical object is its size: a property by which it can be larger or smaller than other objects of the same kind; in technical terms, an ordering of the class of objects to which it belongs.
 a. Magnitude0
 b. Thing
 c. Undefined
 d. Undefined

135. In mathematics, a _____ is the set of all points in three-dimensional space (R^3) which are at distance r from a fixed point of that space, where r is a positive real number called the radius of the _____. The fixed point is called the center or centre, and is not part of the _____ itself.
 a. Sphere0
 b. Thing
 c. Undefined
 d. Undefined

136. A _____ is a unit of length in the metric system, equal to one thousand metres, the current SI base unit of length
 a. Kilometer0
 b. Thing
 c. Undefined
 d. Undefined

137. _____ has many meanings, most of which simply .
 a. Thing
 b. Power0
 c. Undefined
 d. Undefined

138. In geometry, two lines or planes if one falls on the other in such a way as to create congruent adjacent angles. The term may be used as a noun or adjective. Thus, referring to Figure 1, the line AB is the _____ to CD through the point B.
 a. Perpendicular0
 b. Thing
 c. Undefined
 d. Undefined

139. A _____ is a landform that extends above the surrounding terrain in a limited area. A _____ is generally steeper than a hill, but there is no universally accepted standard definition for the height of a _____ or a hill although a _____ usually has an identifiable summit.
 a. Mountain0
 b. Thing
 c. Undefined
 d. Undefined

140. _____ is the force that opposes the relative motion or tendency toward such motion of two surfaces in contact.
 a. Friction0
 b. Thing
 c. Undefined
 d. Undefined

Chapter 4. THE MEAN-VALUE THEOREM AND APPLICATIONS

141. The _____ is one of the classical simple machines; as the name suggests, it is a flat surface whose endpoints are at different heights. By moving an object up an _____ rather than directly from one height to another, the amount of force required is reduced, at the expense of increasing the distance the object must travel. The mechanical advantage of an _____ is the ratio of the length of the sloped surface to the height it spans; this may also be expressed as the cosecant of the angle between the plane and the horizontal.
- a. Thing
- b. Inclined plane0
- c. Undefined
- d. Undefined

142. In topology and related areas of mathematics a _____ or Moore-Smith sequence is a generalization of a sequence, intended to unify the various notions of limit and generalize them to arbitrary topological spaces.
- a. Net0
- b. Thing
- c. Undefined
- d. Undefined

143. _____ is an accounting term which is commonly used in business.
- a. Net profit0
- b. Thing
- c. Undefined
- d. Undefined

144. In mathematics, an _____, mean, or central tendency of a data set refers to a measure of the "middle" or "expected" value of the data set.
- a. Average0
- b. Concept
- c. Undefined
- d. Undefined

145. _____ is the path a moving object follows through space.
- a. Thing
- b. Projectile motion0
- c. Undefined
- d. Undefined

146. Initial objects are also called _____, and terminal objects are also called final.
- a. Thing
- b. Coterminal0
- c. Undefined
- d. Undefined

147. A _____ is a special kind of ratio, indicating a relationship between two measurements with different units, such as miles to gallons or cents to pounds.
- a. Thing
- b. Rate0
- c. Undefined
- d. Undefined

148. U.S. liquid _____ is legally defined as 231 cubic inches, and is equal to 3.785411784 litres or abotu 0.13368 cubic feet. This is the most common definition of a _____. The U.S. fluid ounce is defined as 1/128 of a U.S. _____.
- a. Thing
- b. Gallon0
- c. Undefined
- d. Undefined

149. In linear algebra, the _____ of an n-by-n square matrix A is defined to be the sum of the elements on the main diagonal of A,
- a. Thing
- b. Trace0
- c. Undefined
- d. Undefined

Chapter 4. THE MEAN-VALUE THEOREM AND APPLICATIONS

150. In mathematics, an _____ .
    a. Thing
    b. Ellipse0
    c. Undefined
    d. Undefined

151. The deductive-nomological model is a formalized view of scientific _____ in natural language.
    a. Thing
    b. Explanation0
    c. Undefined
    d. Undefined

152. In mathematics, the _____ f is the collection of all ordered pairs. In particular, graph means the graphical representation of this collection, in the form of a curve or surface, together with axes, etc. Graphing on a Cartesian plane is sometimes referred to as curve sketching.
    a. Graph of a function0
    b. Thing
    c. Undefined
    d. Undefined

153. The word _____ means curving in or hollowed inward.
    a. Concavity0
    b. Thing
    c. Undefined
    d. Undefined

154. A _____ is a polynomial function of the form f(x) = ax^2 + bx +c , where a, b, c are real numbers and a , 0.
    a. Quadratic function0
    b. Event
    c. Undefined
    d. Undefined

155. In mathematics, the additive inverse, or _____ of a number n is the number that, when added to n, yields zero. The additive inverse of n is denoted −n. For example, 7 is −7, because 7 + (−7) = 0, and the additive inverse of −0.3 is 0.3, because −0.3 + 0.3 = 0.
    a. Thing
    b. Opposite0
    c. Undefined
    d. Undefined

156. In mathematics, the _____ of a number n is the number that, when added to n, yields zero. The _____ of n is denoted −n. For example, 7 is −7, because 7 + (−7) = 0, and the _____ of −0.3 is 0.3, because −0.3 + 0.3 = 0.
    a. Additive inverse0
    b. Thing
    c. Undefined
    d. Undefined

157. In Euclidean geometry, an _____ is a closed segment of a differentiable curve in the two-dimensional plane; for example, a circular _____ is a segment of a circle.
    a. Concept
    b. Arc0
    c. Undefined
    d. Undefined

158. _____ are functions which satisfy particular symmetry relations, with respect to taking additive inverses.
    a. Thing
    b. Even function0
    c. Undefined
    d. Undefined

159. _____ is the middle point of a line segment.
    a. Midpoint0
    b. Thing
    c. Undefined
    d. Undefined

Chapter 4. THE MEAN-VALUE THEOREM AND APPLICATIONS

160. In mathematics, there are several meanings of _____ depending on the subject.
 a. Degree0
 b. Thing
 c. Undefined
 d. Undefined

161. An _____ is a straight line or curve A to which another curve B approaches closer and closer as one moves along it. As one moves along B, the space between it and the _____ A becomes smaller and smaller, and can in fact be made as small as one could wish by going far enough along. A curve may or may not touch or cross its _____. In fact, the curve may intersect the _____ an infinite number of times.
 a. Thing
 b. Asymptote0
 c. Undefined
 d. Undefined

162. _____ is a straight line or curve A to which another curve B the one being studied approaches closer and closer as one moves along it.
 a. Thing
 b. Vertical asymptote0
 c. Undefined
 d. Undefined

163. In mathematics, a _____ is any function which can be written as the ratio of two polynomial functions.
 a. Thing
 b. Rational function0
 c. Undefined
 d. Undefined

164. In geometry, an _____ angle is an angle that is not a 90 degree angle, or an angle that is divisible by 90: 180, 270, 360/0
 a. Oblique0
 b. Thing
 c. Undefined
 d. Undefined

165. _____ means "constancy", i.e. if something retains a certain feature even after we change a way of looking at it, then it is symmetric.
 a. Symmetry0
 b. Thing
 c. Undefined
 d. Undefined

166. In business, particularly accounting, a _____ is the time intervals that the accounts, statement, payments, or other calculations cover.
 a. Thing
 b. Period0
 c. Undefined
 d. Undefined

167. An _____ or an extremal point is a point that belongs to the extremity of something.
 a. Thing
 b. Extreme point0
 c. Undefined
 d. Undefined

168. _____ is the fee paid on borrowed money.
 a. Interest0
 b. Thing
 c. Undefined
 d. Undefined

169. A _____ fraction is a fraction in which the absolute value of the numerator is less than the denominator--hence, the absolute value of the fraction is less than 1.

Chapter 4. THE MEAN-VALUE THEOREM AND APPLICATIONS

a. Thing
b. Proper0
c. Undefined
d. Undefined

170. Graphing on a Cartesian plane is sometimes referred to as _____.
a. Thing
b. Curve sketching0
c. Undefined
d. Undefined

171. A _____ is a function that repeats its values after some definite period has been added to its independent variable.
a. Thing
b. Periodic function0
c. Undefined
d. Undefined

172. In Euclidean geometry, a uniform _____ is a linear transformation that enlargers or diminishes objects, and whose _____ factor is the same in all directions. This is also called homothethy.
a. Thing
b. Scale0
c. Undefined
d. Undefined

173. In mathematics, a _____ is a type of conic section defined as the intersection between a right circular conical surface and a plane which cuts through both halves of the cone.
a. Thing
b. Hyperbola0
c. Undefined
d. Undefined

174. A _____ is a one-dimensional picture in which the integers are shown as specially-marked points evenly spaced on a line.
a. Number line0
b. Thing
c. Undefined
d. Undefined

175. A _____ is a set of possible values that a variable can take on in order to satisfy a given set of conditions, which may include equations and inequalities.
a. Thing
b. Solution set0
c. Undefined
d. Undefined

176. _____ is to give an equation $R(x,y) = S(x,y)$ that at least in part has the same graph as $y = f(x)$.
a. Implicit differentiation0
b. Thing
c. Undefined
d. Undefined

177. A _____ is traditionally an infinitesimally small change in a variable.
a. Thing
b. Differential0
c. Undefined
d. Undefined

178. In mathematics, two quantities are called _____ if they vary in such a way that one of the quantities is a constant multiple of the other, or equivalently if they have a constant ratio.
a. Thing
b. Proportional0
c. Undefined
d. Undefined

179. A _____ is a vehicle, missile or aircraft which obtains thrust by the reaction to the ejection of fast moving fluid from within a _____ engine.
   a. Thing
   b. Rocket0
   c. Undefined
   d. Undefined

180. _____ has one 90° internal angle a right angle.
   a. Thing
   b. Right triangle0
   c. Undefined
   d. Undefined

Chapter 5. INTEGRATION

1. In geometry, a _____ is defined as a quadrilateral where all four of its angles are right angles.
   a. Rectangle0
   b. Thing
   c. Undefined
   d. Undefined

2. In mathematics, an _____ is a statement about the relative size or order of two objects.
   a. Inequality0
   b. Thing
   c. Undefined
   d. Undefined

3. A _____ is the result of the addition of a set of numbers. The numbers may be natural numbers, complex numbers, matrices, or still more complicated objects. An infinite _____ is a subtle procedure known as a series.
   a. Sum0
   b. Thing
   c. Undefined
   d. Undefined

4. In mathematics, an inequality is a statement about the relative size or order of two objects. For example 14 > 10, or 14 is _____ 10.
   a. Greater than0
   b. Thing
   c. Undefined
   d. Undefined

5. A _____ function is a function for which, intuitively, small changes in the input result in small changes in the output.
   a. Continuous0
   b. Event
   c. Undefined
   d. Undefined

6. A _____ is 360° or 2δ radians.
   a. Thing
   b. Turn0
   c. Undefined
   d. Undefined

7. In business, particularly accounting, a _____ is the time intervals that the accounts, statement, payments, or other calculations cover.
   a. Period0
   b. Thing
   c. Undefined
   d. Undefined

8. In mathematics and the mathematical sciences, a _____ is a fixed, but possibly unspecified, value. This is in contrast to a variable, which is not fixed.
   a. Thing
   b. Constant0
   c. Undefined
   d. Undefined

9. In mathematics, a set is called _____ if there is a bijection between the set and some set of the form {1, 2, ..., n} where n is a natural number.
   a. Finite0
   b. Thing
   c. Undefined
   d. Undefined

10. In elementary algebra, an _____ is a set that contains every real number between two indicated numbers and may contain the two numbers themselves.
    a. Interval0
    b. Thing
    c. Undefined
    d. Undefined

11. The _____ of measurement are a globally standardized and modernized form of the metric system.

a. Units0
b. Thing
c. Undefined
d. Undefined

12. The mathematical concept of a _____ expresses the intuitive idea of deterministic dependence between two quantities, one of which is viewed as primary and the other as secondary. A _____ then is a way to associate a unique output for each input of a specified type, for example, a real number or an element of a given set.
   a. Function0
   b. Thing
   c. Undefined
   d. Undefined

13. A _____ is a function for which, intuitively, small changes in the input result in small changes in the output.
   a. Continuous function0
   b. Event
   c. Undefined
   d. Undefined

14. _____ is an extension of the concept of a sum.
   a. Definite integral0
   b. Thing
   c. Undefined
   d. Undefined

15. The _____ of a function is an extension of the concept of a sum, and are identified or found through the use of integration.
   a. Integral0
   b. Thing
   c. Undefined
   d. Undefined

16. _____ is a process of combining or accumulating. It may also refer to:
   a. Integration0
   b. Thing
   c. Undefined
   d. Undefined

17. A _____ is a set whose members are members of another set or a set contained within another set.
   a. Subset0
   b. Thing
   c. Undefined
   d. Undefined

18. The _____, the average in everyday English, which is also called the arithmetic _____ (and is distinguished from the geometric _____ or harmonic _____). The average is also called the sample _____. The expected value of a random variable, which is also called the population _____.
   a. Mean0
   b. Thing
   c. Undefined
   d. Undefined

19. Generally, a _____ is a splitting of something into parts.
   a. Partition0
   b. Thing
   c. Undefined
   d. Undefined

20. In geometry, an _____ is a point at which a line segment or ray terminates.
   a. Endpoint0
   b. Thing
   c. Undefined
   d. Undefined

Chapter 5. INTEGRATION

21. A _____ is a negotiable instrument instructing a financial institution to pay a specific amount of a specific currency from a specific demand account held in the maker/depositor's name with that institution. Both the maker and payee may be natural persons or legal entities.
    a. Check0
    b. Thing
    c. Undefined
    d. Undefined

22. _____ was a German mathematician and philosopher. He invented calculus independently of Newton, and his notation is the one in general use since.
    a. Leibniz0
    b. Person
    c. Undefined
    d. Undefined

23. _____ is a function that extends the concept of an ordinary sum
    a. Thing
    b. Integrand0
    c. Undefined
    d. Undefined

24. A _____ is a symbolic representation denoting a quantity or expression. It often represents an "unknown" quantity that has the potential to change.
    a. Thing
    b. Variable0
    c. Undefined
    d. Undefined

25. An _____ is a combination of numbers, operators, grouping symbols and/or free variables and bound variables arranged in a meaningful way which can be evaluated..
    a. Thing
    b. Expression0
    c. Undefined
    d. Undefined

26. The _____ integers are all the integers from zero on upwards.
    a. Thing
    b. Nonnegative0
    c. Undefined
    d. Undefined

27. _____ is a method for approximating the values of integrals.
    a. Thing
    b. Riemann sum0
    c. Undefined
    d. Undefined

28. _____ are objects, characters, or other concrete representations of ideas, concepts, or other abstractions.
    a. Thing
    b. Symbols0
    c. Undefined
    d. Undefined

29. In mathematics, the concept of a _____ tries to capture the intuitive idea of a geometrical one-dimensional and continuous object. A simple example is the circle.
    a. Curve0
    b. Thing
    c. Undefined
    d. Undefined

30. _____ the expected value of a random variable displays the average or central value of the variable. It is a summary value of the distribution of the variable.

a. Thing
b. Determining0
c. Undefined
d. Undefined

31. In mathematical analysis and related areas of mathematics, a set is called _____, if it is, in a certain sense, of finite size.
a. Thing
b. Bounded0
c. Undefined
d. Undefined

32. Continuous functions are of utmost importance in mathematics and applications. However, not all functions are continuous. If a function is not continuous at a point in its domain, one says that it has a _____ there. The set of all points of _____ of a function may be a discrete set, a dense set, or even the entire domain of the function.
a. Thing
b. Discontinuity0
c. Undefined
d. Undefined

33. In mathematics, a _____ function in the sense of algebraic geometry is an everywhere-defined, polynomial function on an algebraic variety V with values in the field K over which V is defined.
a. Thing
b. Regular0
c. Undefined
d. Undefined

34. The _____ are the only integral domain whose positive elements are well-ordered, and in which order is preserved by addition. Like the natural numbers, the _____ form a countably infinite set. The set of all _____ is usually denoted in mathematics by a boldface Z.
a. Thing
b. Integers0
c. Undefined
d. Undefined

35. _____ is a method of mathematical proof typically used to establish that a given statement is true of all natural numbers
a. Mathematical induction0
b. Thing
c. Undefined
d. Undefined

36. In plane geometry, a _____ is a polygon with four equal sides, four right angles, and parallel opposite sides. In algebra, the _____ of a number is that number multiplied by itself.
a. Thing
b. Square0
c. Undefined
d. Undefined

37. A _____ defined function f(x) of a real variable x is a function whose definition is given differently on disjoint subsets of its domain.
a. Piecewise0
b. Thing
c. Undefined
d. Undefined

38. In mathematics, a _____ occurs if there is a bijection between the set and some set of the form 1, 2, ..., n where n is a natural number.
a. Concept
b. Finite set0
c. Undefined
d. Undefined

39. _____ is the middle point of a line segment.

Chapter 5. INTEGRATION

a. Midpoint0
b. Thing
c. Undefined
d. Undefined

40. In mathematics, a _____ is a statement that can be proved on the basis of explicitly stated or previously agreed assumptions.
   a. Thing
   b. Theorem0
   c. Undefined
   d. Undefined

41. _____ is a mathematical subject that includes the study of limits, derivatives, integrals, and power series and constitutes a major part of modern university curriculum.
   a. Thing
   b. Calculus0
   c. Undefined
   d. Undefined

42. In number theory, the _____ of arithmetic (or unique factorization theorem) states that every natural number greater than 1 can be written as a unique product of prime numbers.
   a. Fundamental theorem0
   b. Concept
   c. Undefined
   d. Undefined

43. In mathematics, the _____ inverse, or opposite, of a number n is the number that, when added to n, yields zero. The _____ inverse of n is denoted −n.
   a. Thing
   b. Additive0
   c. Undefined
   d. Undefined

44. In mathematics, a _____ is a demonstration that, assuming certain axioms, some statement is necessarily true.
   a. Proof0
   b. Thing
   c. Undefined
   d. Undefined

45. The _____ is a measurement of how a function changes when the values of its inputs change.
   a. Thing
   b. Derivative0
   c. Undefined
   d. Undefined

46. In mathematics, a _____ may be described informally as a number that can be given by an infinite decimal representation.
   a. Real number0
   b. Thing
   c. Undefined
   d. Undefined

47. _____ is often used to describe the measurement of the steepness, incline, gradient, or grade of a straight line. The _____ is defined as the ratio of the "rise" divided by the "run" between two points on a line, or in other words, the ratio of the altitude change to the horizontal distance between any two points on the line.
   a. Thing
   b. Slope0
   c. Undefined
   d. Undefined

48. An _____ is a straight line or curve A to which another curve B approaches closer and closer as one moves along it. As one moves along B, the space between it and the _____ A becomes smaller and smaller, and can in fact be made as small as one could wish by going far enough along. A curve may or may not touch or cross its _____. In fact, the curve may intersect the _____ an infinite number of times.

Chapter 5. INTEGRATION

    a. Thing
    b. Asymptote0
    c. Undefined
    d. Undefined

49. In mathematics, the _____ of a coordinate system is the point where the axes of the system intersect.
    a. Thing
    b. Origin0
    c. Undefined
    d. Undefined

50. In astronomy, geography, geometry and related sciences and contexts, a plane is said to be _____ at a given point if it is locally perpendicular to the gradient of the gravity field, i.e., with the direction of the gravitational force at that point.
    a. Horizontal0
    b. Thing
    c. Undefined
    d. Undefined

51. The word _____ means curving in or hollowed inward.
    a. Concavity0
    b. Thing
    c. Undefined
    d. Undefined

52. In mathematics, a _____ is the result of multiplying, or an expression that identifies factors to be multiplied.
    a. Thing
    b. Product0
    c. Undefined
    d. Undefined

53. In mathematics, a _____ is the end result of a division problem. It can also be expressed as the number of times the divisor divides into the dividend.
    a. Quotient0
    b. Thing
    c. Undefined
    d. Undefined

54. _____ means "constancy", i.e. if something retains a certain feature even after we change a way of looking at it, then it is symmetric.
    a. Thing
    b. Symmetry0
    c. Undefined
    d. Undefined

55. In mathematics, a _____ of a positive integer n is a way of writing n as a sum of positive integers.
    a. Composition0
    b. Thing
    c. Undefined
    d. Undefined

56. An _____ of a function f is a function F whose derivative is equal to f, i.e., F' = f.
    a. Thing
    b. Antiderivative0
    c. Undefined
    d. Undefined

57. Mathematical _____ is used to represent ideas.
    a. Thing
    b. Notation0
    c. Undefined
    d. Undefined

58. In mathematics, a _____ number is a number which can be expressed as a ratio of two integers. Non-integer _____ numbers (commonly called fractions) are usually written as the vulgar fraction a / b, where b is not zero.

Chapter 5. INTEGRATION

    a. Rational0
    b. Thing
    c. Undefined
    d. Undefined

59. _____, a field in mathematics, is the study of how functions change when their inputs change. The primary object of study in _____ is the derivative.
    a. Differential calculus0
    b. Thing
    c. Undefined
    d. Undefined

60. _____ in calculus is primitive or indefinite integral of a function f is a function F whose derivative is equal to f, i.e., F Œ = f. The process of solving for antiderivatives is _____.
    a. Antidifferentiation0
    b. Thing
    c. Undefined
    d. Undefined

61. In combinatorial mathematics, a _____ is an un-ordered collection of unique elements.
    a. Combination0
    b. Concept
    c. Undefined
    d. Undefined

62. The word _____ comes from the Latin word linearis, which means created by lines.
    a. Thing
    b. Linear0
    c. Undefined
    d. Undefined

63. In statistics, a _____ measure is one which is measuring what is supposed to measure.
    a. Valid0
    b. Thing
    c. Undefined
    d. Undefined

64. A _____ is a deliberate process for transforming one or more inputs into one or more results.
    a. Thing
    b. Calculation0
    c. Undefined
    d. Undefined

65. In acoustics and telecommunication, the _____ of a wave is a component frequency of the signal that is an integer multiple of the fundamental frequency.
    a. Thing
    b. Harmonic0
    c. Undefined
    d. Undefined

66. Simple _____ is the motion of a simple harmonic oscillator, a motion that is neither driven nor damped. Complex _____ is the superposition — linear combination — of several simultaneous simple harmonic motions.
    a. Thing
    b. Harmonic motion0
    c. Undefined
    d. Undefined

67. In economics, economic _____ is simply a state of the world where economic forces are balanced and in the absence of external influences the values of economic variables will not change.
    a. Equilibrium0
    b. Thing
    c. Undefined
    d. Undefined

68. _____ are the basic objects of study in graph theory. Informally speaking, a graph is a set of objects called points, nodes, or vertices connected by links called lines or edges.

Chapter 5. INTEGRATION

a. Thing
b. Graphs0
c. Undefined
d. Undefined

69. In mathematics, _____ are the intuitive idea of a geometrical one-dimensional and continuous object.
   a. Curves0
   b. Thing
   c. Undefined
   d. Undefined

70. In geometry, two sets are called _____ if one can be transformed into the other by an isometry, i.e., a combination of translations, rotations and reflections.
   a. Congruent0
   b. Thing
   c. Undefined
   d. Undefined

71. _____ of calculus is the statement that the two central operations of calculus, differentiation and integration, are inverse operations: if a continuous function is first integrated and then differentiated, the original function is retrieved.
   a. Fundamental Theorem of Calculus0
   b. Thing
   c. Undefined
   d. Undefined

72. _____ is the fee paid on borrowed money.
   a. Interest0
   b. Thing
   c. Undefined
   d. Undefined

73. In calculus, the indefinite integral of a given function i.e. the set of all antiderivatives of the function is always written with a constant, the _____.
   a. Constant of integration0
   b. Thing
   c. Undefined
   d. Undefined

74. Initial objects are also called _____, and terminal objects are also called final.
   a. Coterminal0
   b. Thing
   c. Undefined
   d. Undefined

75. A _____ is a set of numbers that designate location in a given reference system, such as x,y in a planar _____ system or an x,y,z in a three-dimensional _____ system.
   a. Thing
   b. Coordinate0
   c. Undefined
   d. Undefined

76. _____ of an object is its speed in a particular direction.
   a. Thing
   b. Velocity0
   c. Undefined
   d. Undefined

77. In mathematics, the _____ (or modulus) of a real number is its numerical value without regard to its sign.
   a. Absolute value0
   b. Thing
   c. Undefined
   d. Undefined

78. _____ is defined as the rate of change or derivative with respect to time of velocity.

Chapter 5. INTEGRATION

    a. Acceleration0
    b. Thing
    c. Undefined
    d. Undefined

79. A _____ is a special kind of ratio, indicating a relationship between two measurements with different units, such as miles to gallons or cents to pounds.
    a. Thing
    b. Rate0
    c. Undefined
    d. Undefined

80. _____ is the transport of people on a trip/journey or the process or time involved in a person or object moving from one location to another.
    a. Thing
    b. Travel0
    c. Undefined
    d. Undefined

81. _____ was an Italian physicist, mathematician, astronomer, and philosopher who is closely associated with the scientific revolution.
    a. Galileo Galilei0
    b. Person
    c. Undefined
    d. Undefined

82. A _____ is a unit of length, usually used to measure distance, in a number of different systems, including Imperial units, United States customary units and Norwegian/Swedish mil. Its size can vary from system to system, but in each is between 1 and 10 kilometers. In contemporary English contexts _____ refers to either:
    a. Thing
    b. Mile0
    c. Undefined
    d. Undefined

83. In mathematics, a _____ is a two-dimensional manifold or surface that is perfectly flat.
    a. Thing
    b. Plane0
    c. Undefined
    d. Undefined

84. _____ are a measure of time.
    a. Minutes0
    b. Thing
    c. Undefined
    d. Undefined

85. In calculus, the _____ is a formula for the derivative of the composite of two functions.
    a. Concept
    b. Chain rule0
    c. Undefined
    d. Undefined

86. _____ has many meanings, most of which simply .
    a. Thing
    b. Power0
    c. Undefined
    d. Undefined

87. A _____ is traditionally an infinitesimally small change in a variable.
    a. Differential0
    b. Thing
    c. Undefined
    d. Undefined

88. _____ is a trigonemtric function that is important when studying triangles and modeling periodic phenomena, among other applications.

a. Thing
b. Sine0
c. Undefined
d. Undefined

89. A _____ is a set of possible values that a variable can take on in order to satisfy a given set of conditions, which may include equations and inequalities.
    a. Solution set0
    b. Thing
    c. Undefined
    d. Undefined

90. A _____ fraction is a fraction in which the absolute value of the numerator is less than the denominator--hence, the absolute value of the fraction is less than 1.
    a. Thing
    b. Proper0
    c. Undefined
    d. Undefined

91. In Euclidean geometry, a _____ is the set of all points in a plane at a fixed distance, called the radius, from a given point, the center.
    a. Thing
    b. Circle0
    c. Undefined
    d. Undefined

92. In classical geometry, a _____ of a circle or sphere is any line segment from its center to its boundary. By extension, the _____ of a circle or sphere is the length of any such segment. The _____ is half the diameter. In science and engineering the term _____ of curvature is commonly used as a synonym for _____.
    a. Thing
    b. Radius0
    c. Undefined
    d. Undefined

93. A _____ consists of one quarter of the coordinate plane.
    a. Thing
    b. Quadrant0
    c. Undefined
    d. Undefined

94. In mathematics, an _____ .
    a. Thing
    b. Ellipse0
    c. Undefined
    d. Undefined

95. In mathematics, the conjugate _____ or adjoint matrix of an m-by-n matrix A with complex entries is the n-by-m matrix A* obtained from A by taking the transpose and then taking the complex conjugate of each entry.
    a. Pairs0
    b. Thing
    c. Undefined
    d. Undefined

96. Equivalence is the condition of being _____ or essentially equal.
    a. Thing
    b. Equivalent0
    c. Undefined
    d. Undefined

97. In mathematics, a _____ of a k-place relation $L \subseteq X_1 \times ... \times X_k$ is one of the sets X_j, $1 \leq j \leq k$. In the special case where k = 2 and $L \subseteq X_1 \times X_2$ is a function $L : X_1 \to X_2$, it is conventional to refer to X_1 as the _____ of the function and to refer to X_2 as the codomain of the function.

Chapter 5. INTEGRATION

a. Domain0
b. Thing
c. Undefined
d. Undefined

98. In mathematics, an _____, mean, or central tendency of a data set refers to a measure of the "middle" or "expected" value of the data set.
a. Average0
b. Concept
c. Undefined
d. Undefined

99. In linear algebra, the _____ of an n-by-n square matrix A is defined to be the sum of the elements on the main diagonal of A,
a. Thing
b. Trace0
c. Undefined
d. Undefined

100. _____ are functions which satisfy particular symmetry relations, with respect to taking additive inverses.
a. Even function0
b. Thing
c. Undefined
d. Undefined

101. An _____ is an equality that remains true regardless of the values of any variables that appear within it, to distinguish it from an equality which is true under more particular conditions.
a. Identity0
b. Thing
c. Undefined
d. Undefined

102. _____ is the property of a physical object that quantifies the amount of matter and energy it is equivalent to.
a. Mass0
b. Thing
c. Undefined
d. Undefined

103. _____ is mass m per unit volume V.
a. Thing
b. Density0
c. Undefined
d. Undefined

104. In geometry, the _____ of an object is a point in some sense in the middle of the object.
a. Thing
b. Center0
c. Undefined
d. Undefined

105. In physics, the _____ of a system of particles is a specific point at which, for many purposes, the system's mass behaves as if it were concentrated.
a. Thing
b. Center of mass0
c. Undefined
d. Undefined

106. A _____ is any object propelled through space by the applicationp of a force.
a. Projectile0
b. Thing
c. Undefined
d. Undefined

107. In mathematics, the _____ is a conic section generated by the intersection of a right circular conical surface and a plane parallel to a generating straight line of that surface. It can also be defined as locus of points in a plane which are equidistant from a given point.

a. Thing
b. Parabola0
c. Undefined
d. Undefined

108. In mathematics, the _____ of a function is the set of all "output" values produced by that function. Given a function $f : A \to B$, the _____ of f, is defined to be the set $\{x \in B : x = f(a) \text{ for some } a \in A\}$.
   a. Range0
   b. Thing
   c. Undefined
   d. Undefined

109. The _____ or kilogramme is the SI base unit of mass. It is defined as being equal to the mass of the international prototype of the _____.
   a. Kilogram0
   b. Thing
   c. Undefined
   d. Undefined

110. The metre (or _____, see spelling differences) is a measure of length. It is the basic unit of length in the metric system and in the International System of Units (SI), used around the world for general and scientific purposes.
   a. Concept
   b. Meter0
   c. Undefined
   d. Undefined

111. In mathematics, a _____ of a number x is a number r such that $r^2 = x$, or in words, a number r whose square (the result of multiplying the number by itself) is x.
   a. Thing
   b. Square root0
   c. Undefined
   d. Undefined

112. In mathematics, a _____ of a complex-valued function f is a member x of the domain of f such that f(x) vanishes at x, that is, $x : f(x) = 0$.
   a. Thing
   b. Root0
   c. Undefined
   d. Undefined

113. _____ or arithmetics is the oldest and most elementary branch of mathematics, used by almost everyone, for tasks ranging from simple daily counting to advanced science and business calculations.
   a. Thing
   b. Arithmetic0
   c. Undefined
   d. Undefined

114. In mathematics and its applications, a _____ is a system for assigning an n-tuple of numbers or scalars to each point in an n-dimensional space.
   a. Coordinate system0
   b. Concept
   c. Undefined
   d. Undefined

115. In mathematics, the _____ of two sets A and B is the set that contains all elements of A that also belong to B (or equivalently, all elements of B that also belong to A), but no other elements.
   a. Thing
   b. Intersection0
   c. Undefined
   d. Undefined

Chapter 6. APPLICATIONS OF THE INTEGRAL

1. In elementary algebra, an _____ is a set that contains every real number between two indicated numbers and may contain the two numbers themselves.
   a. Thing
   b. Interval0
   c. Undefined
   d. Undefined

2. In mathematics, a _____ is the result of multiplying, or an expression that identifies factors to be multiplied.
   a. Thing
   b. Product0
   c. Undefined
   d. Undefined

3. In mathematics, the _____ f is the collection of all ordered pairs. In particular, graph means the graphical representation of this collection, in the form of a curve or surface, together with axes, etc. Graphing on a Cartesian plane is sometimes referred to as curve sketching.
   a. Graph of a function0
   b. Thing
   c. Undefined
   d. Undefined

4. In geometry, a _____ is defined as a quadrilateral where all four of its angles are right angles.
   a. Rectangle0
   b. Thing
   c. Undefined
   d. Undefined

5. In mathematics, the concept of a _____ tries to capture the intuitive idea of a geometrical one-dimensional and continuous object. A simple example is the circle.
   a. Thing
   b. Curve0
   c. Undefined
   d. Undefined

6. In mathematical analysis and related areas of mathematics, a set is called _____, if it is, in a certain sense, of finite size.
   a. Thing
   b. Bounded0
   c. Undefined
   d. Undefined

7. The mathematical concept of a _____ expresses the intuitive idea of deterministic dependence between two quantities, one of which is viewed as primary and the other as secondary. A _____ then is a way to associate a unique output for each input of a specified type, for example, a real number or an element of a given set.
   a. Thing
   b. Function0
   c. Undefined
   d. Undefined

8. A _____ is the result of the addition of a set of numbers. The numbers may be natural numbers, complex numbers, matrices, or still more complicated objects. An infinite _____ is a subtle procedure known as a series.
   a. Thing
   b. Sum0
   c. Undefined
   d. Undefined

9. In astronomy, geography, geometry and related sciences and contexts, a plane is said to be _____ at a given point if it is locally perpendicular to the gradient of the gravity field, i.e., with the direction of the gravitational force at that point.
   a. Thing
   b. Horizontal0
   c. Undefined
   d. Undefined

10. The _____ of a function is an extension of the concept of a sum, and are identified or found through the use of integration.

Chapter 6. APPLICATIONS OF THE INTEGRAL

    a. Thing
    b. Integral0
    c. Undefined
    d. Undefined

11. _____ is a method for approximating the values of integrals.
    a. Thing
    b. Riemann sum0
    c. Undefined
    d. Undefined

12. In mathematics, the _____ of two sets A and B is the set that contains all elements of A that also belong to B (or equivalently, all elements of B that also belong to A), but no other elements.
    a. Intersection0
    b. Thing
    c. Undefined
    d. Undefined

13. In mathematics, _____ are the intuitive idea of a geometrical one-dimensional and continuous object.
    a. Curves0
    b. Thing
    c. Undefined
    d. Undefined

14. _____ are functions which satisfy particular symmetry relations, with respect to taking additive inverses.
    a. Even function0
    b. Thing
    c. Undefined
    d. Undefined

15. _____ is a function that extends the concept of an ordinary sum
    a. Thing
    b. Integrand0
    c. Undefined
    d. Undefined

16. In mathematics, the _____ is a conic section generated by the intersection of a right circular conical surface and a plane parallel to a generating straight line of that surface. It can also be defined as locus of points in a plane which are equidistant from a given point.
    a. Parabola0
    b. Thing
    c. Undefined
    d. Undefined

17. In mathematics, the _____ of a function is the set of all "output" values produced by that function. Given a function $f : A \to B$, the _____ of f, is defined to be the set $\{x \in B : x = f(a) \text{ for some } a \in A\}$.
    a. Thing
    b. Range0
    c. Undefined
    d. Undefined

18. _____ is a trigonemtric function that is important when studying triangles and modeling periodic phenomena, among other applications.
    a. Thing
    b. Sine0
    c. Undefined
    d. Undefined

19. _____ are the basic objects of study in graph theory. Informally speaking, a graph is a set of objects called points, nodes, or vertices connected by links called lines or edges.
    a. Graphs0
    b. Thing
    c. Undefined
    d. Undefined

Chapter 6. APPLICATIONS OF THE INTEGRAL

20. A _____ is one of the basic shapes of geometry: a polygon with three vertices and three sides which are straight line segments.
    a. Triangle0
    b. Thing
    c. Undefined
    d. Undefined

21. In geometry, a _____ is a special kind of point, usually a corner of a polygon, polyhedron, or higher dimensional polytope. In the geometry of curves a _____ is a point of where the first derivative of curvature is zero. In graph theory, a _____ is the fundamental unit out of which graphs are formed
    a. Vertex0
    b. Thing
    c. Undefined
    d. Undefined

22. _____ is a process of combining or accumulating. It may also refer to:
    a. Thing
    b. Integration0
    c. Undefined
    d. Undefined

23. A _____ is a quadrilateral, which is defined as a shape with four sides, which has a pair of parallel sides.
    a. Thing
    b. Trapezoid0
    c. Undefined
    d. Undefined

24. In mathematics and the mathematical sciences, a _____ is a fixed, but possibly unspecified, value. This is in contrast to a variable, which is not fixed.
    a. Thing
    b. Constant0
    c. Undefined
    d. Undefined

25. _____ is an extension of the concept of a sum.
    a. Definite integral0
    b. Thing
    c. Undefined
    d. Undefined

26. A _____ consists of one quarter of the coordinate plane.
    a. Quadrant0
    b. Thing
    c. Undefined
    d. Undefined

27. In Euclidean geometry, a _____ is the set of all points in a plane at a fixed distance, called the radius, from a given point, the center.
    a. Thing
    b. Circle0
    c. Undefined
    d. Undefined

28. In geometry, a _____ is the intersection of a body in 2-dimensional space with a line, or of a body in 3-dimensional space with a plane
    a. Thing
    b. Cross section0
    c. Undefined
    d. Undefined

29. A _____ is a quantity that denotes the proportional amount or magnitude of one quantity relative to another.
    a. Thing
    b. Ratio0
    c. Undefined
    d. Undefined

Chapter 6. APPLICATIONS OF THE INTEGRAL

30. A _____ is a set of numbers that designate location in a given reference system, such as x,y in a planar _____ system or an x,y,z in a three-dimensional _____ system.
    a. Thing
    b. Coordinate0
    c. Undefined
    d. Undefined

31. An _____ is when two lines intersect somewhere on a plane creating a right angle at intersection
    a. Axes0
    b. Thing
    c. Undefined
    d. Undefined

32. A _____ is a function that assigns a number to subsets of a given set.
    a. Thing
    b. Measure0
    c. Undefined
    d. Undefined

33. In mathematical analysis, _____ are objects which generalize functions and probability distributions.
    a. Thing
    b. Distribution0
    c. Undefined
    d. Undefined

34. A _____ function is a function for which, intuitively, small changes in the input result in small changes in the output.
    a. Continuous0
    b. Event
    c. Undefined
    d. Undefined

35. Two mathematical objects are equal if and only if they are precisely the same in every way. This defines a binary relation, _____, denoted by the sign of _____ "=" in such a way that the statement "x = y" means that x and y are equal.
    a. Thing
    b. Equality0
    c. Undefined
    d. Undefined

36. In mathematics, a _____ is a constant multiplicative factor of a certain object. The object can be such things as a variable, a vector, a function, etc. For example, the _____ of $9x^2$ is 9.
    a. Coefficient0
    b. Thing
    c. Undefined
    d. Undefined

37. The word _____ is used in a variety of ways in mathematics.
    a. Index0
    b. Thing
    c. Undefined
    d. Undefined

38. In mathematics, an _____ is a statement about the relative size or order of two objects.
    a. Thing
    b. Inequality0
    c. Undefined
    d. Undefined

39. _____ is a synonym for information.
    a. Thing
    b. Data0
    c. Undefined
    d. Undefined

40. The _____ of a ring R is defined to be the smallest positive integer n such that $n\, a = 0$, for all a in R.

Chapter 6. APPLICATIONS OF THE INTEGRAL

a. Thing
b. Characteristic0
c. Undefined
d. Undefined

41. In mathematics, _____ geometry was the traditional name for the geometry of three-dimensional Euclidean space — for practical purposes the kind of space we live in.
a. Solid0
b. Thing
c. Undefined
d. Undefined

42. In mathematics, a _____ is a quadric surface, with the following equation in Cartesian coordinates: $(x/_a)^2 + (y/_b)^2 = 1$.
a. Thing
b. Cylinder0
c. Undefined
d. Undefined

43. An _____ is a straight line around which a geometric figure can be rotated.
a. Axis0
b. Thing
c. Undefined
d. Undefined

44. In geometry, two lines or planes if one falls on the other in such a way as to create congruent adjacent angles. The term may be used as a noun or adjective. Thus, referring to Figure 1, the line AB is the _____ to CD through the point B.
a. Perpendicular0
b. Thing
c. Undefined
d. Undefined

45. In mathematics, a _____ is a two-dimensional manifold or surface that is perfectly flat.
a. Thing
b. Plane0
c. Undefined
d. Undefined

46. The _____ of a solid object is the three-dimensional concept of how much space it occupies, often quantified numerically.
a. Thing
b. Volume0
c. Undefined
d. Undefined

47. In mathematics, a _____ is a demonstration that, assuming certain axioms, some statement is necessarily true.
a. Thing
b. Proof0
c. Undefined
d. Undefined

48. Generally, a _____ is a splitting of something into parts.
a. Thing
b. Partition0
c. Undefined
d. Undefined

49. In mathematics, an _____, mean, or central tendency of a data set refers to a measure of the "middle" or "expected" value of the data set.
a. Concept
b. Average0
c. Undefined
d. Undefined

Chapter 6. APPLICATIONS OF THE INTEGRAL

50. The _____, the average in everyday English, which is also called the arithmetic _____ (and is distinguished from the geometric _____ or harmonic _____). The average is also called the sample _____. The expected value of a random variable, which is also called the population _____.
   a. Thing
   b. Mean0
   c. Undefined
   d. Undefined

51. In mathematics, a _____ is a statement that can be proved on the basis of explicitly stated or previously agreed assumptions.
   a. Thing
   b. Theorem0
   c. Undefined
   d. Undefined

52. In plane geometry, a _____ is a polygon with four equal sides, four right angles, and parallel opposite sides. In algebra, the _____ of a number is that number multiplied by itself.
   a. Thing
   b. Square0
   c. Undefined
   d. Undefined

53. In mathematics, an _____ .
   a. Thing
   b. Ellipse0
   c. Undefined
   d. Undefined

54. In geometry, an _____ of a triangle is a straight line through a vertex and perpendicular to (i.e. forming a right angle with) the opposite side or an extension of the opposite side.
   a. Altitude0
   b. Concept
   c. Undefined
   d. Undefined

55. An _____ triange is a triangle with at least two sides of equal length.
   a. Isosceles0
   b. Thing
   c. Undefined
   d. Undefined

56. In classical geometry, a _____ of a circle or sphere is any line segment from its center to its boundary. By extension, the _____ of a circle or sphere is the length of any such segment. The _____ is half the diameter. In science and engineering the term _____ of curvature is commonly used as a synonym for _____.
   a. Radius0
   b. Thing
   c. Undefined
   d. Undefined

57. In mathematics, a _____ is the set of all points in three-dimensional space (R^3) which are at distance r from a fixed point of that space, where r is a positive real number called the radius of the _____. The fixed point is called the center or centre, and is not part of the _____ itself.
   a. Sphere0
   b. Thing
   c. Undefined
   d. Undefined

58. A _____ is a three-dimensional geometric shape formed by straight lines through a fixed point (vertex) to the points of a fixed curve (directrix)
   a. Concept
   b. Cone0
   c. Undefined
   d. Undefined

Chapter 6. APPLICATIONS OF THE INTEGRAL

59. In geometry, an _____ polygon is a polygon which has all sides of the same length.
   a. Thing
   b. Equilateral0
   c. Undefined
   d. Undefined

60. An _____ is a triangle in which all sides are of equal length.
   a. Thing
   b. Equilateral triangle0
   c. Undefined
   d. Undefined

61. The _____ of a right triangle is the triangle's longest side; the side opposite the right angle.
   a. Hypotenuse0
   b. Thing
   c. Undefined
   d. Undefined

62. _____ has one 90° internal angle a right angle.
   a. Right triangle0
   b. Thing
   c. Undefined
   d. Undefined

63. _____ is the portion of a solid – normally a cone or pyramid – which lies between two parallel planes cutting the solid.
   a. Truncated pyramid0
   b. Thing
   c. Undefined
   d. Undefined

64. _____ is a three-dimensional geometric shape formed by straight lines through a fixed point vertex to the points of a fixed curve directrix.
   a. Right circular cone0
   b. Thing
   c. Undefined
   d. Undefined

65. The _____ of measurement are a globally standardized and modernized form of the metric system.
   a. Units0
   b. Thing
   c. Undefined
   d. Undefined

66. The _____ is an imaginary line on the Earth's surface equidistant from the North Pole and South Pole.
   a. Thing
   b. Equator0
   c. Undefined
   d. Undefined

67. In mathematics, _____ are two-dimensional manifolds or surfaces that are perfectly flat.
   a. Planes0
   b. Thing
   c. Undefined
   d. Undefined

68. In geometry, a _____ (Greek words diairo = divide and metro = measure) of a circle is any straight line segment that passes through the centre and whose endpoints are on the circular boundary, or, in more modern usage, the length of such a line segment. When using the word in the more modern sense, one speaks of the _____ rather than a _____, because all diameters of a circle have the same length. This length is twice the radius. The _____ of a circle is also the longest chord that the circle has.
   a. Diameter0
   b. Thing
   c. Undefined
   d. Undefined

94   *Chapter 6. APPLICATIONS OF THE INTEGRAL*

69. _____ are a measure of time.
    a. Minutes0
    b. Thing
    c. Undefined
    d. Undefined

70. _____ is the state of being greater than any finite real or natural number, however large.
    a. Infinite0
    b. Thing
    c. Undefined
    d. Undefined

71. In mathematics, a set is called _____ if there is a bijection between the set and some set of the form {1, 2, ..., n} where n is a natural number.
    a. Finite0
    b. Thing
    c. Undefined
    d. Undefined

72. The _____ integers are all the integers from zero on upwards.
    a. Nonnegative0
    b. Thing
    c. Undefined
    d. Undefined

73. A _____ is a movement of an object in a circular motion. A two-dimensional object rotates around a center (or point) of _____. A three-dimensional object rotates around a line called an axis. If the axis of _____ is within the body, the body is said to rotate upon itself, or spin—which implies relative speed and perhaps free-movement with angular momentum. A circular motion about an external point, e.g. the Earth about the Sun, is called an orbit or more properly an orbital revolution.
    a. Thing
    b. Rotation0
    c. Undefined
    d. Undefined

74. A _____ is a function for which, intuitively, small changes in the input result in small changes in the output.
    a. Event
    b. Continuous function0
    c. Undefined
    d. Undefined

75. In geometry, a line _____ is a part of a line that is bounded by two end points, and contains every point on the line between its end points.
    a. Concept
    b. Segment0
    c. Undefined
    d. Undefined

76. _____ is a means of calculating the volume of a solid of revolution, when integrating along an axis perpendicular to the axis of revolution.
    a. Shell method0
    b. Thing
    c. Undefined
    d. Undefined

77. A _____ surface is the surface or face of a solid on its sides. It can also be defined as any face or surface that is not a base.
    a. Lateral0
    b. Thing
    c. Undefined
    d. Undefined

78. A _____ is a part of a line that is bounded by two end points, and contains every point on the line between its end points.

Chapter 6. APPLICATIONS OF THE INTEGRAL

    a. Thing
    b. Line segment0
    c. Undefined
    d. Undefined

79. In topology, the _____ are subsets S of a topological space X is the set of points which can be approached both from S and from the outside of S.
    a. Boundaries0
    b. Thing
    c. Undefined
    d. Undefined

80. A _____ is a deliberate process for transforming one or more inputs into one or more results.
    a. Thing
    b. Calculation0
    c. Undefined
    d. Undefined

81. In geometry, the _____ of an object is a point in some sense in the middle of the object.
    a. Thing
    b. Center0
    c. Undefined
    d. Undefined

82. An _____ of a function f is a function F whose derivative is equal to f, i.e., F' = f.
    a. Antiderivative0
    b. Thing
    c. Undefined
    d. Undefined

83. In geometry, a _____ is a surface of revolution generated by revolving a circle in three dimensional space about an axis coplanar with the circle, which does not touch the circle. Examples of tori include the surfaces of doughnuts and inner tubes. A circle rotated about a chord of the circle is called a _____ in some contexts, but this is not a common usage in mathematics. The shape produced when a circle is rotated about a chord resembles a round cushion. _____ was the Latin word for a cushion of this shape.
    a. Thing
    b. Torus0
    c. Undefined
    d. Undefined

84. _____ is a mathematical subject that includes the study of limits, derivatives, integrals, and power series and constitutes a major part of modern university curriculum.
    a. Thing
    b. Calculus0
    c. Undefined
    d. Undefined

85. In number theory, the _____ of arithmetic (or unique factorization theorem) states that every natural number greater than 1 can be written as a unique product of prime numbers.
    a. Concept
    b. Fundamental theorem0
    c. Undefined
    d. Undefined

86. _____ of calculus is the statement that the two central operations of calculus, differentiation and integration, are inverse operations: if a continuous function is first integrated and then differentiated, the original function is retrieved.
    a. Thing
    b. Fundamental Theorem of Calculus0
    c. Undefined
    d. Undefined

87. In physics, the _____ of a system of particles is a specific point at which, for many purposes, the system's mass behaves as if it were concentrated.

96   Chapter 6. APPLICATIONS OF THE INTEGRAL

    a. Thing
    c. Undefined
    b. Center of mass0
    d. Undefined

88. In geometry, the _____ or barycenter of an object X in n-dimensional space is the intersection of all hyperplanes that divide X into two parts of equal moment about the hyperplane
    a. Thing
    c. Undefined
    b. Centroid0
    d. Undefined

89. _____ is the property of a physical object that quantifies the amount of matter and energy it is equivalent to.
    a. Thing
    c. Undefined
    b. Mass0
    d. Undefined

90. A _____ signifies a point or points of probability on a subject e.g., the _____ of creativity, which allows for the formation of rule or norm or law by interpretation of the phenomena events that can be created.
    a. Principle0
    c. Undefined
    b. Thing
    d. Undefined

91. _____ means "constancy", i.e. if something retains a certain feature even after we change a way of looking at it, then it is symmetric.
    a. Symmetry0
    c. Undefined
    b. Thing
    d. Undefined

92. _____ of a two-dimensional figure is a line such that, if a perpendicular is constructed, any two points lying on the perpendicular at equal distances from the _____ are identical.
    a. Axis of symmetry0
    c. Undefined
    b. Thing
    d. Undefined

93. In set theory and other branches of mathematics, the _____ of a collection of sets is the set that contains everything that belongs to any of the sets, but nothing else.
    a. Thing
    c. Undefined
    b. Union0
    d. Undefined

94. A _____ is a mathematical statement which follows easily from a previously proven statement, typically a mathematical theorem.
    a. Corollary0
    c. Undefined
    b. Thing
    d. Undefined

95. _____ was a Hellenized Egyptian born in Alexandria, Egypt. He is best known for his work, Synagoge. It is a compendium of mathematics of which eight volumes survive. It covers a wide range of topics, including geometry, recreational mathematics, doubling the cube, polygons and polyhedra.
    a. Person
    c. Undefined
    b. Pappus of Alexandria0
    d. Undefined

96. The _____ is the distance around a closed curve. _____ is a kind of perimeter.

Chapter 6. APPLICATIONS OF THE INTEGRAL

    a. Thing   b. Circumference0
    c. Undefined   d. Undefined

97. In Euclidean geometry, an _____ is a closed segment of a differentiable curve in the two-dimensional plane; for example, a circular _____ is a segment of a circle.
    a. Concept   b. Arc0
    c. Undefined   d. Undefined

98. In mathematics, a _____ is an algebraic structure in which addition and multiplication are defined and have properties listed below.
    a. Ring0   b. Thing
    c. Undefined   d. Undefined

99. _____ is mass m per unit volume V.
    a. Density0   b. Thing
    c. Undefined   d. Undefined

100. In mathematics, a _____ is an n-tuple with n being 3.
    a. Thing   b. Triple0
    c. Undefined   d. Undefined

101. In physics, _____ is an influence that may cause an object to accelerate. It may be experienced as a lift, a push, or a pull. The actual acceleration of the body is determined by the vector sum of all forces acting on it, known as net _____ or resultant _____.
    a. Force0   b. Thing
    c. Undefined   d. Undefined

102. In mathematics, the additive inverse, or _____ of a number n is the number that, when added to n, yields zero. The additive inverse of n is denoted −n. For example, 7 is −7, because 7 + (−7) = 0, and the additive inverse of −0.3 is 0.3, because −0.3 + 0.3 = 0.
    a. Opposite0   b. Thing
    c. Undefined   d. Undefined

103. In mathematics, the _____ of a number n is the number that, when added to n, yields zero. The _____ of n is denoted −n. For example, 7 is −7, because 7 + (−7) = 0, and the _____ of −0.3 is 0.3, because −0.3 + 0.3 = 0.
    a. Thing   b. Additive inverse0
    c. Undefined   d. Undefined

104. In economics, economic _____ is simply a state of the world where economic forces are balanced and in the absence of external influences the values of economic variables will not change.
    a. Equilibrium0   b. Thing
    c. Undefined   d. Undefined

105. In mathematics, the _____ of a coordinate system is the point where the axes of the system intersect.

98 **Chapter 6. APPLICATIONS OF THE INTEGRAL**

    a. Origin0
    c. Undefined
    b. Thing
    d. Undefined

106. Sir Isaac _____, was an English physicist, mathematician, astronomer, natural philosopher, and alchemist, regarded by many as the greatest figure in the history of science
    a. Newton0
    c. Undefined
    b. Person
    d. Undefined

107. _____ is the SI unit of energy.
    a. Thing
    c. Undefined
    b. Joule0
    d. Undefined

108. The _____ or kilogramme is the SI base unit of mass. It is defined as being equal to the mass of the international prototype of the _____.
    a. Thing
    c. Undefined
    b. Kilogram0
    d. Undefined

109. _____ is defined as the rate of change or derivative with respect to time of velocity.
    a. Thing
    c. Undefined
    b. Acceleration0
    d. Undefined

110. The metre (or _____, see spelling differences) is a measure of length. It is the basic unit of length in the metric system and in the International System of Units (SI), used around the world for general and scientific purposes.
    a. Concept
    c. Undefined
    b. Meter0
    d. Undefined

111. In mathematics a _____ is a function which defines a distance between elements of a set.
    a. Metric0
    c. Undefined
    b. Thing
    d. Undefined

112. The _____ is a decimalized system of measurement based on the metre and the gram.
    a. Concept
    c. Undefined
    b. Metric system0
    d. Undefined

113. _____ is the eighteenth letter of the Greek alphabet.
    a. Thing
    c. Undefined
    b. Sigma0
    d. Undefined

114. A _____ is a special kind of ratio, indicating a relationship between two measurements with different units, such as miles to gallons or cents to pounds.
    a. Rate0
    c. Undefined
    b. Thing
    d. Undefined

115. In mathematics, science including computer science, linguistics and engineering, an _____ is, generally speaking, an independent variable or input to a function.

Chapter 6. APPLICATIONS OF THE INTEGRAL

a. Thing
b. Argument0
c. Undefined
d. Undefined

116. The _____ rule, also known as a slipstick, is a mechanical analog computer, consisting of at least two finely divided scales, most often a fixed outer pair and a movable inner one, with a sliding window called the cursor.
a. Slide0
b. Thing
c. Undefined
d. Undefined

117. The _____ is one of the classical simple machines; as the name suggests, it is a flat surface whose endpoints are at different heights. By moving an object up an _____ rather than directly from one height to another, the amount of force required is reduced, at the expense of increasing the distance the object must travel. The mechanical advantage of an _____ is the ratio of the length of the sloped surface to the height it spans; this may also be expressed as the cosecant of the angle between the plane and the horizontal.
a. Inclined plane0
b. Thing
c. Undefined
d. Undefined

118. U.S. liquid _____ is legally defined as 231 cubic inches, and is equal to 3.785411784 litres or abotu 0.13368 cubic feet. This is the most common definition of a _____. The U.S. fluid ounce is defined as 1/128 of a U.S. _____.
a. Gallon0
b. Thing
c. Undefined
d. Undefined

119. A _____ is a symbolic representation denoting a quantity or expression. It often represents an "unknown" quantity that has the potential to change.
a. Thing
b. Variable0
c. Undefined
d. Undefined

120. _____ of an object is its speed in a particular direction.
a. Velocity0
b. Thing
c. Undefined
d. Undefined

121. A _____ is a unit of length, usually used to measure distance, in a number of different systems, including Imperial units, United States customary units and Norwegian/Swedish mil. Its size can vary from system to system, but in each is between 1 and 10 kilometers. In contemporary English contexts _____ refers to either:
a. Mile0
b. Thing
c. Undefined
d. Undefined

122. _____ is the estimation of a physical quantity such as distance, energy, temperature, or time.
a. Measurement0
b. Thing
c. Undefined
d. Undefined

123. _____ has many meanings, most of which simply .
a. Power0
b. Thing
c. Undefined
d. Undefined

Chapter 6. APPLICATIONS OF THE INTEGRAL

124. In mathematics, a matrix can be thought of as each row or _____ being a vector. Hence, a space formed by row vectors or _____ vectors are said to be a row space or a _____ space.
    a. Column0
    b. Concept
    c. Undefined
    d. Undefined

125. _____ is the middle point of a line segment.
    a. Thing
    b. Midpoint0
    c. Undefined
    d. Undefined

126. An _____ (isosceles trapezium in British English) is a quadrilateral with a line of symmetry bisecting one pair of opposite sides, making it automatically a trapezoid. Also, an _____'s base angles are congruent.
    a. Isosceles trapezoid0
    b. Concept
    c. Undefined
    d. Undefined

127. In a right triangle, the _____ of the triangle are the two sides that are perpendicular to each other, as opposed to the hypotenuse.
    a. Thing
    b. Legs0
    c. Undefined
    d. Undefined

128. _____ is often used to describe the measurement of the steepness, incline, gradient, or grade of a straight line. The _____ is defined as the ratio of the "rise" divided by the "run" between two points on a line, or in other words, the ratio of the altitude change to the horizontal distance between any two points on the line.
    a. Thing
    b. Slope0
    c. Undefined
    d. Undefined

129. _____, a field in mathematics, is the study of how functions change when their inputs change. The primary object of study in _____ is the derivative.
    a. Thing
    b. Differential calculus0
    c. Undefined
    d. Undefined

130. The word _____ means curving in or hollowed inward.
    a. Thing
    b. Concavity0
    c. Undefined
    d. Undefined

131. _____ are flexible, elastic objects used to store mechanical energy.
    a. Springs0
    b. Thing
    c. Undefined
    d. Undefined

Chapter 7. THE TRANSCENDENTAL FUNCTIONS

1. In mathematics, a _____ is a constant multiplicative factor of a certain object. The object can be such things as a variable, a vector, a function, etc. For example, the _____ of $9x^2$ is 9.
   a. Coefficient0
   b. Thing
   c. Undefined
   d. Undefined

2. In mathematics, a _____ is an expression that is constructed from one or more variables and constants, using only the operations of addition, subtraction, multiplication, and constant positive whole number exponents. is a _____. Note in particular that division by an expression containing a variable is not in general allowed in polynomials. [1]
   a. Polynomial0
   b. Thing
   c. Undefined
   d. Undefined

3. The mathematical concept of a _____ expresses the intuitive idea of deterministic dependence between two quantities, one of which is viewed as primary and the other as secondary. A _____ then is a way to associate a unique output for each input of a specified type, for example, a real number or an element of a given set.
   a. Thing
   b. Function0
   c. Undefined
   d. Undefined

4. In mathematics, a _____ number is a real or complex number which is not algebraic, that is, not a solution of a non-zero polynomial equation, with rational coefficients.
   a. Thing
   b. Transcendental0
   c. Undefined
   d. Undefined

5. _____ element of an element x with respect to a binary operation * with identity element e is an element y such that x * y = y * x = e. In particular,
   a. Inverse0
   b. Thing
   c. Undefined
   d. Undefined

6. In mathematics, a _____ of a k-place relation $L \subseteq X_1 \times ... \times X_k$ is one of the sets X_j, $1 \leq j \leq k$. In the special case where k = 2 and $L \subseteq X_1 \times X_2$ is a function $L : X_1 \to X_2$, it is conventional to refer to X_1 as the _____ of the function and to refer to X_2 as the codomain of the function.
   a. Thing
   b. Domain0
   c. Undefined
   d. Undefined

7. In mathematics and the mathematical sciences, a _____ is a fixed, but possibly unspecified, value. This is in contrast to a variable, which is not fixed.
   a. Constant0
   b. Thing
   c. Undefined
   d. Undefined

8. _____ is a function whose values do not vary and thus are constant.
   a. Thing
   b. Constant function0
   c. Undefined
   d. Undefined

9. A _____ is a polynomial function of the form $f(x) = ax^2 + bx + c$, where a, b, c are real numbers and a , 0.
   a. Quadratic function0
   b. Event
   c. Undefined
   d. Undefined

Chapter 7. THE TRANSCENDENTAL FUNCTIONS

10. A _____ is a three-dimensional solid object bounded by six square faces, facets, or sides, with three meeting at each vertex.
    a. Thing
    b. Cube0
    c. Undefined
    d. Undefined

11. The _____ integers are all the integers from zero on upwards.
    a. Thing
    b. Nonnegative0
    c. Undefined
    d. Undefined

12. In plane geometry, a _____ is a polygon with four equal sides, four right angles, and parallel opposite sides. In algebra, the _____ of a number is that number multiplied by itself.
    a. Square0
    b. Thing
    c. Undefined
    d. Undefined

13. In mathematics, a _____ of a number x is a number r such that $r^2 = x$, or in words, a number r whose square (the result of multiplying the number by itself) is x.
    a. Thing
    b. Square root0
    c. Undefined
    d. Undefined

14. In mathematics, a _____ of a complex-valued function f is a member x of the domain of f such that f(x) vanishes at x, that is, x : f (x) = 0.
    a. Root0
    b. Thing
    c. Undefined
    d. Undefined

15. In astronomy, geography, geometry and related sciences and contexts, a plane is said to be _____ at a given point if it is locally perpendicular to the gradient of the gravity field, i.e., with the direction of the gravitational force at that point.
    a. Thing
    b. Horizontal0
    c. Undefined
    d. Undefined

16. _____ is a test used to determine if a function is injective, surjective or bijective.
    a. Horizontal line test0
    b. Thing
    c. Undefined
    d. Undefined

17. Acid _____ ratio measures the ability of a company to use its near cash or quick assets to immediately extinguish its current liabilities.
    a. Thing
    b. Test0
    c. Undefined
    d. Undefined

18. In mathematics, a _____ is a statement that can be proved on the basis of explicitly stated or previously agreed assumptions.
    a. Theorem0
    b. Thing
    c. Undefined
    d. Undefined

19. In mathematics, a _____ is a demonstration that, assuming certain axioms, some statement is necessarily true.

Chapter 7. THE TRANSCENDENTAL FUNCTIONS

a. Proof0
b. Thing
c. Undefined
d. Undefined

20. In mathematics, the _____ of a function is the set of all "output" values produced by that function. Given a function $f : A \to B$, the _____ of f, is defined to be the set $\{x \in B : x = f(a)$ for some $a \in A\}$.
    a. Range0
    b. Thing
    c. Undefined
    d. Undefined

21. Mathematical _____ is used to represent ideas.
    a. Thing
    b. Notation0
    c. Undefined
    d. Undefined

22. An _____ is a function which does the reverse of a given function.
    a. Inverse function0
    b. Thing
    c. Undefined
    d. Undefined

23. In mathematics, the multiplicative inverse of a number x, denoted 1/x or x^{-1}, is the number which, when multiplied by x, yields 1. The multiplicative inverse of x is also called the _____ of x.
    a. Reciprocal0
    b. Thing
    c. Undefined
    d. Undefined

24. The _____, the average in everyday English, which is also called the arithmetic _____ (and is distinguished from the geometric _____ or harmonic _____). The average is also called the sample _____. The expected value of a random variable, which is also called the population _____.
    a. Mean0
    b. Thing
    c. Undefined
    d. Undefined

25. _____ are the basic objects of study in graph theory. Informally speaking, a graph is a set of objects called points, nodes, or vertices connected by links called lines or edges.
    a. Thing
    b. Graphs0
    c. Undefined
    d. Undefined

26. A _____ is a deliberate process for transforming one or more inputs into one or more results.
    a. Calculation0
    b. Thing
    c. Undefined
    d. Undefined

27. _____ are objects, characters, or other concrete representations of ideas, concepts, or other abstractions.
    a. Symbols0
    b. Thing
    c. Undefined
    d. Undefined

28. The word _____ comes from the Latin word linearis, which means created by lines.
    a. Linear0
    b. Thing
    c. Undefined
    d. Undefined

29. A _____ is a first degree polynomial mathematical function of the form: $f(x) = mx + b$ where m and b are real constants and x is a real variable.

Chapter 7. THE TRANSCENDENTAL FUNCTIONS

    a. Thing
    b. Linear function0
    c. Undefined
    d. Undefined

30. The _____ is a measurement of how a function changes when the values of its inputs change.
    a. Thing
    b. Derivative0
    c. Undefined
    d. Undefined

31. In Euclidean geometry, a uniform _____ is a linear transformation that enlargers or diminishes objects, and whose _____ factor is the same in all directions. This is also called homothethy.
    a. Thing
    b. Scale0
    c. Undefined
    d. Undefined

32. In calculus, the _____ is a formula for the derivative of the composite of two functions.
    a. Chain rule0
    b. Concept
    c. Undefined
    d. Undefined

33. In mathematics, a _____ (also spelled reflexion) is a map that transforms an object into its mirror image.
    a. Reflection0
    b. Concept
    c. Undefined
    d. Undefined

34. _____, a field in mathematics, is the study of how functions change when their inputs change. The primary object of study in _____ is the derivative.
    a. Differential calculus0
    b. Thing
    c. Undefined
    d. Undefined

35. In trigonometry, the _____ is a function defined as $\tan x = \sin x / \cos x$. The function is so-named because it can be defined as the length of a certain segment of a _____ (in the geometric sense) to the unit circle. In plane geometry, a line is _____ to a curve, at some point, if both line and curve pass through the point with the same direction.
    a. Thing
    b. Tangent0
    c. Undefined
    d. Undefined

36. _____ has two distinct but etymologically-related meanings: one in geometry and one in trigonometry.
    a. Tangent line0
    b. Thing
    c. Undefined
    d. Undefined

37. _____ is often used to describe the measurement of the steepness, incline, gradient, or grade of a straight line. The _____ is defined as the ratio of the "rise" divided by the "run" between two points on a line, or in other words, the ratio of the altitude change to the horizontal distance between any two points on the line.
    a. Slope0
    b. Thing
    c. Undefined
    d. Undefined

38. In geometry, _____ lines are two lines that share one or more common points.
    a. Thing
    b. Intersecting0
    c. Undefined
    d. Undefined

Chapter 7. THE TRANSCENDENTAL FUNCTIONS

39. _____ was a German mathematician and philosopher. He invented calculus independently of Newton, and his notation is the one in general use since.
   a. Person
   b. Leibniz0
   c. Undefined
   d. Undefined

40. _____ named in honor of the 17th century German philosopher and mathematician Gottfried Wilhelm Leibniz, was originally the use of expressions such as dx and dy and to represent "infinitely small" or infinitesimal increments of quantities x and y, just as Äx and Äy represent finite increments of x and y respectively.
   a. Leibniz notation0
   b. Thing
   c. Undefined
   d. Undefined

41. A _____ is a special kind of ratio, indicating a relationship between two measurements with different units, such as miles to gallons or cents to pounds.
   a. Thing
   b. Rate0
   c. Undefined
   d. Undefined

42. In mathematics, a _____ of a positive integer n is a way of writing n as a sum of positive integers.
   a. Thing
   b. Composition0
   c. Undefined
   d. Undefined

43. The _____ functions is determined by the nesting of two or more functions to form a single new function.
   a. Composition of two0
   b. Thing
   c. Undefined
   d. Undefined

44. A _____ function is a function for which, intuitively, small changes in the input result in small changes in the output.
   a. Event
   b. Continuous0
   c. Undefined
   d. Undefined

45. _____ is a set of numbers, in the broadest sense of the word, together with one or more operations, such as addition or multiplication.
   a. Number system0
   b. Thing
   c. Undefined
   d. Undefined

46. In mathematics, a _____ of a number x is the exponent y of the power by such that $x = b^y$. The value used for the base b must be neither 0 nor 1, nor a root of 1 in the case of the extension to complex numbers, and is typically 10, e, or 2.
   a. Logarithm0
   b. Thing
   c. Undefined
   d. Undefined

47. _____ has many meanings, most of which simply .
   a. Thing
   b. Power0
   c. Undefined
   d. Undefined

48. _____ is a mathematical subject that includes the study of limits, derivatives, integrals, and power series and constitutes a major part of modern university curriculum.

a. Thing
b. Calculus0
c. Undefined
d. Undefined

49. In mathematics, _____ is an elementary arithmetic operation. When one of the numbers is a whole number, _____ is the repeated sum of the other number.
    a. Multiplication0
    b. Thing
    c. Undefined
    d. Undefined

50. In mathematics, a _____ is the result of multiplying, or an expression that identifies factors to be multiplied.
    a. Product0
    b. Thing
    c. Undefined
    d. Undefined

51. A _____ is the result of the addition of a set of numbers. The numbers may be natural numbers, complex numbers, matrices, or still more complicated objects. An infinite _____ is a subtle procedure known as a series.
    a. Sum0
    b. Thing
    c. Undefined
    d. Undefined

52. _____ is an adjective usually refering to being in the centre.
    a. Thing
    b. Central0
    c. Undefined
    d. Undefined

53. In mathematics, a _____ is the end result of a division problem. It can also be expressed as the number of times the divisor divides into the dividend.
    a. Thing
    b. Quotient0
    c. Undefined
    d. Undefined

54. The function difference divided by the point difference is known as the _____
    a. Thing
    b. Difference quotient0
    c. Undefined
    d. Undefined

55. A _____ is the part of a fraction that tells how many equal parts make up a whole, and which is used in the name of the fraction: "halves", "thirds", "fourths" or "quarters", "fifths" and so on.
    a. Denominator0
    b. Concept
    c. Undefined
    d. Undefined

56. In mathematics, a _____ number is a number which can be expressed as a ratio of two integers. Non-integer _____ numbers (commonly called fractions) are usually written as the vulgar fraction a / b, where b is not zero.
    a. Rational0
    b. Thing
    c. Undefined
    d. Undefined

57. In common philosophical language, a proposition or _____, is the content of an assertion, that is, it is true-or-false and defined by the meaning of a particular piece of language.
    a. Concept
    b. Statement0
    c. Undefined
    d. Undefined

Chapter 7. THE TRANSCENDENTAL FUNCTIONS

58. In elementary algebra, an _____ is a set that contains every real number between two indicated numbers and may contain the two numbers themselves.
    a. Thing
    b. Interval0
    c. Undefined
    d. Undefined

59. A _____ of a number is the product of that number with any integer.
    a. Thing
    b. Multiple0
    c. Undefined
    d. Undefined

60. In mathematics, an inequality is a statement about the relative size or order of two objects. For example 14 > 10, or 14 is _____ 10.
    a. Thing
    b. Greater than0
    c. Undefined
    d. Undefined

61. An _____ of a product of sums expresses it as a sum of products by using the fact that multiplication distributes over addition.
    a. Expansion0
    b. Thing
    c. Undefined
    d. Undefined

62. In mathematics, _____ (i.e. an irrational number) occurs when any real number that is not a rational number — that is, it is a number which cannot be expressed as m/n, where m and n are integers.
    a. Thing
    b. Irrationality0
    c. Undefined
    d. Undefined

63. In mathematics, the concept of a _____ tries to capture the intuitive idea of a geometrical one-dimensional and continuous object. A simple example is the circle.
    a. Curve0
    b. Thing
    c. Undefined
    d. Undefined

64. A _____ is traditionally an infinitesimally small change in a variable.
    a. Thing
    b. Differential0
    c. Undefined
    d. Undefined

65. Leonhard _____ was a pioneering Swiss mathematician and physicist, who spent most of his life in Russia and Germany.
    a. Euler0
    b. Person
    c. Undefined
    d. Undefined

66. The _____ implies that on any great circle around the world, the temperature, pressure, elevation, carbon dioxide concentration, or anything else that varies continuously, there will always exist two antipodal points that share the same value for that variable.
    a. Intermediate Value Theorem0
    b. Thing
    c. Undefined
    d. Undefined

67. _____ are functions which satisfy particular symmetry relations, with respect to taking additive inverses.

Chapter 7. THE TRANSCENDENTAL FUNCTIONS

    a. Thing
    b. Even function0
    c. Undefined
    d. Undefined

68. In mathematics, _____ is a part of the set theoretic notion of function.
    a. Image0
    b. Thing
    c. Undefined
    d. Undefined

69. Any point where a graph makes contact with an coordinate axis is called an _____ of the graph
    a. Thing
    b. Intercept0
    c. Undefined
    d. Undefined

70. The word _____ means curving in or hollowed inward.
    a. Concavity0
    b. Thing
    c. Undefined
    d. Undefined

71. An _____ is a straight line or curve A to which another curve B approaches closer and closer as one moves along it. As one moves along B, the space between it and the _____ A becomes smaller and smaller, and can in fact be made as small as one could wish by going far enough along. A curve may or may not touch or cross its _____. In fact, the curve may intersect the _____ an infinite number of times.
    a. Asymptote0
    b. Thing
    c. Undefined
    d. Undefined

72. _____ is a straight line or curve A to which another curve B the one being studied approaches closer and closer as one moves along it.
    a. Vertical asymptote0
    b. Thing
    c. Undefined
    d. Undefined

73. The _____ of a function is an extension of the concept of a sum, and are identified or found through the use of integration.
    a. Thing
    b. Integral0
    c. Undefined
    d. Undefined

74. _____ is a process of combining or accumulating. It may also refer to:
    a. Thing
    b. Integration0
    c. Undefined
    d. Undefined

75. A _____ is a negotiable instrument instructing a financial institution to pay a specific amount of a specific currency from a specific demand account held in the maker/depositor's name with that institution. Both the maker and payee may be natural persons or legal entities.
    a. Thing
    b. Check0
    c. Undefined
    d. Undefined

76. An _____ of a function f is a function F whose derivative is equal to f, i.e., F' = f.
    a. Thing
    b. Antiderivative0
    c. Undefined
    d. Undefined

Chapter 7. THE TRANSCENDENTAL FUNCTIONS

77. A _____ is a numeral used to indicate a count. The most common use of the word today is to name the part of a fraction that tells the number or count of equal parts.
    a. Thing
    b. Numerator0
    c. Undefined
    d. Undefined

78. _____ is a function that extends the concept of an ordinary sum
    a. Thing
    b. Integrand0
    c. Undefined
    d. Undefined

79. A _____ is a set of possible values that a variable can take on in order to satisfy a given set of conditions, which may include equations and inequalities.
    a. Thing
    b. Solution set0
    c. Undefined
    d. Undefined

80. In statistics, a _____ measure is one which is measuring what is supposed to measure.
    a. Valid0
    b. Thing
    c. Undefined
    d. Undefined

81. The _____ governs the differentiation of products of differentiable functions.
    a. Product rule0
    b. Thing
    c. Undefined
    d. Undefined

82. In mathematics, the _____(e) for L-functions are a class of summation formulae, expressing sums taken over the complex number zeroes of a given L-function, typically in terms of quantities studied by number theory by use of the theory of special functions.
    a. Explicit formula0
    b. Thing
    c. Undefined
    d. Undefined

83. In mathematics, factorization (British English: factorisation) or factoring is the decomposition of an object (for example, a number, a polynomial, or a matrix) into a product of other objects, or _____, which when multiplied together give the original.
    a. Thing
    b. Factors0
    c. Undefined
    d. Undefined

84. In mathematics, _____ are the intuitive idea of a geometrical one-dimensional and continuous object.
    a. Curves0
    b. Thing
    c. Undefined
    d. Undefined

85. In mathematical analysis and related areas of mathematics, a set is called _____, if it is, in a certain sense, of finite size.
    a. Thing
    b. Bounded0
    c. Undefined
    d. Undefined

86. A _____ consists of one quarter of the coordinate plane.

Chapter 7. THE TRANSCENDENTAL FUNCTIONS

    a. Thing
    b. Quadrant0
    c. Undefined
    d. Undefined

87. _____ is defined as the rate of change or derivative with respect to time of velocity.
    a. Acceleration0
    b. Thing
    c. Undefined
    d. Undefined

88. The _____ is a method of finding the derivative of a function that is the quotient of two other functions for which derivatives exist.
    a. Quotient rule0
    b. Thing
    c. Undefined
    d. Undefined

89. The term _____ refers to the largest and the smallest element of a set.
    a. Thing
    b. Extreme value0
    c. Undefined
    d. Undefined

90. In mathematics, an _____, mean, or central tendency of a data set refers to a measure of the "middle" or "expected" value of the data set.
    a. Average0
    b. Concept
    c. Undefined
    d. Undefined

91. In mathematics, _____ growth occurs when the growth rate of a function is always proportional to the function's current size.
    a. Exponential0
    b. Thing
    c. Undefined
    d. Undefined

92. _____ is one of the most important functions in mathematics. A function commonly used to study growth and decay
    a. Exponential function0
    b. Thing
    c. Undefined
    d. Undefined

93. In mathematics, maxima and minima, known collectively as extrema, are the largest value maximum or smallest value minimum, that a function takes in a point either within a given neighborhood local _____ or on the function domain in its entirety global _____.
    a. Extremum0
    b. Thing
    c. Undefined
    d. Undefined

94. _____ of an object is its speed in a particular direction.
    a. Thing
    b. Velocity0
    c. Undefined
    d. Undefined

95. In mathematics, the _____ of two sets A and B is the set that contains all elements of A that also belong to B (or equivalently, all elements of B that also belong to A), but no other elements.
    a. Intersection0
    b. Thing
    c. Undefined
    d. Undefined

Chapter 7. THE TRANSCENDENTAL FUNCTIONS

96. An _____ is a combination of numbers, operators, grouping symbols and/or free variables and bound variables arranged in a meaningful way which can be evaluated..
   a. Expression0
   b. Thing
   c. Undefined
   d. Undefined

97. In mathematics, an _____ number is any real number that is not a rational number- that is, it is a number which cannot be expressed as a fraction m/n, where m and n are integers.
   a. Thing
   b. Irrational0
   c. Undefined
   d. Undefined

98. An _____ is an equality that remains true regardless of the values of any variables that appear within it, to distinguish it from an equality which is true under more particular conditions.
   a. Identity0
   b. Thing
   c. Undefined
   d. Undefined

99. _____ traditionally refers to the statistical process of determining comparable scores on different forms of an exam
   a. Thing
   b. Equating0
   c. Undefined
   d. Undefined

100. A _____ is a mathematical statement which follows easily from a previously proven statement, typically a mathematical theorem.
   a. Corollary0
   b. Thing
   c. Undefined
   d. Undefined

101. _____ is the design, analysis, and/or construction of works for practical purposes.
   a. Engineering0
   b. Thing
   c. Undefined
   d. Undefined

102. _____, Greek for "knowledge of nature," is the branch of science concerned with the discovery and characterization of universal laws which govern matter, energy, space, and time.
   a. Thing
   b. Physics0
   c. Undefined
   d. Undefined

103. _____ means "constancy", i.e. if something retains a certain feature even after we change a way of looking at it, then it is symmetric.
   a. Symmetry0
   b. Thing
   c. Undefined
   d. Undefined

104. _____ is the chance that something is likely to happen or be the case.
   a. Probability0
   b. Thing
   c. Undefined
   d. Undefined

105. _____ is a mathematical science pertaining to the collection, analysis, interpretation or explanation, and presentation of data. It is applicable to a wide variety of academic disciplines, from the physical and social sciences to the humanities.

112 *Chapter 7. THE TRANSCENDENTAL FUNCTIONS*

    a. Statistics0
    c. Undefined
    b. Thing
    d. Undefined

106. A _____ is a set of numbers that designate location in a given reference system, such as x,y in a planar _____ system or an x,y,z in a three-dimensional _____ system.
    a. Coordinate0
    c. Undefined
    b. Thing
    d. Undefined

107. In mathematics, the _____ of a coordinate system is the point where the axes of the system intersect.
    a. Thing
    c. Undefined
    b. Origin0
    d. Undefined

108. In mathematics, two quantities are called _____ if they vary in such a way that one of the quantities is a constant multiple of the other, or equivalently if they have a constant ratio.
    a. Proportional0
    c. Undefined
    b. Thing
    d. Undefined

109. In geometry, a _____ is a special kind of point, usually a corner of a polygon, polyhedron, or higher dimensional polytope. In the geometry of curves a _____ is a point of where the first derivative of curvature is zero. In graph theory, a _____ is the fundamental unit out of which graphs are formed
    a. Thing
    c. Undefined
    b. Vertex0
    d. Undefined

110. In geometry, a _____ is defined as a quadrilateral where all four of its angles are right angles.
    a. Rectangle0
    c. Undefined
    b. Thing
    d. Undefined

111. The _____ of a solid object is the three-dimensional concept of how much space it occupies, often quantified numerically.
    a. Thing
    c. Undefined
    b. Volume0
    d. Undefined

112. In mathematics, _____ geometry was the traditional name for the geometry of three-dimensional Euclidean space — for practical purposes the kind of space we live in.
    a. Thing
    c. Undefined
    b. Solid0
    d. Undefined

113. _____ is a means of calculating the volume of a solid of revolution, when integrating along an axis perpendicular to the axis of revolution.
    a. Thing
    c. Undefined
    b. Shell method0
    d. Undefined

114. _____ is an extension of the concept of a sum.
    a. Definite integral0
    c. Undefined
    b. Thing
    d. Undefined

Chapter 7. THE TRANSCENDENTAL FUNCTIONS 113

115. In mathematics, a _____ is a mathematical statement which appears likely to be true, but has not been formally proven to be true under the rules of mathematical logic.
 a. Concept
 b. Conjecture0
 c. Undefined
 d. Undefined

116. In mathematics, a _____ is a number which can be expressed as a ratio of two integers. Non-integer rational numbers (commonly called fractions) are usually written as the vulgar fraction a / b, where b is not zero.
 a. Concept
 b. Rational Number0
 c. Undefined
 d. Undefined

117. _____ is a mathematical operation, written a^n, involving two numbers, the base a and the exponent n.
 a. Exponentiating0
 b. Thing
 c. Undefined
 d. Undefined

118. _____ is a mathematical operation, written a^n, involving two numbers, the base a and the exponent n.
 a. Thing
 b. Exponentiation0
 c. Undefined
 d. Undefined

119. A _____ is a symbolic representation denoting a quantity or expression. It often represents an "unknown" quantity that has the potential to change.
 a. Thing
 b. Variable0
 c. Undefined
 d. Undefined

120. _____ is the fee paid on borrowed money.
 a. Thing
 b. Interest0
 c. Undefined
 d. Undefined

121. _____ is the logarithm to the base e, where e is an irrational constant approximately equal to 2.718281828459.
 a. Thing
 b. Natural logarithm0
 c. Undefined
 d. Undefined

122. In mathematics, _____ occurs when the growth rate of a function is always proportional to the function's current size.
 a. Exponential growth0
 b. Thing
 c. Undefined
 d. Undefined

123. In business, particularly accounting, a _____ is the time intervals that the accounts, statement, payments, or other calculations cover.
 a. Period0
 b. Thing
 c. Undefined
 d. Undefined

124. _____ is a kind of property which exists as magnitude or multitude. It is among the basic classes of things along with quality, substance, change, and relation.
 a. Thing
 b. Amount0
 c. Undefined
 d. Undefined

Chapter 7. THE TRANSCENDENTAL FUNCTIONS

125. In mathematics, the _____ inverse, or opposite, of a number n is the number that, when added to n, yields zero. The _____ inverse of n is denoted −n.
 a. Thing
 b. Additive0
 c. Undefined
 d. Undefined

126. In mathematics, the _____ inverse of a number x, denoted 1/x or x^{-1}, is the number which, when multiplied by x, yields 1. The _____ inverse of x is also called the reciprocal of x.
 a. Multiplicative0
 b. Thing
 c. Undefined
 d. Undefined

127. Initial objects are also called _____, and terminal objects are also called final.
 a. Thing
 b. Coterminal0
 c. Undefined
 d. Undefined

128. _____ is a set, with some particular properties and usually some additional structure, such as the operations of addition or multiplication, for instance.
 a. Thing
 b. Space0
 c. Undefined
 d. Undefined

129. In sociology and biology a _____ is the collection of people or organisms of a particular species living in a given geographic area or space, usually measured by a census.
 a. Thing
 b. Population0
 c. Undefined
 d. Undefined

130. _____ is change in population over time, and can be quantified as the change in the number of individuals in a population per unit time.
 a. Population growth0
 b. Thing
 c. Undefined
 d. Undefined

131. Equivalence is the condition of being _____ or essentially equal.
 a. Equivalent0
 b. Thing
 c. Undefined
 d. Undefined

132. The _____ is the total number of human beings alive on the planet Earth at a given time.
 a. Thing
 b. World population0
 c. Undefined
 d. Undefined

133. _____ is the process in which an unstable atomic nucleus loses energy by emitting radiation in the form of particles or electromagnetic waves.
 a. Radioactive decay0
 b. Thing
 c. Undefined
 d. Undefined

134. _____ is a subset of a population.
 a. Thing
 b. Sample0
 c. Undefined
 d. Undefined

Chapter 7. THE TRANSCENDENTAL FUNCTIONS 115

135. _____ Any process by which a specified characteristic usually amplitude of the output of a device is prevented from exceeding a predetermined value.
   a. Limiting0
   b. Thing
   c. Undefined
   d. Undefined

136. An _____ is the fee paid on borrow money.
   a. Interest rate0
   b. Concept
   c. Undefined
   d. Undefined

137. _____ or investing is a term with several closely-related meanings in business management, finance and economics, related to saving or deferring consumption.
   a. Thing
   b. Investment0
   c. Undefined
   d. Undefined

138. _____ generally derives from name. A _____ quantity e.g., length, diameter, volume, voltage, value is generally the quantity according to which some item has been named or is generally referred to.
   a. Nominal0
   b. Thing
   c. Undefined
   d. Undefined

139. An _____ is an increase, either of some fixed amount, for example added regularly, or of a variable amount.
   a. Thing
   b. Increment0
   c. Undefined
   d. Undefined

140. _____ interest refers to the fact that whenever interest is calculated, it is based not only on the original principal, but also on any unpaid interest that has been added to the principal.
   a. Thing
   b. Compound0
   c. Undefined
   d. Undefined

141. _____ refers to the fact that whenever interest is calculated, it is based not only on the original principal, but also on any unpaid interest that has been added to the principal. The more frequently interest is compounded, the faster the balance grows.
   a. Compound interest0
   b. Concept
   c. Undefined
   d. Undefined

142. In calculus, the _____ is a theorem regarding the limit of a function. The theorem asserts that if two functions approach the same limit at a point, and if a third function is "squeezed" between those functions, then the third function also approaches that limit at that point.
   a. Thing
   b. Squeeze Theorem0
   c. Undefined
   d. Undefined

143. The _____ is the period of time required for a quantity to double in size or value.
   a. Thing
   b. Doubling time0
   c. Undefined
   d. Undefined

144. The act of _____ is the calculated approximation of a result which is usable even if input data may be incomplete, uncertain, or noisy.

116 *Chapter 7. THE TRANSCENDENTAL FUNCTIONS*

    a. Thing
    c. Undefined
    b. Estimating0
    d. Undefined

145. In mathematics, a _____ of an integer n, also called a factor of n, is an integer which evenly divides n without leaving a remainder.
    a. Thing
    c. Undefined
    b. Divisor0
    d. Undefined

146. In mathematics, a _____ is an n-tuple with n being 3.
    a. Triple0
    c. Undefined
    b. Thing
    d. Undefined

147. In the scientific method, an _____ (Latin: ex-+-periri, "of (or from) trying"), is a set of actions and observations, performed in the context of solving a particular problem or question, in order to support or falsify a hypothesis or research concerning phenomena.
    a. Thing
    c. Undefined
    b. Experiment0
    d. Undefined

148. _____ is a synonym for information.
    a. Data0
    c. Undefined
    b. Thing
    d. Undefined

149. A _____ is a statement or claimt that a particular event will occur in the future in more certain terms than a forecast.
    a. Thing
    c. Undefined
    b. Prediction0
    d. Undefined

150. A _____ is a unit of length, usually used to measure distance, in a number of different systems, including Imperial units, United States customary units and Norwegian/Swedish mil. Its size can vary from system to system, but in each is between 1 and 10 kilometers. In contemporary English contexts _____ refers to either:
    a. Mile0
    c. Undefined
    b. Thing
    d. Undefined

151. _____ are a measure of time.
    a. Thing
    c. Undefined
    b. Minutes0
    d. Undefined

152. The metre (or _____, see spelling differences) is a measure of length. It is the basic unit of length in the metric system and in the International System of Units (SI), used around the world for general and scientific purposes.
    a. Meter0
    c. Undefined
    b. Concept
    d. Undefined

153. In geometry, an _____ of a triangle is a straight line through a vertex and perpendicular to (i.e. forming a right angle with) the opposite side or an extension of the opposite side.

Chapter 7. THE TRANSCENDENTAL FUNCTIONS

a. Concept
b. Altitude0
c. Undefined
d. Undefined

154. _____ of a single or multiple future payments is the nominal amounts of money to change hands at some future date, discounted to account for the time value of money, and other factors such as investment risk.
a. Present value0
b. Thing
c. Undefined
d. Undefined

155. _____ measures the nominal future sum of money that a given sum of money is "worth" at a specified time in the future assuming a certain interest rate; this value does not include corrections for inflation or other factors that affect the true value of money in the future.
a. Thing
b. Future value0
c. Undefined
d. Undefined

156. _____ is a unit of speed, expressing the number of international miles covered per hour.
a. Thing
b. Miles per hour0
c. Undefined
d. Undefined

157. _____ is a radiometric dating method that uses the naturally occurring isotope carbon-14 to determine the age of carbonaceous materials up to about 60,000 years.
a. Thing
b. Radiocarbon dating0
c. Undefined
d. Undefined

158. A _____ is a quantity that denotes the proportional amount or magnitude of one quantity relative to another.
a. Ratio0
b. Thing
c. Undefined
d. Undefined

159. In mathematics, the _____ functions are functions of an angle; they are important when studying triangles and modeling periodic phenomena, among many other applications.
a. Thing
b. Trigonometric0
c. Undefined
d. Undefined

160. The _____ are functions of an angle; they are important when studying triangles and modeling periodic phenomena, among many other applications.
a. Thing
b. Trigonometric functions0
c. Undefined
d. Undefined

161. In mathematics, the _____ are the inverse functions of the trigonometric functions.
a. Inverse trigonometric functions0
b. Thing
c. Undefined
d. Undefined

162. _____ is a trigonemtric function that is important when studying triangles and modeling periodic phenomena, among other applications.
a. Sine0
b. Thing
c. Undefined
d. Undefined

Chapter 7. THE TRANSCENDENTAL FUNCTIONS

163. In Euclidean geometry, an _____ is a closed segment of a differentiable curve in the two-dimensional plane; for example, a circular _____ is a segment of a circle.
   a. Arc0
   b. Concept
   c. Undefined
   d. Undefined

164. The _____ is a unit of plane angle. It is represented by the symbol "rad" or, more rarely, by the superscript c (for "circular measure"). For example, an angle of 1.2 radians would be written "1.2 rad" or "1.2c" (second symbol can produce confusion with centigrads).
   a. Radian0
   b. Thing
   c. Undefined
   d. Undefined

165. _____ is a unit of plane angle, equal to 180/δ degrees, or about 57.2958 degrees
   a. Radian measure0
   b. Thing
   c. Undefined
   d. Undefined

166. A _____ is a function that assigns a number to subsets of a given set.
   a. Measure0
   b. Thing
   c. Undefined
   d. Undefined

167. Angles smaller than a right angle are called _____ angles (less than 90 degrees).
   a. Concept
   b. Acute0
   c. Undefined
   d. Undefined

168. In mathematics, a _____ may be described informally as a number that can be given by an infinite decimal representation.
   a. Real number0
   b. Thing
   c. Undefined
   d. Undefined

169. _____ is a trigonometric function that is the reciprocal of cosine.
   a. Secant0
   b. Thing
   c. Undefined
   d. Undefined

170. _____ is a term in Trigonometry used to describe the secant of the complement of a cirlce.
   a. Thing
   b. Cosecant0
   c. Undefined
   d. Undefined

171. The _____ of an angle is the ratio of the length of the adjacent side to the length of the hypotenuse.
   a. Concept
   b. Cosine0
   c. Undefined
   d. Undefined

172. _____ is the ratio of the adjacent to the opposite side of a right-angled triangle
   a. Thing
   b. Cotangent0
   c. Undefined
   d. Undefined

173. In mathematics, a function f is _____ of a function g if f whenever A and B are complementary angles. This definition typically applies to trigonometric functions.

Chapter 7. THE TRANSCENDENTAL FUNCTIONS

a. Cofunction0
b. Thing
c. Undefined
d. Undefined

174. A _____ is one of the basic shapes of geometry: a polygon with three vertices and three sides which are straight line segments.
  a. Thing
  b. Triangle0
  c. Undefined
  d. Undefined

175. _____ has one 90° internal angle a right angle.
  a. Right triangle0
  b. Thing
  c. Undefined
  d. Undefined

176. In geometry, two lines or planes if one falls on the other in such a way as to create congruent adjacent angles. The term may be used as a noun or adjective. Thus, referring to Figure 1, the line AB is the _____ to CD through the point B.
  a. Thing
  b. Perpendicular0
  c. Undefined
  d. Undefined

177. Generally, a _____ is a splitting of something into parts.
  a. Thing
  b. Partition0
  c. Undefined
  d. Undefined

178. _____ is the transport of people on a trip/journey or the process or time involved in a person or object moving from one location to another.
  a. Thing
  b. Travel0
  c. Undefined
  d. Undefined

179. _____ is electromagnetic radiation with a wavelength that is visible to the eye (visible _____) or, in a technical or scientific context, electromagnetic radiation of any wavelength.
  a. Light0
  b. Thing
  c. Undefined
  d. Undefined

180. The _____ in a vacuum is an important physical constant denoted by the letter c for constant or the Latin word celeritas meaning "swiftness
  a. Speed of light0
  b. Thing
  c. Undefined
  d. Undefined

181. The word _____ is used in a variety of ways in mathematics.
  a. Index0
  b. Thing
  c. Undefined
  d. Undefined

182. In geometry, the relations of _____ are those such as 'lies on' between points and lines (as in 'point P lies on line L'), and 'intersects' (as in 'line L_1 intersects line L_2', in three-dimensional space). That is, they are the binary relations describing how subsets meet.
  a. Thing
  b. Incidence0
  c. Undefined
  d. Undefined

Chapter 7. THE TRANSCENDENTAL FUNCTIONS

183. In mathematics, a _____ is a two-dimensional manifold or surface that is perfectly flat.
 a. Plane0
 b. Thing
 c. Undefined
 d. Undefined

184. A _____ given two distinct points A and B on the _____, is the set of points C on the line containing points A and B such that A is not strictly between C and B.
 a. Thing
 b. Ray0
 c. Undefined
 d. Undefined

185. In combinatorial mathematics, a _____ is an un-ordered collection of unique elements.
 a. Combination0
 b. Concept
 c. Undefined
 d. Undefined

186. A _____ is 360° or 2δ radians.
 a. Thing
 b. Turn0
 c. Undefined
 d. Undefined

187. A _____ is an analog of an ordinary trigonometric, or circular, function.
 a. Hyperbolic function0
 b. Thing
 c. Undefined
 d. Undefined

188. _____ is a reaction force applied by a stretched string on the objects which stretch it.
 a. Thing
 b. Tension0
 c. Undefined
 d. Undefined

189. _____ is mass m per unit volume V.
 a. Density0
 b. Thing
 c. Undefined
 d. Undefined

190. In physics, _____ is an influence that may cause an object to accelerate. It may be experienced as a lift, a push, or a pull. The actual acceleration of the body is determined by the vector sum of all forces acting on it, known as net _____ or resultant _____.
 a. Force0
 b. Thing
 c. Undefined
 d. Undefined

191. _____ is the shape of a hanging flexible chain or cable when supported at its ends and acted upon by a uniform gravitational force. The chain is steepest near the points of suspension because this part of the chain has the most weight pulling down on it. Toward the bottom, the slope of the chain decreases because the chain is supporting less weight.
 a. Thing
 b. Catenary0
 c. Undefined
 d. Undefined

192. In geometry, the _____ of an object is a point in some sense in the middle of the object.
 a. Center0
 b. Thing
 c. Undefined
 d. Undefined

Chapter 7. THE TRANSCENDENTAL FUNCTIONS

193. In mathematics and its applications, a _____ is a system for assigning an n-tuple of numbers or scalars to each point in an n-dimensional space.
   a. Coordinate system0
   b. Concept
   c. Undefined
   d. Undefined

194. _____ is a special mathematical relationship between two quantities. Two quantities are called proportional if they vary in such a way that one of the quantities is a constant multiple of the other, or equivalently if they have a constant ratio.
   a. Proportionality0
   b. Thing
   c. Undefined
   d. Undefined

195. In finance, the _____, the rule of 71, the rule of 70 and the rule of 69.3 all refer to a method for estimating an investment's doubling time, or halving time. These rules apply to exponential growth and decay respectively, and are therefore used for compound interest as opposed to simple interest calculations.
   a. Rule of 720
   b. Thing
   c. Undefined
   d. Undefined

Chapter 8. TECHNIQUES OF INTEGRATION

1. In mathematics and the mathematical sciences, a _____ is a fixed, but possibly unspecified, value. This is in contrast to a variable, which is not fixed.
   a. Constant0
   b. Thing
   c. Undefined
   d. Undefined

2. The _____ of a function is an extension of the concept of a sum, and are identified or found through the use of integration.
   a. Integral0
   b. Thing
   c. Undefined
   d. Undefined

3. _____ is a trigonemtric function that is important when studying triangles and modeling periodic phenomena, among other applications.
   a. Sine0
   b. Thing
   c. Undefined
   d. Undefined

4. A _____ is a set of numbers that designate location in a given reference system, such as x,y in a planar _____ system or an x,y,z in a three-dimensional _____ system.
   a. Thing
   b. Coordinate0
   c. Undefined
   d. Undefined

5. In mathematics and its applications, a _____ is a system for assigning an n-tuple of numbers or scalars to each point in an n-dimensional space.
   a. Concept
   b. Coordinate system0
   c. Undefined
   d. Undefined

6. _____ are the basic objects of study in graph theory. Informally speaking, a graph is a set of objects called points, nodes, or vertices connected by links called lines or edges.
   a. Graphs0
   b. Thing
   c. Undefined
   d. Undefined

7. In mathematical analysis and related areas of mathematics, a set is called _____, if it is, in a certain sense, of finite size.
   a. Thing
   b. Bounded0
   c. Undefined
   d. Undefined

8. In mathematics, the _____ of two sets A and B is the set that contains all elements of A that also belong to B (or equivalently, all elements of B that also belong to A), but no other elements.
   a. Thing
   b. Intersection0
   c. Undefined
   d. Undefined

9. In elementary algebra, an _____ is a set that contains every real number between two indicated numbers and may contain the two numbers themselves.
   a. Interval0
   b. Thing
   c. Undefined
   d. Undefined

10. The _____ of measurement are a globally standardized and modernized form of the metric system.

Chapter 8. TECHNIQUES OF INTEGRATION

    a. Units0
    c. Undefined
    b. Thing
    d. Undefined

11. The _____ of a solid object is the three-dimensional concept of how much space it occupies, often quantified numerically.
    a. Thing
    c. Undefined
    b. Volume0
    d. Undefined

12. In mathematics, _____ geometry was the traditional name for the geometry of three-dimensional Euclidean space — for practical purposes the kind of space we live in.
    a. Thing
    c. Undefined
    b. Solid0
    d. Undefined

13. _____ are cubes in which all sides are of the same length and all face perpendicular to each other including an atom at each corner of the unigt cell.
    a. Thing
    c. Undefined
    b. Cubic units0
    d. Undefined

14. In mathematics, a _____ is the result of multiplying, or an expression that identifies factors to be multiplied.
    a. Product0
    c. Undefined
    b. Thing
    d. Undefined

15. _____ is a process of combining or accumulating. It may also refer to:
    a. Integration0
    c. Undefined
    b. Thing
    d. Undefined

16. The _____ is a measurement of how a function changes when the values of its inputs change.
    a. Derivative0
    c. Undefined
    b. Thing
    d. Undefined

17. In mathematics, the concept of a _____ tries to capture the intuitive idea of a geometrical one-dimensional and continuous object. A simple example is the circle.
    a. Thing
    c. Undefined
    b. Curve0
    d. Undefined

18. A _____ fraction is a fraction in which the absolute value of the numerator is less than the denominator--hence, the absolute value of the fraction is less than 1.
    a. Proper0
    c. Undefined
    b. Thing
    d. Undefined

19. An _____ of a function f is a function F whose derivative is equal to f, i.e., F' = f.
    a. Thing
    c. Undefined
    b. Antiderivative0
    d. Undefined

20. In mathematics, the _____ functions are functions of an angle; they are important when studying triangles and modeling periodic phenomena, among many other applications.

a. Trigonometric0
b. Thing
c. Undefined
d. Undefined

21. The _____ are functions of an angle; they are important when studying triangles and modeling periodic phenomena, among many other applications.
   a. Trigonometric functions0
   b. Thing
   c. Undefined
   d. Undefined

22. In mathematics, _____ growth occurs when the growth rate of a function is always proportional to the function's current size.
   a. Exponential0
   b. Thing
   c. Undefined
   d. Undefined

23. _____ is a function that extends the concept of an ordinary sum
   a. Integrand0
   b. Thing
   c. Undefined
   d. Undefined

24. In mathematics, a _____ is an expression that is constructed from one or more variables and constants, using only the operations of addition, subtraction, multiplication, and constant positive whole number exponents. is a _____. Note in particular that division by an expression containing a variable is not in general allowed in polynomials. [1]
   a. Thing
   b. Polynomial0
   c. Undefined
   d. Undefined

25. The mathematical concept of a _____ expresses the intuitive idea of deterministic dependence between two quantities, one of which is viewed as primary and the other as secondary. A _____ then is a way to associate a unique output for each input of a specified type, for example, a real number or an element of a given set.
   a. Function0
   b. Thing
   c. Undefined
   d. Undefined

26. In chemistry, a _____ is substance made by combining two or more different materials in such a way that no chemical reaction occurs.
   a. Mixture0
   b. Thing
   c. Undefined
   d. Undefined

27. In calculus, the _____ is a formula for the derivative of the composite of two functions.
   a. Chain rule0
   b. Concept
   c. Undefined
   d. Undefined

28. In mathematics, a _____ is a statement that can be proved on the basis of explicitly stated or previously agreed assumptions.
   a. Theorem0
   b. Thing
   c. Undefined
   d. Undefined

29. _____ is a mathematical subject that includes the study of limits, derivatives, integrals, and power series and constitutes a major part of modern university curriculum.

Chapter 8. TECHNIQUES OF INTEGRATION

a. Thing
b. Calculus0
c. Undefined
d. Undefined

30. In number theory, the _____ of arithmetic (or unique factorization theorem) states that every natural number greater than 1 can be written as a unique product of prime numbers.
a. Concept
b. Fundamental theorem0
c. Undefined
d. Undefined

31. _____ of calculus is the statement that the two central operations of calculus, differentiation and integration, are inverse operations: if a continuous function is first integrated and then differentiated, the original function is retrieved.
a. Thing
b. Fundamental Theorem of Calculus0
c. Undefined
d. Undefined

32. In mathematics, a _____ of a number x is the exponent y of the power by such that $x = b^y$. The value used for the base b must be neither 0 nor 1, nor a root of 1 in the case of the extension to complex numbers, and is typically 10, e, or 2.
a. Logarithm0
b. Thing
c. Undefined
d. Undefined

33. _____ element of an element x with respect to a binary operation * with identity element e is an element y such that $x * y = y * x = e$. In particular,
a. Inverse0
b. Thing
c. Undefined
d. Undefined

34. In mathematics, the _____ are the inverse functions of the trigonometric functions.
a. Inverse trigonometric functions0
b. Thing
c. Undefined
d. Undefined

35. In mathematics, _____ is the substitution of trigonometric functions for other expressions.
a. Thing
b. Trigonometric substitution0
c. Undefined
d. Undefined

36. In geometry, the _____ or barycenter of an object X in n-dimensional space is the intersection of all hyperplanes that divide X into two parts of equal moment about the hyperplane
a. Thing
b. Centroid0
c. Undefined
d. Undefined

37. An _____ is when two lines intersect somewhere on a plane creating a right angle at intersection
a. Thing
b. Axes0
c. Undefined
d. Undefined

38. _____ is the property of a physical object that quantifies the amount of matter and energy it is equivalent to.
a. Mass0
b. Thing
c. Undefined
d. Undefined

39. _____ is mass m per unit volume V.

Chapter 8. TECHNIQUES OF INTEGRATION

    a. Thing
    c. Undefined
    b. Density0
    d. Undefined

40. In geometry, the _____ of an object is a point in some sense in the middle of the object.
    a. Center0
    b. Thing
    c. Undefined
    d. Undefined

41. In physics, the _____ of a system of particles is a specific point at which, for many purposes, the system's mass behaves as if it were concentrated.
    a. Thing
    b. Center of mass0
    c. Undefined
    d. Undefined

42. In mathematics, _____ refers to the rewriting of an expression into a simpler form.
    a. Thing
    b. Reduction0
    c. Undefined
    d. Undefined

43. In mathematics, a _____ is a constant multiplicative factor of a certain object. The object can be such things as a variable, a vector, a function, etc. For example, the _____ of $9x^2$ is 9.
    a. Coefficient0
    b. Thing
    c. Undefined
    d. Undefined

44. In mathematics, there are several meanings of _____ depending on the subject.
    a. Thing
    b. Degree0
    c. Undefined
    d. Undefined

45. A _____ function is a function for which, intuitively, small changes in the input result in small changes in the output.
    a. Continuous0
    b. Event
    c. Undefined
    d. Undefined

46. An _____ is an equality that remains true regardless of the values of any variables that appear within it, to distinguish it from an equality which is true under more particular conditions.
    a. Identity0
    b. Thing
    c. Undefined
    d. Undefined

47. A _____ is a special kind of ratio, indicating a relationship between two measurements with different units, such as miles to gallons or cents to pounds.
    a. Thing
    b. Rate0
    c. Undefined
    d. Undefined

48. _____ is the fee paid on borrowed money.
    a. Interest0
    b. Thing
    c. Undefined
    d. Undefined

49. _____ of a single or multiple future payments is the nominal amounts of money to change hands at some future date, discounted to account for the time value of money, and other factors such as investment risk.

Chapter 8. TECHNIQUES OF INTEGRATION

    a. Present value0   b. Thing
    c. Undefined   d. Undefined

50.   An _____ is the fee paid on borrow money.
    a. Interest rate0   b. Concept
    c. Undefined   d. Undefined

51.   _____ or investing is a term with several closely-related meanings in business management, finance and economics, related to saving or deferring consumption.
    a. Investment0   b. Thing
    c. Undefined   d. Undefined

52.   _____ measures the nominal future sum of money that a given sum of money is "worth" at a specified time in the future assuming a certain interest rate; this value does not include corrections for inflation or other factors that affect the true value of money in the future.
    a. Future value0   b. Thing
    c. Undefined   d. Undefined

53.   _____ is a business term for the amount of money that a company receives from its activities in a given period, mostly from sales of products and/or services to customers
    a. Revenue0   b. Thing
    c. Undefined   d. Undefined

54.   Generally, a _____ is a splitting of something into parts.
    a. Partition0   b. Thing
    c. Undefined   d. Undefined

55.   The term _____, or axiom, indicates a starting assumption from which other statements are logically derived.
    a. Postulate0   b. Thing
    c. Undefined   d. Undefined

56.   The _____ of an angle is the ratio of the length of the adjacent side to the length of the hypotenuse.
    a. Cosine0   b. Concept
    c. Undefined   d. Undefined

57.   The _____ are the only integral domain whose positive elements are well-ordered, and in which order is preserved by addition. Like the natural numbers, the _____ form a countably infinite set. The set of all _____ is usually denoted in mathematics by a boldface Z .
    a. Integers0   b. Thing
    c. Undefined   d. Undefined

58.   _____ has many meanings, most of which simply .
    a. Power0   b. Thing
    c. Undefined   d. Undefined

128 Chapter 8. TECHNIQUES OF INTEGRATION

59. A _____ is the result of the addition of a set of numbers. The numbers may be natural numbers, complex numbers, matrices, or still more complicated objects. An infinite _____ is a subtle procedure known as a series.
    a. Thing
    b. Sum0
    c. Undefined
    d. Undefined

60. Equivalence is the condition of being _____ or essentially equal.
    a. Equivalent0
    b. Thing
    c. Undefined
    d. Undefined

61. _____ is the ratio of the adjacent to the opposite side of a right-angled triangle
    a. Thing
    b. Cotangent0
    c. Undefined
    d. Undefined

62. In trigonometry, the _____ is a function defined as $\tan x = \sin x / \cos x$. The function is so-named because it can be defined as the length of a certain segment of a _____ (in the geometric sense) to the unit circle. In plane geometry, a line is _____ to a curve, at some point, if both line and curve pass through the point with the same direction.
    a. Tangent0
    b. Thing
    c. Undefined
    d. Undefined

63. _____ is a trigonometric function that is the reciprocal of cosine.
    a. Secant0
    b. Thing
    c. Undefined
    d. Undefined

64. In mathematics, _____ are the intuitive idea of a geometrical one-dimensional and continuous object.
    a. Curves0
    b. Thing
    c. Undefined
    d. Undefined

65. A _____ is a set of possible values that a variable can take on in order to satisfy a given set of conditions, which may include equations and inequalities.
    a. Thing
    b. Solution set0
    c. Undefined
    d. Undefined

66. _____ is the symbol used to indicate the nth root of a number
    a. Thing
    b. Radical0
    c. Undefined
    d. Undefined

67. In geometry, a line _____ is a part of a line that is bounded by two end points, and contains every point on the line between its end points.
    a. Segment0
    b. Concept
    c. Undefined
    d. Undefined

68. In classical geometry, a _____ of a circle or sphere is any line segment from its center to its boundary. By extension, the _____ of a circle or sphere is the length of any such segment. The _____ is half the diameter. In science and engineering the term _____ of curvature is commonly used as a synonym for _____.

Chapter 8. TECHNIQUES OF INTEGRATION

    a. Thing
    b. Radius0
    c. Undefined
    d. Undefined

69. A circular _____ or circle _____ also known as a pie piece is the portion of a circle enclosed by two radii and an arc.
    a. Sector0
    b. Thing
    c. Undefined
    d. Undefined

70. _____ is an adjective usually refering to being in the centre.
    a. Thing
    b. Central0
    c. Undefined
    d. Undefined

71. In Euclidean geometry, a _____ is the set of all points in a plane at a fixed distance, called the radius, from a given point, the center.
    a. Thing
    b. Circle0
    c. Undefined
    d. Undefined

72. The _____ is a unit of plane angle. It is represented by the symbol "rad" or, more rarely, by the superscript c (for "circular measure"). For example, an angle of 1.2 radians would be written "1.2 rad" or "1.2c" (second symbol can produce confusion with centigrads).
    a. Radian0
    b. Thing
    c. Undefined
    d. Undefined

73. In mathematics, a _____ is a type of conic section defined as the intersection between a right circular conical surface and a plane which cuts through both halves of the cone.
    a. Hyperbola0
    b. Thing
    c. Undefined
    d. Undefined

74. In geometry, a _____ is a surface of revolution generated by revolving a circle in three dimensional space about an axis coplanar with the circle, which does not touch the circle. Examples of tori include the surfaces of doughnuts and inner tubes. A circle rotated about a chord of the circle is called a _____ in some contexts, but this is not a common usage in mathematics. The shape produced when a circle is rotated about a chord resembles a round cushion. _____ was the Latin word for a cushion of this shape.
    a. Thing
    b. Torus0
    c. Undefined
    d. Undefined

75. In mathematics, a _____ number is a number which can be expressed as a ratio of two integers. Non-integer _____ numbers (commonly called fractions) are usually written as the vulgar fraction a / b, where b is not zero.
    a. Rational0
    b. Thing
    c. Undefined
    d. Undefined

76. In mathematics, a _____ is any function which can be written as the ratio of two polynomial functions.
    a. Thing
    b. Rational function0
    c. Undefined
    d. Undefined

Chapter 8. TECHNIQUES OF INTEGRATION

77. In algebra, the _____ decomposition or _____ expansion is used to reduce the degree of either the numerator or the denominator of a rational function.
   a. Partial fraction0
   b. Thing
   c. Undefined
   d. Undefined

78. _____ is a means of calculating the volume of a solid of revolution, when integrating along an axis perpendicular to the axis of revolution.
   a. Thing
   b. Shell method0
   c. Undefined
   d. Undefined

79. In mathematics, a _____ is the end result of a division problem. It can also be expressed as the number of times the divisor divides into the dividend.
   a. Thing
   b. Quotient0
   c. Undefined
   d. Undefined

80. A _____ is a numeral used to indicate a count. The most common use of the word today is to name the part of a fraction that tells the number or count of equal parts.
   a. Numerator0
   b. Thing
   c. Undefined
   d. Undefined

81. A _____ is the part of a fraction that tells how many equal parts make up a whole, and which is used in the name of the fraction: "halves", "thirds", "fourths" or "quarters", "fifths" and so on.
   a. Concept
   b. Denominator0
   c. Undefined
   d. Undefined

82. In mathematics, an inequality is a statement about the relative size or order of two objects. For example 14 > 10, or 14 is _____ 10.
   a. Thing
   b. Greater than0
   c. Undefined
   d. Undefined

83. In mathematics, _____ is an elementary arithmetic operation. When one of the numbers is a whole number, _____ is the repeated sum of the other number.
   a. Multiplication0
   b. Thing
   c. Undefined
   d. Undefined

84. _____ refers to the reduction of the body of a formerly living organism into simpler forms of matter.
   a. Decomposing0
   b. Thing
   c. Undefined
   d. Undefined

85. There are two simple _____ the greatest common factor and least common multiple: standard factorization and prime factorization.
   a. Methods for finding0
   b. Thing
   c. Undefined
   d. Undefined

86. A _____ is the sum of a whole number and a proper fraction.

Chapter 8. TECHNIQUES OF INTEGRATION

a. Thing
b. Mixed number0
c. Undefined
d. Undefined

87. _____ or arithmetics is the oldest and most elementary branch of mathematics, used by almost everyone, for tasks ranging from simple daily counting to advanced science and business calculations.
a. Thing
b. Arithmetic0
c. Undefined
d. Undefined

88. A _____ is traditionally an infinitesimally small change in a variable.
a. Thing
b. Differential0
c. Undefined
d. Undefined

89. A _____ is a mathematical equation for an unknown function of one or several variables which relates the values of the function itself and of its derivatives of various orders.
a. Differential equation0
b. Thing
c. Undefined
d. Undefined

90. _____, or Rationalisation in mathematics is the process of removing a square root or imaginary number from the denominator of a fraction.
a. Thing
b. Rationalizing0
c. Undefined
d. Undefined

91. _____ is a mathematical operation, written a^n, involving two numbers, the base a and the exponent n.
a. Thing
b. Exponentiating0
c. Undefined
d. Undefined

92. _____ is a mathematical operation, written a^n, involving two numbers, the base a and the exponent n.
a. Thing
b. Exponentiation0
c. Undefined
d. Undefined

93. The _____, the average in everyday English, which is also called the arithmetic _____ (and is distinguished from the geometric _____ or harmonic _____). The average is also called the sample _____. The expected value of a random variable, which is also called the population _____.
a. Thing
b. Mean0
c. Undefined
d. Undefined

94. _____ is an extension of the concept of a sum.
a. Definite integral0
b. Thing
c. Undefined
d. Undefined

95. The act of _____ is the calculated approximation of a result which is usable even if input data may be incomplete, uncertain, or noisy.
a. Thing
b. Estimating0
c. Undefined
d. Undefined

96. A _____ is a quadrilateral, which is defined as a shape with four sides, which has a pair of parallel sides.

Chapter 8. TECHNIQUES OF INTEGRATION

    a. Trapezoid0
    b. Thing
    c. Undefined
    d. Undefined

97. _____ constitutes a broad family of algorithms for calculating the numerical value of a definite integral, and by extension, the term is also sometimes used to describe the numerical solution of differential equations.
    a. Numerical integration0
    b. Thing
    c. Undefined
    d. Undefined

98. In geometry, a _____ is defined as a quadrilateral where all four of its angles are right angles.
    a. Rectangle0
    b. Thing
    c. Undefined
    d. Undefined

99. In mathematics, the _____ is a conic section generated by the intersection of a right circular conical surface and a plane parallel to a generating straight line of that surface. It can also be defined as locus of points in a plane which are equidistant from a given point.
    a. Thing
    b. Parabola0
    c. Undefined
    d. Undefined

100. _____ is the middle point of a line segment.
    a. Midpoint0
    b. Thing
    c. Undefined
    d. Undefined

101. Three or more points that lie on the same line are called _____.
    a. Thing
    b. Collinear0
    c. Undefined
    d. Undefined

102. In mathematics, a _____ case is a limiting case in which a class of object changes its nature so as to belong to another, usually simpler, class.
    a. Thing
    b. Degenerate0
    c. Undefined
    d. Undefined

103. _____ the American term is a way to approximately calculate the definite integral
    a. Trapezoidal Rule0
    b. Thing
    c. Undefined
    d. Undefined

104. _____ is the process of reducing the number of significant digits in a number.
    a. Rounding0
    b. Concept
    c. Undefined
    d. Undefined

105. In mathematics, the word _____ is used informally to refer to certain distinct bodies of knowledge about mathematics.
    a. Theoretical0
    b. Thing
    c. Undefined
    d. Undefined

106. Deductive _____ is the kind of _____ in which the conclusion is necessitated by, or reached from, previously known facts (the premises).

Chapter 8. TECHNIQUES OF INTEGRATION

    a. Reasoning0
    b. Thing
    c. Undefined
    d. Undefined

107. _____ is the study of algorithms for the problems of continuous mathematics as distinguished from discrete mathematics.
    a. Thing
    b. Numerical analysis0
    c. Undefined
    d. Undefined

108. In mathematics, an _____ is a statement about the relative size or order of two objects.
    a. Thing
    b. Inequality0
    c. Undefined
    d. Undefined

109. A _____ is a negotiable instrument instructing a financial institution to pay a specific amount of a specific currency from a specific demand account held in the maker/depositor's name with that institution. Both the maker and payee may be natural persons or legal entities.
    a. Check0
    b. Thing
    c. Undefined
    d. Undefined

110. The word _____ comes from the Latin word linearis, which means created by lines.
    a. Linear0
    b. Thing
    c. Undefined
    d. Undefined

111. _____ is a method for approximating the values of integrals.
    a. Thing
    b. Riemann sum0
    c. Undefined
    d. Undefined

112. In mathematics, the _____ also called the Gauss _____ is a non-elementary function which occurs in probability, statistics and partial differential equations.
    a. Thing
    b. Error function0
    c. Undefined
    d. Undefined

113. _____ is the design, analysis, and/or construction of works for practical purposes.
    a. Engineering0
    b. Thing
    c. Undefined
    d. Undefined

114. _____ is a mathematical science pertaining to the collection, analysis, interpretation or explanation, and presentation of data. It is applicable to a wide variety of academic disciplines, from the physical and social sciences to the humanities.
    a. Statistics0
    b. Thing
    c. Undefined
    d. Undefined

115. _____ is the chance that something is likely to happen or be the case.
    a. Thing
    b. Probability0
    c. Undefined
    d. Undefined

Chapter 8. TECHNIQUES OF INTEGRATION

116. In mathematics, _____ occurs when the growth rate of a function is always proportional to the function's current size.
   a. Thing
   b. Exponential growth0
   c. Undefined
   d. Undefined

117. A _____ is an object that is attached to a pivot point so that it can swing freely.
   a. Thing
   b. Pendulum0
   c. Undefined
   d. Undefined

118. In topology, the _____ are subsets S of a topological space X is the set of points which can be approached both from S and from the outside of S.
   a. Thing
   b. Boundaries0
   c. Undefined
   d. Undefined

119. A _____ is an equation in which each term is either a constant or the product of a constant times the first power of a variable.
   a. Linear equation0
   b. Thing
   c. Undefined
   d. Undefined

120. In calculus, the indefinite integral of a given function i.e. the set of all antiderivatives of the function is always written with a constant, the _____.
   a. Constant of integration0
   b. Thing
   c. Undefined
   d. Undefined

121. _____ is a function that is chosen to facilitate the solving of a given ordinary differential equation. Consider an ordinary differential equation of the form
   a. Thing
   b. Integrating factor0
   c. Undefined
   d. Undefined

122. Initial objects are also called _____, and terminal objects are also called final.
   a. Thing
   b. Coterminal0
   c. Undefined
   d. Undefined

123. In mathematics, in the field of differential equations, an initial value problem is a differential equation together with specified value, called the _____, of the unknown function at a given point in the domain of the solution.
   a. Initial condition0
   b. Thing
   c. Undefined
   d. Undefined

124. A _____ is an abstract model that uses mathematical language to describe the behavior of a system. Eykhoff defined a _____ as 'a representation of the essential aspects of an existing system which presents knowledge of that system in usable form'.
   a. Thing
   b. Mathematical model0
   c. Undefined
   d. Undefined

125. Sir Isaac _____, was an English physicist, mathematician, astronomer, natural philosopher, and alchemist, regarded by many as the greatest figure in the history of science

Chapter 8. TECHNIQUES OF INTEGRATION

a. Newton0
b. Person
c. Undefined
d. Undefined

126. In mathematics, two quantities are called _____ if they vary in such a way that one of the quantities is a constant multiple of the other, or equivalently if they have a constant ratio.
    a. Thing
    b. Proportional0
    c. Undefined
    d. Undefined

127. _____ is a physical property of a system that underlies the common notions of hot and cold; something that is hotter has the greater _____.
    a. Temperature0
    b. Thing
    c. Undefined
    d. Undefined

128. _____ is a special mathematical relationship between two quantities. Two quantities are called proportional if they vary in such a way that one of the quantities is a constant multiple of the other, or equivalently if they have a constant ratio.
    a. Proportionality0
    b. Thing
    c. Undefined
    d. Undefined

129. _____ is the application of tools and a processing medium to the transformation of raw materials into finished goods for sale.
    a. Manufacturing0
    b. Thing
    c. Undefined
    d. Undefined

130. U.S. liquid _____ is legally defined as 231 cubic inches, and is equal to 3.785411784 litres or abotu 0.13368 cubic feet. This is the most common definition of a _____. The U.S. fluid ounce is defined as 1/128 of a U.S. _____.
    a. Gallon0
    b. Thing
    c. Undefined
    d. Undefined

131. _____ is a kind of property which exists as magnitude or multitude. It is among the basic classes of things along with quality, substance, change, and relation.
    a. Thing
    b. Amount0
    c. Undefined
    d. Undefined

132. _____ is the weakest of the four fundamental forces of bature, as described by Issac Newton
    a. Thing
    b. Gravitational force0
    c. Undefined
    d. Undefined

133. In physics, _____ is an influence that may cause an object to accelerate. It may be experienced as a lift, a push, or a pull. The actual acceleration of the body is determined by the vector sum of all forces acting on it, known as net _____ or resultant _____.
    a. Thing
    b. Force0
    c. Undefined
    d. Undefined

134. _____ of an object is its speed in a particular direction.

Chapter 8. TECHNIQUES OF INTEGRATION

    a. Thing
    b. Velocity0
    c. Undefined
    d. Undefined

135. In mathematics, the additive inverse, or _____ of a number n is the number that, when added to n, yields zero. The additive inverse of n is denoted −n. For example, 7 is −7, because 7 + (−7) = 0, and the additive inverse of −0.3 is 0.3, because −0.3 + 0.3 = 0.
    a. Thing
    b. Opposite0
    c. Undefined
    d. Undefined

136. In mathematics, the _____ of a number n is the number that, when added to n, yields zero. The _____ of n is denoted −n. For example, 7 is −7, because 7 + (−7) = 0, and the _____ of −0.3 is 0.3, because −0.3 + 0.3 = 0.
    a. Additive inverse0
    b. Thing
    c. Undefined
    d. Undefined

137. _____ is the difference of electrical potential between two points of an electrical or electronic circuit, expressed in volts
    a. Thing
    b. Voltage0
    c. Undefined
    d. Undefined

138. The ratio of the magnetic flux to the current is called the _____, or more accurately self-_____ of the circuit.
    a. Inductance0
    b. Thing
    c. Undefined
    d. Undefined

139. _____ are a measure of time.
    a. Thing
    b. Minutes0
    c. Undefined
    d. Undefined

140. In sociology and biology a _____ is the collection of people or organisms of a particular species living in a given geographic area or space, usually measured by a census.
    a. Thing
    b. Population0
    c. Undefined
    d. Undefined

141. _____ is change in population over time, and can be quantified as the change in the number of individuals in a population per unit time.
    a. Thing
    b. Population growth0
    c. Undefined
    d. Undefined

142. _____ systems represent systems whose behavior is not expressible as a sum of the behaviors of its descriptors.
    a. Thing
    b. Nonlinear0
    c. Undefined
    d. Undefined

143. In mathematics, a _____ is a two-dimensional manifold or surface that is perfectly flat.
    a. Thing
    b. Plane0
    c. Undefined
    d. Undefined

Chapter 8. TECHNIQUES OF INTEGRATION

144. In mathematics, a _____ is a curve in a Euclidian plane. The most frequently studied types are the smooth _____, and the algebraic _____.
    a. Plane curve0
    b. Thing
    c. Undefined
    d. Undefined

145. In astronomy, geography, geometry and related sciences and contexts, a plane is said to be _____ at a given point if it is locally perpendicular to the gradient of the gravity field, i.e., with the direction of the gravitational force at that point.
    a. Horizontal0
    b. Thing
    c. Undefined
    d. Undefined

146. _____ is a differential equation together with specified value, called the initial condition, of the unknown function at a given point in the domain of the solution.
    a. Initial value problem0
    b. Thing
    c. Undefined
    d. Undefined

147. _____ is the path a moving object follows through space.
    a. Thing
    b. Projectile motion0
    c. Undefined
    d. Undefined

148. _____ is often used to describe the measurement of the steepness, incline, gradient, or grade of a straight line. The _____ is defined as the ratio of the "rise" divided by the "run" between two points on a line, or in other words, the ratio of the altitude change to the horizontal distance between any two points on the line.
    a. Slope0
    b. Thing
    c. Undefined
    d. Undefined

149. In mathematics, _____ is synonymous with perpendicular when used as a simple adjective that is not part of any longer phrase with a standard definition. It means at right angles. It comes from the Greek á½€Ï Î¸ÏŒÏ, orthos, meaning "straight", used by Euclid to mean right; and Î³Ï‰Î½Î¯Î± gonia, meaning angle. Two streets that cross each other at a right angle are _____ to one another.
    a. Thing
    b. Orthogonal0
    c. Undefined
    d. Undefined

150. In mathematics, a _____ is a family of curves in the plane that intersect a given family of curves at right angles.
    a. Orthogonal trajectory0
    b. Thing
    c. Undefined
    d. Undefined

151. In geometry and trigonometry, a _____ is defined as an angle between two straight intersecting lines of ninety degrees, or one-quarter of a circle.
    a. Thing
    b. Right angle0
    c. Undefined
    d. Undefined

152. An _____ is a combination of numbers, operators, grouping symbols and/or free variables and bound variables arranged in a meaningful way which can be evaluated..
    a. Thing
    b. Expression0
    c. Undefined
    d. Undefined

Chapter 8. TECHNIQUES OF INTEGRATION

153. In mathematics, an _____ .
 a. Thing
 b. Ellipse0
 c. Undefined
 d. Undefined

154. _____ interest refers to the fact that whenever interest is calculated, it is based not only on the original principal, but also on any unpaid interest that has been added to the principal.
 a. Thing
 b. Compound0
 c. Undefined
 d. Undefined

155. _____ is defined as the rate of change or derivative with respect to time of velocity.
 a. Acceleration0
 b. Thing
 c. Undefined
 d. Undefined

156. The _____ or kilogramme is the SI base unit of mass. It is defined as being equal to the mass of the international prototype of the _____.
 a. Thing
 b. Kilogram0
 c. Undefined
 d. Undefined

157. The metre (or _____, see spelling differences) is a measure of length. It is the basic unit of length in the metric system and in the International System of Units (SI), used around the world for general and scientific purposes.
 a. Concept
 b. Meter0
 c. Undefined
 d. Undefined

158. In plane geometry, a _____ is a polygon with four equal sides, four right angles, and parallel opposite sides. In algebra, the _____ of a number is that number multiplied by itself.
 a. Thing
 b. Square0
 c. Undefined
 d. Undefined

159. In mathematics, a _____ number is a real or complex number which is not algebraic, that is, not a solution of a non-zero polynomial equation, with rational coefficients.
 a. Transcendental0
 b. Thing
 c. Undefined
 d. Undefined

160. An _____ is a straight line or curve A to which another curve B approaches closer and closer as one moves along it. As one moves along B, the space between it and the _____ A becomes smaller and smaller, and can in fact be made as small as one could wish by going far enough along. A curve may or may not touch or cross its _____. In fact, the curve may intersect the _____ an infinite number of times.
 a. Thing
 b. Asymptote0
 c. Undefined
 d. Undefined

161. The term _____ refers to the largest and the smallest element of a set.
 a. Extreme value0
 b. Thing
 c. Undefined
 d. Undefined

162. The word _____ means curving in or hollowed inward.

Chapter 8. TECHNIQUES OF INTEGRATION

   a. Thing
   c. Undefined
   b. Concavity0
   d. Undefined

163. In business, particularly accounting, a _____ is the time intervals that the accounts, statement, payments, or other calculations cover.
   a. Thing
   c. Undefined
   b. Period0
   d. Undefined

164. _____ is a subset of a population.
   a. Thing
   c. Undefined
   b. Sample0
   d. Undefined

140 *Chapter 9. THE CONIC SECTIONS; POLAR COORDINATES; PARAMETRIC EQUATIONS*

1. In Euclidean geometry, a _____ is moving every point a constant distance in a specified direction.
   a. Translation0
   b. Concept
   c. Undefined
   d. Undefined

2. In mathematics, a _____ is a demonstration that, assuming certain axioms, some statement is necessarily true.
   a. Thing
   b. Proof0
   c. Undefined
   d. Undefined

3. In mathematics, the _____ of a coordinate system is the point where the axes of the system intersect.
   a. Origin0
   b. Thing
   c. Undefined
   d. Undefined

4. In mathematics, the _____ is a conic section generated by the intersection of a right circular conical surface and a plane parallel to a generating straight line of that surface. It can also be defined as locus of points in a plane which are equidistant from a given point.
   a. Thing
   b. Parabola0
   c. Undefined
   d. Undefined

5. In geometry, two lines or planes if one falls on the other in such a way as to create congruent adjacent angles. The term may be used as a noun or adjective. Thus, referring to Figure 1, the line AB is the _____ to CD through the point B.
   a. Thing
   b. Perpendicular0
   c. Undefined
   d. Undefined

6. _____ is a three-dimensional geometric shape formed by straight lines through a fixed point vertex to the points of a fixed curve directrix.
   a. Right circular cone0
   b. Thing
   c. Undefined
   d. Undefined

7. In mathematics, a _____ is a two-dimensional manifold or surface that is perfectly flat.
   a. Thing
   b. Plane0
   c. Undefined
   d. Undefined

8. A _____ is a three-dimensional geometric shape formed by straight lines through a fixed point (vertex) to the points of a fixed curve (directrix)
   a. Concept
   b. Cone0
   c. Undefined
   d. Undefined

9. In mathematics, a _____ section is a curve that can be formed by intersecting a cone with a plane.
   a. Thing
   b. Conic0
   c. Undefined
   d. Undefined

10. In mathematics, the _____ of two sets A and B is the set that contains all elements of A that also belong to B (or equivalently, all elements of B that also belong to A), but no other elements.
    a. Intersection0
    b. Thing
    c. Undefined
    d. Undefined

11. In mathematics, an _____ .

Chapter 9. THE CONIC SECTIONS; POLAR COORDINATES; PARAMETRIC EQUATIONS

a. Thing
b. Ellipse0
c. Undefined
d. Undefined

12. In mathematics, a _____ is a type of conic section defined as the intersection between a right circular conical surface and a plane which cuts through both halves of the cone.
a. Hyperbola0
b. Thing
c. Undefined
d. Undefined

13. In Euclidean geometry, a _____ is the set of all points in a plane at a fixed distance, called the radius, from a given point, the center.
a. Thing
b. Circle0
c. Undefined
d. Undefined

14. An _____ is a straight line around which a geometric figure can be rotated.
a. Thing
b. Axis0
c. Undefined
d. Undefined

15. In mathematics, an _____ on a real vector space is a choice of which ordered bases are "positively" oriented, or right-handed, and which are "negatively" oriented, or left-handed.
a. Thing
b. Orientation0
c. Undefined
d. Undefined

16. In geometry, _____ lines are two lines that share one or more common points.
a. Thing
b. Intersecting0
c. Undefined
d. Undefined

17. In geometry, a _____ is a special kind of point, usually a corner of a polygon, polyhedron, or higher dimensional polytope. In the geometry of curves a _____ is a point of where the first derivative of curvature is zero. In graph theory, a _____ is the fundamental unit out of which graphs are formed
a. Thing
b. Vertex0
c. Undefined
d. Undefined

18. A _____ is a set of numbers that designate location in a given reference system, such as x,y in a planar _____ system or an x,y,z in a three-dimensional _____ system.
a. Thing
b. Coordinate0
c. Undefined
d. Undefined

19. An _____ is when two lines intersect somewhere on a plane creating a right angle at intersection
a. Thing
b. Axes0
c. Undefined
d. Undefined

20. In astronomy, geography, geometry and related sciences and contexts, a plane is said to be _____ at a given point if it is locally perpendicular to the gradient of the gravity field, i.e., with the direction of the gravitational force at that point.
a. Thing
b. Horizontal0
c. Undefined
d. Undefined

142   Chapter 9. THE CONIC SECTIONS; POLAR COORDINATES; PARAMETRIC EQUATIONS

21. The _____ of measurement are a globally standardized and modernized form of the metric system.
    a. Thing
    b. Units0
    c. Undefined
    d. Undefined

22. In mathematics, the concept of a _____ tries to capture the intuitive idea of a geometrical one-dimensional and continuous object. A simple example is the circle.
    a. Thing
    b. Curve0
    c. Undefined
    d. Undefined

23. A _____ signifies a point or points of probability on a subject e.g., the _____ of creativity, which allows for the formation of rule or norm or law by interpretation of the phenomena events that can be created.
    a. Thing
    b. Principle0
    c. Undefined
    d. Undefined

24. In mathematics, a _____ (also spelled reflexion) is a map that transforms an object into its mirror image.
    a. Concept
    b. Reflection0
    c. Undefined
    d. Undefined

25. _____ is electromagnetic radiation with a wavelength that is visible to the eye (visible _____) or, in a technical or scientific context, electromagnetic radiation of any wavelength.
    a. Thing
    b. Light0
    c. Undefined
    d. Undefined

26. In geometry, the relations of _____ are those such as 'lies on' between points and lines (as in 'point P lies on line L'), and 'intersects' (as in 'line L_1 intersects line L_2', in three-dimensional space). That is, they are the binary relations describing how subsets meet.
    a. Incidence0
    b. Thing
    c. Undefined
    d. Undefined

27. A _____ is one of the basic shapes of geometry: a polygon with three vertices and three sides which are straight line segments.
    a. Thing
    b. Triangle0
    c. Undefined
    d. Undefined

28. An _____ triange is a triangle with at least two sides of equal length.
    a. Isosceles0
    b. Thing
    c. Undefined
    d. Undefined

29. The _____, the average in everyday English, which is also called the arithmetic _____ (and is distinguished from the geometric _____ or harmonic _____). The average is also called the sample _____. The expected value of a random variable, which is also called the population _____.
    a. Thing
    b. Mean0
    c. Undefined
    d. Undefined

30. In geometry and physics, _____ are half-lines that continue forever in one direction.

Chapter 9. THE CONIC SECTIONS; POLAR COORDINATES; PARAMETRIC EQUATIONS 143

    a. Thing   b. Rays0
    c. Undefined   d. Undefined

31.   In geometry, a _____ is defined as a quadrilateral where all four of its angles are right angles.
    a. Thing   b. Rectangle0
    c. Undefined   d. Undefined

32.   In trigonometry, the _____ is a function defined as $\tan x = \sin x / \cos x$. The function is so-named because it can be defined as the length of a certain segment of a _____ (in the geometric sense) to the unit circle. In plane geometry, a line is _____ to a curve, at some point, if both line and curve pass through the point with the same direction.
    a. Tangent0   b. Thing
    c. Undefined   d. Undefined

33.   _____ has two distinct but etymologically-related meanings: one in geometry and one in trigonometry.
    a. Tangent line0   b. Thing
    c. Undefined   d. Undefined

34.   In mathematics, the additive inverse, or _____ of a number n is the number that, when added to n, yields zero. The additive inverse of n is denoted −n. For example, 7 is −7, because 7 + (−7) = 0, and the additive inverse of −0.3 is 0.3, because −0.3 + 0.3 = 0.
    a. Thing   b. Opposite0
    c. Undefined   d. Undefined

35.   In mathematics, the _____ of a number n is the number that, when added to n, yields zero. The _____ of n is denoted −n. For example, 7 is −7, because 7 + (−7) = 0, and the _____ of −0.3 is 0.3, because −0.3 + 0.3 = 0.
    a. Additive inverse0   b. Thing
    c. Undefined   d. Undefined

36.   In geometry, a line _____ is a part of a line that is bounded by two end points, and contains every point on the line between its end points.
    a. Segment0   b. Concept
    c. Undefined   d. Undefined

37.   In a conic section, the _____ is the chord parallel to the directrix through the focus, with the symbol 2l.
    a. Latus rectum0   b. Thing
    c. Undefined   d. Undefined

38.   A _____ is a part of a line that is bounded by two end points, and contains every point on the line between its end points.
    a. Line segment0   b. Thing
    c. Undefined   d. Undefined

39.   In mathematical analysis and related areas of mathematics, a set is called _____, if it is, in a certain sense, of finite size.

144   Chapter 9. THE CONIC SECTIONS; POLAR COORDINATES; PARAMETRIC EQUATIONS

    a. Thing
    b. Bounded0
    c. Undefined
    d. Undefined

40. In geometry, the _____ or barycenter of an object X in n-dimensional space is the intersection of all hyperplanes that divide X into two parts of equal moment about the hyperplane
    a. Centroid0
    b. Thing
    c. Undefined
    d. Undefined

41. The _____ of a solid object is the three-dimensional concept of how much space it occupies, often quantified numerically.
    a. Volume0
    b. Thing
    c. Undefined
    d. Undefined

42. In mathematics, _____ geometry was the traditional name for the geometry of three-dimensional Euclidean space — for practical purposes the kind of space we live in.
    a. Solid0
    b. Thing
    c. Undefined
    d. Undefined

43. In mathematics and the mathematical sciences, a _____ is a fixed, but possibly unspecified, value. This is in contrast to a variable, which is not fixed.
    a. Constant0
    b. Thing
    c. Undefined
    d. Undefined

44. In geometry, an _____ polygon is a polygon which has all sides of the same length.
    a. Thing
    b. Equilateral0
    c. Undefined
    d. Undefined

45. An _____ is a triangle in which all sides are of equal length.
    a. Equilateral triangle0
    b. Thing
    c. Undefined
    d. Undefined

46. In Euclidean geometry, a uniform _____ is a linear transformation that enlargers or diminishes objects, and whose _____ factor is the same in all directions. This is also called homothethy.
    a. Scale0
    b. Thing
    c. Undefined
    d. Undefined

47. In mathematics, an inequality is a statement about the relative size or order of two objects. For example 14 > 10, or 14 is _____ 10.
    a. Thing
    b. Greater than0
    c. Undefined
    d. Undefined

48. In geometry, the _____ are a pair of special points used in describing conic sections. The four types of conic sections are the circle, parabola, ellipse, and hyperbola.
    a. Foci0
    b. Thing
    c. Undefined
    d. Undefined

Chapter 9. THE CONIC SECTIONS; POLAR COORDINATES; PARAMETRIC EQUATIONS

49. In linear algebra, the _____ of an n-by-n square matrix A is defined to be the sum of the elements on the main diagonal of A,
   a. Trace0
   b. Thing
   c. Undefined
   d. Undefined

50. In linear algebra, a _____ of a matrix A is the determinant of some smaller square matrix, cut down from A.
   a. Minor0
   b. Thing
   c. Undefined
   d. Undefined

51. In geometry, _____, or general position for a set of points, or other configuration, means the general case situation, as opposed to some more special or coincidental cases that are possible.
   a. Standard position0
   b. Thing
   c. Undefined
   d. Undefined

52. In geometry, the _____ of an object is a point in some sense in the middle of the object.
   a. Center0
   b. Thing
   c. Undefined
   d. Undefined

53. In plane geometry, a _____ is a polygon with four equal sides, four right angles, and parallel opposite sides. In algebra, the _____ of a number is that number multiplied by itself.
   a. Square0
   b. Thing
   c. Undefined
   d. Undefined

54. _____, either of the curved-bracket punctuation marks that together make a set of _____
   a. Thing
   b. Parentheses0
   c. Undefined
   d. Undefined

55. An _____ is a straight line or curve A to which another curve B approaches closer and closer as one moves along it. As one moves along B, the space between it and the _____ A becomes smaller and smaller, and can in fact be made as small as one could wish by going far enough along. A curve may or may not touch or cross its _____. In fact, the curve may intersect the _____ an infinite number of times.
   a. Thing
   b. Asymptote0
   c. Undefined
   d. Undefined

56. _____ is the middle point of a line segment.
   a. Thing
   b. Midpoint0
   c. Undefined
   d. Undefined

57. In classical geometry, a _____ of a circle or sphere is any line segment from its center to its boundary. By extension, the _____ of a circle or sphere is the length of any such segment. The _____ is half the diameter. In science and engineering the term _____ of curvature is commonly used as a synonym for _____.
   a. Thing
   b. Radius0
   c. Undefined
   d. Undefined

58. In mathematics, science including computer science, linguistics and engineering, an _____ is, generally speaking, an independent variable or input to a function.

146   Chapter 9. THE CONIC SECTIONS; POLAR COORDINATES; PARAMETRIC EQUATIONS

    a. Thing
    b. Argument0
    c. Undefined
    d. Undefined

59. A _____ is a deliberate process for transforming one or more inputs into one or more results.
   a. Thing
   b. Calculation0
   c. Undefined
   d. Undefined

60. _____ of an object is its speed in a particular direction.
   a. Velocity0
   b. Thing
   c. Undefined
   d. Undefined

61. In mathematics, the _____ of a function is the set of all "output" values produced by that function. Given a function $f : A \to B$, the _____ of f, is defined to be the set $\{x \in B : x = f(a) \text{ for some } a \in A\}$.
   a. Thing
   b. Range0
   c. Undefined
   d. Undefined

62. _____ is the process of planning, recording, and controlling the movement of a craft or vehicle from one place to another.
   a. Thing
   b. Navigation0
   c. Undefined
   d. Undefined

63. In mathematics, a _____ is the result of multiplying, or an expression that identifies factors to be multiplied.
   a. Product0
   b. Thing
   c. Undefined
   d. Undefined

64. _____ are external two-dimensional outlines, with the appearance or configuration of some thing - in contrast to the matter or content or substance of which it is composed.
   a. Thing
   b. Shapes0
   c. Undefined
   d. Undefined

65. _____ is a parameter associated with every conic section.
   a. Thing
   b. Eccentricity0
   c. Undefined
   d. Undefined

66. In mathematics and its applications, a _____ is a system for assigning an n-tuple of numbers or scalars to each point in an n-dimensional space.
   a. Coordinate system0
   b. Concept
   c. Undefined
   d. Undefined

67. A frame of _____ is a particular perspective from which the universe is observed.
   a. Thing
   b. Reference0
   c. Undefined
   d. Undefined

68. In functional analysis and related areas of mathematics the _____ set of a given subset of a vector space is a certain set in the dual space.

Chapter 9. THE CONIC SECTIONS; POLAR COORDINATES; PARAMETRIC EQUATIONS

a. Polar0
b. Thing
c. Undefined
d. Undefined

69. A _____ is a particular perspective from which the universe is observed.
    a. Thing
    b. Frame of reference0
    c. Undefined
    d. Undefined

70. In geometry and trigonometry, a _____ is defined as an angle between two straight intersecting lines of ninety degrees, or one-quarter of a circle.
    a. Right angle0
    b. Thing
    c. Undefined
    d. Undefined

71. The _____ is a unit of plane angle. It is represented by the symbol "rad" or, more rarely, by the superscript c (for "circular measure"). For example, an angle of 1.2 radians would be written "1.2 rad" or "1.2c" (second symbol can produce confusion with centigrads).
    a. Thing
    b. Radian0
    c. Undefined
    d. Undefined

72. A _____ given two distinct points A and B on the _____, is the set of points C on the line containing points A and B such that A is not strictly between C and B.
    a. Ray0
    b. Thing
    c. Undefined
    d. Undefined

73. In mathematics, the conjugate _____ or adjoint matrix of an m-by-n matrix A with complex entries is the n-by-m matrix A* obtained from A by taking the transpose and then taking the complex conjugate of each entry.
    a. Thing
    b. Pairs0
    c. Undefined
    d. Undefined

74. A _____ of a number is the product of that number with any integer.
    a. Thing
    b. Multiple0
    c. Undefined
    d. Undefined

75. A _____ consists of one quarter of the coordinate plane.
    a. Quadrant0
    b. Thing
    c. Undefined
    d. Undefined

76. The _____ are the only integral domain whose positive elements are well-ordered, and in which order is preserved by addition. Like the natural numbers, the _____ form a countably infinite set. The set of all _____ is usually denoted in mathematics by a boldface Z .
    a. Integers0
    b. Thing
    c. Undefined
    d. Undefined

77. _____ is a trigonemtric function that is important when studying triangles and modeling periodic phenomena, among other applications.

148   *Chapter 9. THE CONIC SECTIONS; POLAR COORDINATES; PARAMETRIC EQUATIONS*

   a. Sine0
   b. Thing
   c. Undefined
   d. Undefined

78. In mathematics, _____ is an elementary arithmetic operation. When one of the numbers is a whole number, _____ is the repeated sum of the other number.
   a. Thing
   b. Multiplication0
   c. Undefined
   d. Undefined

79. _____ means "constancy", i.e. if something retains a certain feature even after we change a way of looking at it, then it is symmetric.
   a. Thing
   b. Symmetry0
   c. Undefined
   d. Undefined

80. In mathematics, the _____ of Bernoulli is an eight-shaped algebraic curve described by a Cartesian equation
   a. Thing
   b. Lemniscate0
   c. Undefined
   d. Undefined

81. The _____ of an angle is the ratio of the length of the adjacent side to the length of the hypotenuse.
   a. Cosine0
   b. Concept
   c. Undefined
   d. Undefined

82. The _____ is a statement about a general triangle which relates the lengths of its sides to the cosine of one of its angles.
   a. Thing
   b. Law of cosines0
   c. Undefined
   d. Undefined

83. Acid _____ ratio measures the ability of a company to use its near cash or quick assets to immediately extinguish its current liabilities.
   a. Thing
   b. Test0
   c. Undefined
   d. Undefined

84. In mathematics, a _____ is a connected curve that does not intersect itself and ends at the same point in which it starts.
   a. Closed curve0
   b. Thing
   c. Undefined
   d. Undefined

85. In business, particularly accounting, a _____ is the time intervals that the accounts, statement, payments, or other calculations cover.
   a. Thing
   b. Period0
   c. Undefined
   d. Undefined

86. The mathematical concept of a _____ expresses the intuitive idea of deterministic dependence between two quantities, one of which is viewed as primary and the other as secondary. A _____ then is a way to associate a unique output for each input of a specified type, for example, a real number or an element of a given set.

Chapter 9. THE CONIC SECTIONS; POLAR COORDINATES; PARAMETRIC EQUATIONS

a. Function0
b. Thing
c. Undefined
d. Undefined

87. In elementary algebra, an _____ is a set that contains every real number between two indicated numbers and may contain the two numbers themselves.
a. Thing
b. Interval0
c. Undefined
d. Undefined

88. The term _____ refers to the largest and the smallest element of a set.
a. Thing
b. Extreme value0
c. Undefined
d. Undefined

89. In mathematics, _____ are the intuitive idea of a geometrical one-dimensional and continuous object.
a. Thing
b. Curves0
c. Undefined
d. Undefined

90. In geometry, the _____ is an epicycloid with one cusp. That is, a _____ is a curve that can be produced as the path of a point on the circumference of a circle as that circle rolls around another fixed circle with the same radius.
a. Thing
b. Cardioid0
c. Undefined
d. Undefined

91. A _____ is a movement of an object in a circular motion. A two-dimensional object rotates around a center (or point) of _____. A three-dimensional object rotates around a line called an axis. If the axis of _____ is within the body, the body is said to rotate upon itself, or spinâ€"which implies relative speed and perhaps free-movement with angular momentum. A circular motion about an external point, e.g. the Earth about the Sun, is called an orbit or more properly an orbital revolution.
a. Thing
b. Rotation0
c. Undefined
d. Undefined

92. A _____ function curves downwards. The graph of a _____ function of one variable remains above its tangents and below its cords.
a. Convex0
b. Thing
c. Undefined
d. Undefined

93. In mathematics, a _____ is a heart-shaped mathematical curve. The cardioid is considered a special case, with a cusp.
a. Limagon0
b. Thing
c. Undefined
d. Undefined

94. In computer programs, an important form of control flow is the _____.
a. Inner loop0
b. Thing
c. Undefined
d. Undefined

95. The _____ of a mathematical object is its size: a property by which it can be larger or smaller than other objects of the same kind; in technical terms, an ordering of the class of objects to which it belongs.

Chapter 9. THE CONIC SECTIONS; POLAR COORDINATES; PARAMETRIC EQUATIONS

    a. Thing
    b. Magnitude0
    c. Undefined
    d. Undefined

96. In statistics, a _____ measure is one which is measuring what is supposed to measure.
    a. Valid0
    b. Thing
    c. Undefined
    d. Undefined

97. In mathematical analysis, _____ are objects which generalize functions and probability distributions.
    a. Distribution0
    b. Thing
    c. Undefined
    d. Undefined

98. In physics, a _____ may refer to the scalar _____ or to the vector _____.
    a. Thing
    b. Potential0
    c. Undefined
    d. Undefined

99. In physics, _____ is an influence that may cause an object to accelerate. It may be experienced as a lift, a push, or a pull. The actual acceleration of the body is determined by the vector sum of all forces acting on it, known as net _____ or resultant _____.
    a. Thing
    b. Force0
    c. Undefined
    d. Undefined

100. _____ are the basic objects of study in graph theory. Informally speaking, a graph is a set of objects called points, nodes, or vertices connected by links called lines or edges.
    a. Graphs0
    b. Thing
    c. Undefined
    d. Undefined

101. In mathematics, a _____ is a mathematical statement which appears likely to be true, but has not been formally proven to be true under the rules of mathematical logic.
    a. Concept
    b. Conjecture0
    c. Undefined
    d. Undefined

102. A circular _____ or circle _____ also known as a pie piece is the portion of a circle enclosed by two radii and an arc.
    a. Thing
    b. Sector0
    c. Undefined
    d. Undefined

103. _____ is an adjective usually refering to being in the centre.
    a. Thing
    b. Central0
    c. Undefined
    d. Undefined

104. In mathematics, an _____ is a statement about the relative size or order of two objects.
    a. Inequality0
    b. Thing
    c. Undefined
    d. Undefined

105. In topology, the _____ are subsets S of a topological space X is the set of points which can be approached both from S and from the outside of S.

Chapter 9. THE CONIC SECTIONS; POLAR COORDINATES; PARAMETRIC EQUATIONS

a. Boundaries0
b. Thing
c. Undefined
d. Undefined

106. A _____ function is a function for which, intuitively, small changes in the input result in small changes in the output.
a. Event
b. Continuous0
c. Undefined
d. Undefined

107. Generally, a _____ is a splitting of something into parts.
a. Partition0
b. Thing
c. Undefined
d. Undefined

108. _____ is a process of combining or accumulating. It may also refer to:
a. Integration0
b. Thing
c. Undefined
d. Undefined

109. _____ is a cubic curve generated by increasing or diminishing the radius vector of a variable point Q on a straight line AB by the distance QC of the point from the foot of the perpendicular drawn from the origin to the fixed line.
a. Strophoid0
b. Thing
c. Undefined
d. Undefined

110. In mathematics, a _____ may be described informally as a number that can be given by an infinite decimal representation.
a. Thing
b. Real number0
c. Undefined
d. Undefined

111. _____ is either of the two parts into which a plane divides the three-dimensional space. More generally, a _____ is either of the two parts into which a hyperplane divides an affine space.
a. Half-space0
b. Thing
c. Undefined
d. Undefined

112. In Euclidean geometry, an _____ is a closed segment of a differentiable curve in the two-dimensional plane; for example, a circular _____ is a segment of a circle.
a. Arc0
b. Concept
c. Undefined
d. Undefined

113. In mathematics, a _____ of a k-place relation $L \subseteq X_1 \times ... \times X_k$ is one of the sets X_j, $1 \leq j \leq k$. In the special case where k = 2 and $L \subseteq X_1 \times X_2$ is a function $L : X_1 \to X_2$, it is conventional to refer to X_1 as the _____ of the function and to refer to X_2 as the codomain of the function.
a. Thing
b. Domain0
c. Undefined
d. Undefined

114. An _____ is an equality that remains true regardless of the values of any variables that appear within it, to distinguish it from an equality which is true under more particular conditions.

152 *Chapter 9. THE CONIC SECTIONS; POLAR COORDINATES; PARAMETRIC EQUATIONS*

    a. Thing
    b. Identity0
    c. Undefined
    d. Undefined

115. A _____ is the quantity that defines certain relatively constant characteristics of systems or functions..
    a. Parameter0
    b. Thing
    c. Undefined
    d. Undefined

116. _____ is the transport of people on a trip/journey or the process or time involved in a person or object moving from one location to another.
    a. Thing
    b. Travel0
    c. Undefined
    d. Undefined

117. A _____ is an annuity that has no definite end, or a stream of cash payments that continues forever.
    a. Perpetuity0
    b. Thing
    c. Undefined
    d. Undefined

118. A _____ is a negotiable instrument instructing a financial institution to pay a specific amount of a specific currency from a specific demand account held in the maker/depositor's name with that institution. Both the maker and payee may be natural persons or legal entities.
    a. Check0
    b. Thing
    c. Undefined
    d. Undefined

119. The word _____ comes from the Latin word linearis, which means created by lines.
    a. Linear0
    b. Thing
    c. Undefined
    d. Undefined

120. _____ is a circle with a unit radius, i.e., a circle whose radius is 1.
    a. Thing
    b. Unit circle0
    c. Undefined
    d. Undefined

121. In mathematics, a _____ curve is the graph of the system of parametric equations, which describes complex harmonic motion.
    a. Thing
    b. Lissajous0
    c. Undefined
    d. Undefined

122. _____ statistics are statistics that estimate population parameters.
    a. Parametric0
    b. Thing
    c. Undefined
    d. Undefined

123. In mathematics, _____ bear slight similarity to functions: they allow one to use arbitrary values, called parameters, in place of independent variables in equations, which in turn provide values for dependent variables. A simple kinematical example is when one uses a time parameter to determine the position, velocity, and other information about a body in motion.
    a. Thing
    b. Parametric equations0
    c. Undefined
    d. Undefined

Chapter 9. THE CONIC SECTIONS; POLAR COORDINATES; PARAMETRIC EQUATIONS

124. In mathematics, _____ expressions is used to reduce the expression into the lowest possible term.
   a. Simplifying0
   b. Thing
   c. Undefined
   d. Undefined

125. _____ is a mathematical subject that includes the study of limits, derivatives, integrals, and power series and constitutes a major part of modern university curriculum.
   a. Thing
   b. Calculus0
   c. Undefined
   d. Undefined

126. _____ was an Italian physicist, mathematician, astronomer, and philosopher who is closely associated with the scientific revolution.
   a. Galileo Galilei0
   b. Person
   c. Undefined
   d. Undefined

127. A _____ is any object propelled through space by the applicationp of a force.
   a. Projectile0
   b. Thing
   c. Undefined
   d. Undefined

128. _____ is the path a moving object follows through space.
   a. Thing
   b. Projectile motion0
   c. Undefined
   d. Undefined

129. _____ is defined as the rate of change or derivative with respect to time of velocity.
   a. Acceleration0
   b. Thing
   c. Undefined
   d. Undefined

130. A _____ is a function that assigns a number to subsets of a given set.
   a. Thing
   b. Measure0
   c. Undefined
   d. Undefined

131. Initial objects are also called _____, and terminal objects are also called final.
   a. Coterminal0
   b. Thing
   c. Undefined
   d. Undefined

132. In mathematics, the word _____ is used informally to refer to certain distinct bodies of knowledge about mathematics.
   a. Thing
   b. Theoretical0
   c. Undefined
   d. Undefined

133. In the scientific method, an _____ (Latin: ex-+-periri, "of (or from) trying"), is a set of actions and observations, performed in the context of solving a particular problem or question, in order to support or falsify a hypothesis or research concerning phenomena.
   a. Thing
   b. Experiment0
   c. Undefined
   d. Undefined

154   Chapter 9. THE CONIC SECTIONS; POLAR COORDINATES; PARAMETRIC EQUATIONS

134. _____ is often used to describe the measurement of the steepness, incline, gradient, or grade of a straight line. The _____ is defined as the ratio of the "rise" divided by the "run" between two points on a line, or in other words, the ratio of the altitude change to the horizontal distance between any two points on the line.
   a. Thing
   b. Slope0
   c. Undefined
   d. Undefined

135. In mathematics, a _____ in elementary terms is any of a variety of different functions from geometry, such as rotations, reflections and translations.
   a. Thing
   b. Transformation0
   c. Undefined
   d. Undefined

136. A quadratic equation with real solutions, called roots, which may be real or complex, is given by the _____: $x = \frac{-b \pm \sqrt{b^2 - 4ac}}{2a}$.
   a. Quadratic formula0
   b. Thing
   c. Undefined
   d. Undefined

137. In set theory and other branches of mathematics, the _____ of a collection of sets is the set that contains everything that belongs to any of the sets, but nothing else.
   a. Union0
   b. Thing
   c. Undefined
   d. Undefined

138. In mathematics, a set is called _____ if there is a bijection between the set and some set of the form {1, 2, ..., n} where n is a natural number.
   a. Finite0
   b. Thing
   c. Undefined
   d. Undefined

139. The _____ is a measurement of how a function changes when the values of its inputs change.
   a. Thing
   b. Derivative0
   c. Undefined
   d. Undefined

140. A _____ is the result of the addition of a set of numbers. The numbers may be natural numbers, complex numbers, matrices, or still more complicated objects. An infinite _____ is a subtle procedure known as a series.
   a. Thing
   b. Sum0
   c. Undefined
   d. Undefined

141. _____ also called rectification of a curve—was historically difficult.
   a. Arc length0
   b. Thing
   c. Undefined
   d. Undefined

142. In mathematics, a _____ is a statement that can be proved on the basis of explicitly stated or previously agreed assumptions.
   a. Theorem0
   b. Thing
   c. Undefined
   d. Undefined

143. _____ means in succession or back-to-back

Chapter 9. THE CONIC SECTIONS; POLAR COORDINATES; PARAMETRIC EQUATIONS

a. Consecutive0
b. Thing
c. Undefined
d. Undefined

144. The _____ of a function is an extension of the concept of a sum, and are identified or found through the use of integration.
   a. Integral0
   b. Thing
   c. Undefined
   d. Undefined

145. _____ is a method for approximating the values of integrals.
   a. Riemann sum0
   b. Thing
   c. Undefined
   d. Undefined

146. The _____ is the distance around a closed curve. _____ is a kind of perimeter.
   a. Thing
   b. Circumference0
   c. Undefined
   d. Undefined

147. In calculus, the _____ is a formula for the derivative of the composite of two functions.
   a. Concept
   b. Chain rule0
   c. Undefined
   d. Undefined

148. In mathematics, a _____ is a curve in a Euclidian plane. The most frequently studied types are the smooth _____, and the algebraic _____.
   a. Thing
   b. Plane curve0
   c. Undefined
   d. Undefined

149. A _____ is a special kind of ratio, indicating a relationship between two measurements with different units, such as miles to gallons or cents to pounds.
   a. Thing
   b. Rate0
   c. Undefined
   d. Undefined

150. In geometry, an _____ is a point at which a line segment or ray terminates.
   a. Thing
   b. Endpoint0
   c. Undefined
   d. Undefined

151. In mathematics, _____ is a part of the set theoretic notion of function.
   a. Thing
   b. Image0
   c. Undefined
   d. Undefined

152. _____ was a highly influential French philosopher, mathematician, scientist, and writer. Dubbed the "Founder of Modern Philosophy", and the "Father of Modern Mathematics". His theories provided the basis for the calculus of Newton and Leibniz, by applying infinitesimal calculus to the tangent line problem, thus permitting the evolution of that branch of modern mathematics
   a. Descartes0
   b. Person
   c. Undefined
   d. Undefined

153. _____ is a function that extends the concept of an ordinary sum

156 *Chapter 9. THE CONIC SECTIONS; POLAR COORDINATES; PARAMETRIC EQUATIONS*

a. Integrand0
b. Thing
c. Undefined
d. Undefined

154. An _____ of a function f is a function F whose derivative is equal to f, i.e., F' = f.
a. Antiderivative0
b. Thing
c. Undefined
d. Undefined

155. _____ is the shape of a hanging flexible chain or cable when supported at its ends and acted upon by a uniform gravitational force. The chain is steepest near the points of suspension because this part of the chain has the most weight pulling down on it. Toward the bottom, the slope of the chain decreases because the chain is supporting less weight.
a. Thing
b. Catenary0
c. Undefined
d. Undefined

156. In mathematics, a _____ is the set of all points in three-dimensional space (R^3) which are at distance r from a fixed point of that space, where r is a positive real number called the radius of the _____. The fixed point is called the center or centre, and is not part of the _____ itself.
a. Sphere0
b. Thing
c. Undefined
d. Undefined

157. _____, a field in mathematics, is the study of how functions change when their inputs change. The primary object of study in _____ is the derivative.
a. Thing
b. Differential calculus0
c. Undefined
d. Undefined

158. A _____ is a symbolic representation denoting a quantity or expression. It often represents an "unknown" quantity that has the potential to change.
a. Variable0
b. Thing
c. Undefined
d. Undefined

159. In physics, the _____ of a system of particles is a specific point at which, for many purposes, the system's mass behaves as if it were concentrated.
a. Thing
b. Center of mass0
c. Undefined
d. Undefined

160. _____ is the property of a physical object that quantifies the amount of matter and energy it is equivalent to.
a. Thing
b. Mass0
c. Undefined
d. Undefined

161. _____ of a two-dimensional figure is a line such that, if a perpendicular is constructed, any two points lying on the perpendicular at equal distances from the _____ are identical.
a. Axis of symmetry0
b. Thing
c. Undefined
d. Undefined

162. Sir Isaac _____, was an English physicist, mathematician, astronomer, natural philosopher, and alchemist, regarded by many as the greatest figure in the history of science

Chapter 9. THE CONIC SECTIONS; POLAR COORDINATES; PARAMETRIC EQUATIONS 157

    a. Newton0   b. Person
    c. Undefined   d. Undefined

163. _____ was a German mathematician and philosopher. He invented calculus independently of Newton, and his notation is the one in general use since.
    a. Leibniz0   b. Person
    c. Undefined   d. Undefined

164. _____ is an extension of the concept of a sum.
    a. Thing   b. Definite integral0
    c. Undefined   d. Undefined

165. The _____ of a right circular cone is the distance from any point on the circle to the apex of the cone.
    a. Thing   b. Slant height0
    c. Undefined   d. Undefined

166. A _____ surface is the surface or face of a solid on its sides. It can also be defined as any face or surface that is not a base.
    a. Lateral0   b. Thing
    c. Undefined   d. Undefined

167. In mathematics, a _____ is an algebraic structure in which addition and multiplication are defined and have properties listed below.
    a. Thing   b. Ring0
    c. Undefined   d. Undefined

168. A _____ is the curve defined by the path of a point on the edge of circular wheel as the wheel rolls along a straight line.
    a. Cycloid0   b. Thing
    c. Undefined   d. Undefined

169. In mathematics, _____ are two-dimensional manifolds or surfaces that are perfectly flat.
    a. Thing   b. Planes0
    c. Undefined   d. Undefined

170. An _____ is a type of quadric surface that is a higher dimensional analogue of an ellipse.
    a. Ellipsoid0   b. Thing
    c. Undefined   d. Undefined

171. _____ is mass m per unit volume V.
    a. Thing   b. Density0
    c. Undefined   d. Undefined

158 Chapter 9. THE CONIC SECTIONS; POLAR COORDINATES; PARAMETRIC EQUATIONS

172. In geometry, a _____ is a surface of revolution generated by revolving a circle in three dimensional space about an axis coplanar with the circle, which does not touch the circle. Examples of tori include the surfaces of doughnuts and inner tubes. A circle rotated about a chord of the circle is called a _____ in some contexts, but this is not a common usage in mathematics. The shape produced when a circle is rotated about a chord resembles a round cushion. _____ was the Latin word for a cushion of this shape.
- a. Thing
- b. Torus0
- c. Undefined
- d. Undefined

173. _____ is the force that opposes the relative motion or tendency toward such motion of two surfaces in contact.
- a. Friction0
- b. Thing
- c. Undefined
- d. Undefined

174. _____ is the weakest of the four fundamental forces of bature, as described by Issac Newton
- a. Thing
- b. Gravitational force0
- c. Undefined
- d. Undefined

175. In acoustics and telecommunication, the _____ of a wave is a component frequency of the signal that is an integer multiple of the fundamental frequency.
- a. Thing
- b. Harmonic0
- c. Undefined
- d. Undefined

176. Simple _____ is the motion of a simple harmonic oscillator, a motion that is neither driven nor damped. Complex _____ is the superposition — linear combination — of several simultaneous simple harmonic motions.
- a. Thing
- b. Harmonic motion0
- c. Undefined
- d. Undefined

177. _____ is a kind of property which exists as magnitude or multitude. It is among the basic classes of things along with quality, substance, change, and relation.
- a. Thing
- b. Amount0
- c. Undefined
- d. Undefined

178. _____ is a field of mathematics that deals with functionals, as opposed to ordinary calculus which deals with functions. Such functionals can for example be formed as integrals involving an unknown function and its derivatives. The interest is in extremal functions: those making the functional attain a maximum or minimum value.
- a. Calculus of variations0
- b. Thing
- c. Undefined
- d. Undefined

179. _____ is the property of two events happening at the same time in at least one reference frame.
- a. Simultaneous0
- b. Thing
- c. Undefined
- d. Undefined

180. In mathematics, a _____ are a curve which emanates from a central point, getting progressively farther away as it revolves around the point.
- a. Thing
- b. Spirals0
- c. Undefined
- d. Undefined

Chapter 9. THE CONIC SECTIONS; POLAR COORDINATES; PARAMETRIC EQUATIONS

181. _____ is a concept in traditional logic referring to a "type of immediate inference in which from a given proposition another proposition is inferred which has as its subject the predicate of the original proposition and as its predicate the subject of the original proposition (the quality of the proposition being retained)."
- a. Conversion0
- b. Concept
- c. Undefined
- d. Undefined

182. A _____ is a function for which, intuitively, small changes in the input result in small changes in the output.
- a. Event
- b. Continuous function0
- c. Undefined
- d. Undefined

Chapter 10. SEQUENCES: INDETERMINATE FORMS; IMPROPER INTEGRALS

1. In a large distribution of data it is often easier to understand the data if it is grouped into intervals where each _____ can contain more than one data value. Distributions are often reduced to 10 to 20 intervals.
   - a. Interval1
   - b. ACTRAN
   - c. Undefined
   - d. Undefined

2. At times we must contend with variables that assume a large number of values. In this case it is typical to create _____ of values of the variable and then make a frequency tally of the number of observations falling within each interval. As is the case with any data reduction technique, detail is lost.
   - a. Intervals1
   - b. ACTRAN
   - c. Undefined
   - d. Undefined

3. There are properties of objects that do assume one and only value, and we refer to these characteristics as constants. _____, then, are the invariables that differentiate one class of objects from another.
   - a. 15 theorem
   - b. Constants1
   - c. Undefined
   - d. Undefined

4. A measure of variability, the _____ is the distance from the lowest to the highest score.
   - a. 15 theorem
   - b. Range1
   - c. Undefined
   - d. Undefined

5. The very fact that we are measuring objects with respect to some characteristic implies that the objects differ in that characteristic; or stated in another way, that the characteristic can take on a number of different values. These properties or characteristics of an object that can assume two or more different values are referred to as a _____.
   - a. 15 theorem
   - b. Variable1
   - c. Undefined
   - d. Undefined

6. An _____ is an indication of the value of an unknown quantity based on observed data. More formally, an _____ is the particular value of an estimator that is obtained from a particular sample of data and used to indicate the value of a parameter.
   - a. ACTRAN
   - b. Estimate1
   - c. Undefined
   - d. Undefined

7. An _____ is any process or study, which results in the collection of data, the outcome of which is unknown. In statistics, the term is usually restricted to situations in which the researcher has control over some of the conditions under which the _____ takes place.
   - a. Experiment1
   - b. ACTRAN
   - c. Undefined
   - d. Undefined

8. The probability of correctly rejecting a false Ho is referred to as _____.
   - a. 15 theorem
   - b. Power1
   - c. Undefined
   - d. Undefined

9. The most important measure of central tendency, and one of the basic building blocks of all statistical analysis, is the arithmetic _____. It is simply the sum of all the set of values divided by the number of values involved. As a measure of central tendency, it is affected by extreme scores, and it assumes a ratio scale of measurement.

Chapter 10. SEQUENCES: INDETERMINATE FORMS; IMPROPER INTEGRALS

   a. 15 theorem
   c. Undefined
   b. Mean1
   d. Undefined

10. A statistic calculated by multiplying the data values together and taking the N-th root of the result., the _____ is often used as a measure of central tendency for skewed distributions.
   a. Geometric mean1
   c. Undefined
   b. 15 theorem
   d. Undefined

11. The goal of most inferential statistical analyses is to be able to generalize or apply the findings to the entire population and not just to the sample. The concept of _____ requires that the researcher determine some level of probability that the findings were due to chance or that they actually describe the population. The value of the probability that the findings were due to chance is usually reported when the findings of an analysis is reported.
   a. Generalization1
   c. Undefined
   b. 15 theorem
   d. Undefined

12. A number that does not change in value in a given situation is a _____.
   a. 15 theorem
   c. Undefined
   b. Constant1
   d. Undefined

13. Statistical analysis, sometimes referred to simply as _____, is concerned with the definition and collection, organization, and interpretation of data according to well-defined procedures. The term itself, _____, is a defining characteristic of a sample, such as a sample mean, or sample standard deviation.
   a. 15 theorem
   c. Undefined
   b. Statistics1
   d. Undefined

14. A _____ provides a quantitative description of the likely occurrence of a particular event. _____ is conventionally expressed on a scale from 0 to 1; a rare event has a _____ close to 0, a very common event has a _____ close to 1. _____ is calculated as the ratio of the number of favorable events to the total number of possible events.
   a. Probability1
   c. Undefined
   b. 15 theorem
   d. Undefined

15. _____, the height of the curve for a given value of X; closely related to the probability of an observation in an interval around X.
   a. 15 theorem
   c. Undefined
   b. Density1
   d. Undefined

16. The _____ of a continuous random variable is a function, which can be integrated to obtain the probability that the random variable takes a value in a given interval.
   a. Probability Density Function1
   c. Undefined
   b. 15 theorem
   d. Undefined

17. A measure of variability in a distribution, the _____ is the square root of the variance. The _____ measures the variability of scores around the mean: the standardized difference. It is the square root of the mean square error.

a. Standard deviation1
b. 15 theorem
c. Undefined
d. Undefined

18. A _____ refers to the distance or difference between any score in a distribution of data from the mean.
   a. 15 theorem
   b. Deviation1
   c. Undefined
   d. Undefined

Chapter 11. INFINITE SERIES

1. The Greek letter _____ indicates summation.
   a. 15 theorem
   b. Sigma1
   c. Undefined
   d. Undefined

2. The very fact that we are measuring objects with respect to some characteristic implies that the objects differ in that characteristic; or stated in another way, that the characteristic can take on a number of different values. These properties or characteristics of an object that can assume two or more different values are referred to as a _____.
   a. 15 theorem
   b. Variable1
   c. Undefined
   d. Undefined

3. A number that does not change in value in a given situation is a _____.
   a. Constant1
   b. 15 theorem
   c. Undefined
   d. Undefined

4. The most important measure of central tendency, and one of the basic building blocks of all statistical analysis, is the arithmetic _____. It is simply the sum of all the set of values divided by the number of values involved. As a measure of central tendency, it is affected by extreme scores, and it assumes a ratio scale of measurement.
   a. Mean1
   b. 15 theorem
   c. Undefined
   d. Undefined

5. In a large distribution of data it is often easier to understand the data if it is grouped into intervals where each _____ can contain more than one data value. Distributions are often reduced to 10 to 20 intervals.
   a. ACTRAN
   b. Interval1
   c. Undefined
   d. Undefined

6. At times we must contend with variables that assume a large number of values. In this case it is typical to create _____ of values of the variable and then make a frequency tally of the number of observations falling within each interval. As is the case with any data reduction technique, detail is lost.
   a. Intervals1
   b. ACTRAN
   c. Undefined
   d. Undefined

7. An _____ is an indication of the value of an unknown quantity based on observed data. More formally, an _____ is the particular value of an estimator that is obtained from a particular sample of data and used to indicate the value of a parameter.
   a. ACTRAN
   b. Estimate1
   c. Undefined
   d. Undefined

8. By _____ we mean an average calculated by taking into account not only the frequencies of the values of a variable but also some other factor such as their variance. The _____ of observed data is the result of dividing the sum of the products of each observed value, the number of times it occurs, and this other factor by the total number of observations
   a. Weighted average1
   b. 15 theorem
   c. Undefined
   d. Undefined

9. A _____ is a subset or portion of a population. Samples are extremely important in the field of statistical analysis, since due to economic and practical constraints we usually cannot make measurements on every single member of the particular population.

a. 15 theorem
c. Undefined
b. Sample1
d. Undefined

10. The probability of correctly rejecting a false Ho is referred to as _____.
   a. Power1
   b. 15 theorem
   c. Undefined
   d. Undefined

11. The same statistical principles apply to the evaluation of observed _____ between sets of data. The field of statistics provides the necessary techniques for making statements of our certainty that there are real as opposed to chance differences.
   a. Differences1
   b. 15 theorem
   c. Undefined
   d. Undefined

12. A _____ is simply a polynomial with two terms.
   a. Binomial1
   b. 15 theorem
   c. Undefined
   d. Undefined

13. The goal of most inferential statistical analyses is to be able to generalize or apply the findings to the entire population and not just to the sample. The concept of _____ requires that the researcher determine some level of probability that the findings were due to chance or that they actually describe the population. The value of the probability that the findings were due to chance is usually reported when the findings of an analysis is reported.
   a. 15 theorem
   b. Generalization1
   c. Undefined
   d. Undefined

14. There are properties of objects that do assume one and only value, and we refer to these characteristics as constants. _____, then, are the invariables that differentiate one class of objects from another.
   a. Constants1
   b. 15 theorem
   c. Undefined
   d. Undefined

15. The _____ refers to the amount of change in Y for a 1 unit change in X; or in-other-words, the rate of change in the predicted value as a function of a change in the predictor variable.
   a. Slope1
   b. 15 theorem
   c. Undefined
   d. Undefined

Chapter 12. VECTORS

1. A _____ is a scheme for the numerical representation of the values of a variable. The interpretation we place upon the numbers of the scale, rather than the numbers themselves, makes the _____ useful. The most common scales are nominal, ordinal, interval
   - a. Scale1
   - b. 15 theorem
   - c. Undefined
   - d. Undefined

2. _____ is implied when data values are distributed in the same way above and below the middle of the sample.
   - a. Symmetry1
   - b. 15 theorem
   - c. Undefined
   - d. Undefined

3. The _____ is often confused with the median. The Median is a statistic for the distribution whereas the _____ provides a statistic for an interval; it is the center of the interval; the arithmetic average of the upper and lower limits.
   - a. Midpoint1
   - b. 15 theorem
   - c. Undefined
   - d. Undefined

4. _____ is used synonymously for variable.
   - a. Factor1
   - b. 15 theorem
   - c. Undefined
   - d. Undefined

5. The most important measure of central tendency, and one of the basic building blocks of all statistical analysis, is the arithmetic _____. It is simply the sum of all the set of values divided by the number of values involved. As a measure of central tendency, it is affected by extreme scores, and it assumes a ratio scale of measurement.
   - a. 15 theorem
   - b. Mean1
   - c. Undefined
   - d. Undefined

6. A number that does not change in value in a given situation is a _____.
   - a. 15 theorem
   - b. Constant1
   - c. Undefined
   - d. Undefined

7. The goal of most inferential statistical analyses is to be able to generalize or apply the findings to the entire population and not just to the sample. The concept of _____ requires that the researcher determine some level of probability that the findings were due to chance or that they actually describe the population. The value of the probability that the findings were due to chance is usually reported when the findings of an analysis is reported.
   - a. Generalization1
   - b. 15 theorem
   - c. Undefined
   - d. Undefined

8. The probability of correctly rejecting a false Ho is referred to as _____.
   - a. 15 theorem
   - b. Power1
   - c. Undefined
   - d. Undefined

9. A _____ is a value used to represent a certain population characteristic. Because of the impracticality of measuring an entire population to determine this value, parameters are usually estimated.
   - a. Parameter1
   - b. 15 theorem
   - c. Undefined
   - d. Undefined

10. The defining characteristics of populations are called _____. Observations must be made on every single member of the population in question in order to precisely state the value of _____.

a. Parameters1
b. 15 theorem
c. Undefined
d. Undefined

11. The value of Y when X is 0 is the _____.
a. ACTRAN
b. Intercept1
c. Undefined
d. Undefined

Chapter 13. VECTOR CALCULUS

1. In a large distribution of data it is often easier to understand the data if it is grouped into intervals where each _____ can contain more than one data value. Distributions are often reduced to 10 to 20 intervals.
   - a. ACTRAN
   - b. Interval1
   - c. Undefined
   - d. Undefined

2. A number that does not change in value in a given situation is a _____.
   - a. Constant1
   - b. 15 theorem
   - c. Undefined
   - d. Undefined

3. There are properties of objects that do assume one and only value, and we refer to these characteristics as constants. _____, then, are the invariables that differentiate one class of objects from another.
   - a. Constants1
   - b. 15 theorem
   - c. Undefined
   - d. Undefined

4. An _____ is any process or study, which results in the collection of data, the outcome of which is unknown. In statistics, the term is usually restricted to situations in which the researcher has control over some of the conditions under which the _____ takes place.
   - a. ACTRAN
   - b. Experiment1
   - c. Undefined
   - d. Undefined

5. A _____ is a value used to represent a certain population characteristic. Because of the impracticality of measuring an entire population to determine this value, parameters are usually estimated.
   - a. Parameter1
   - b. 15 theorem
   - c. Undefined
   - d. Undefined

6. A measure of variability, the _____ is the distance from the lowest to the highest score.
   - a. 15 theorem
   - b. Range1
   - c. Undefined
   - d. Undefined

7. The most important measure of central tendency, and one of the basic building blocks of all statistical analysis, is the arithmetic _____. It is simply the sum of all the set of values divided by the number of values involved. As a measure of central tendency, it is affected by extreme scores, and it assumes a ratio scale of measurement.
   - a. Mean1
   - b. 15 theorem
   - c. Undefined
   - d. Undefined

8. An _____ is an indication of the value of an unknown quantity based on observed data. More formally, an _____ is the particular value of an estimator that is obtained from a particular sample of data and used to indicate the value of a parameter.
   - a. ACTRAN
   - b. Estimate1
   - c. Undefined
   - d. Undefined

9. The _____ refers to the amount of change in Y for a 1 unit change in X; or in-other-words, the rate of change in the predicted value as a function of a change in the predictor variable.
   - a. Slope1
   - b. 15 theorem
   - c. Undefined
   - d. Undefined

Chapter 13. VECTOR CALCULUS

10. By _____ we mean collecting observations made upon our environment -- observations, which are the results of measurements using clocks, balances, measuring rods, counting operations, or other objectively defined measuring instruments or procedures. _____ may mean simply counting the number of times a particular property occurs.
   a. Data1
   b. 15 theorem
   c. Undefined
   d. Undefined

11. _____ refer to any data source, whether individuals, physical or biological things, geographic locations, time periods, or events; that is, anything upon which observations can be made.
   a. ACTRAN
   b. Objects1
   c. Undefined
   d. Undefined

12. The probability of correctly rejecting a false Ho is referred to as _____.
   a. 15 theorem
   b. Power1
   c. Undefined
   d. Undefined

Chapter 14. FUNCTIONS OF SEVERAL VARIABLES

1. _____ are characteristics or properties of an object that can take on one or more different values.
   a. 15 theorem
   b. Variables1
   c. Undefined
   d. Undefined

2. A measure of variability, the _____ is the distance from the lowest to the highest score.
   a. Range1
   b. 15 theorem
   c. Undefined
   d. Undefined

3. The very fact that we are measuring objects with respect to some characteristic implies that the objects differ in that characteristic; or stated in another way, that the characteristic can take on a number of different values. These properties or characteristics of an object that can assume two or more different values are referred to as a _____.
   a. Variable1
   b. 15 theorem
   c. Undefined
   d. Undefined

4. A number that does not change in value in a given situation is a _____.
   a. Constant1
   b. 15 theorem
   c. Undefined
   d. Undefined

5. In a large distribution of data it is often easier to understand the data if it is grouped into intervals where each _____ can contain more than one data value. Distributions are often reduced to 10 to 20 intervals.
   a. Interval1
   b. ACTRAN
   c. Undefined
   d. Undefined

6. There are properties of objects that do assume one and only value, and we refer to these characteristics as constants. _____, then, are the invariables that differentiate one class of objects from another.
   a. 15 theorem
   b. Constants1
   c. Undefined
   d. Undefined

7. _____ is implied when data values are distributed in the same way above and below the middle of the sample.
   a. Symmetry1
   b. 15 theorem
   c. Undefined
   d. Undefined

8. An _____ is any process or study, which results in the collection of data, the outcome of which is unknown. In statistics, the term is usually restricted to situations in which the researcher has control over some of the conditions under which the _____ takes place.
   a. Experiment1
   b. ACTRAN
   c. Undefined
   d. Undefined

9. The most important measure of central tendency, and one of the basic building blocks of all statistical analysis, is the arithmetic _____. It is simply the sum of all the set of values divided by the number of values involved. As a measure of central tendency, it is affected by extreme scores, and it assumes a ratio scale of measurement.
   a. Mean1
   b. 15 theorem
   c. Undefined
   d. Undefined

10. The _____ refers to the amount of change in Y for a 1 unit change in X; or in-other-words, the rate of change in the predicted value as a function of a change in the predictor variable.

a. 15 theorem
c. Undefined

b. Slope1
d. Undefined

11. The goal of most inferential statistical analyses is to be able to generalize or apply the findings to the entire population and not just to the sample. The concept of _____ requires that the researcher determine some level of probability that the findings were due to chance or that they actually describe the population. The value of the probability that the findings were due to chance is usually reported when the findings of an analysis is reported.

a. Generalization1
c. Undefined

b. 15 theorem
d. Undefined

12. A _____ provides a quantitative description of the likely occurrence of a particular event. _____ is conventionally expressed on a scale from 0 to 1; a rare event has a _____ close to 0, a very common event has a _____ close to 1. _____ is calculated as the ratio of the number of favorable events to the total number of possible events.

a. 15 theorem
c. Undefined

b. Probability1
d. Undefined

Chapter 15. GRADIENTS; EXTREME VALUES; DIFFERENTIALS

1. The very fact that we are measuring objects with respect to some characteristic implies that the objects differ in that characteristic; or stated in another way, that the characteristic can take on a number of different values. These properties or characteristics of an object that can assume two or more different values are referred to as a _____.
   a. Variable1
   b. 15 theorem
   c. Undefined
   d. Undefined

2. _____ are characteristics or properties of an object that can take on one or more different values.
   a. 15 theorem
   b. Variables1
   c. Undefined
   d. Undefined

3. In a large distribution of data it is often easier to understand the data if it is grouped into intervals where each _____ can contain more than one data value. Distributions are often reduced to 10 to 20 intervals.
   a. Interval1
   b. ACTRAN
   c. Undefined
   d. Undefined

4. The same statistical principles apply to the evaluation of observed _____ between sets of data. The field of statistics provides the necessary techniques for making statements of our certainty that there are real as opposed to chance differences.
   a. 15 theorem
   b. Differences1
   c. Undefined
   d. Undefined

5. The _____ refers to the amount of change in Y for a 1 unit change in X; or in-other-words, the rate of change in the predicted value as a function of a change in the predictor variable.
   a. 15 theorem
   b. Slope1
   c. Undefined
   d. Undefined

6. _____, the height of the curve for a given value of X; closely related to the probability of an observation in an interval around X.
   a. Density1
   b. 15 theorem
   c. Undefined
   d. Undefined

7. A number that does not change in value in a given situation is a _____.
   a. Constant1
   b. 15 theorem
   c. Undefined
   d. Undefined

8. A _____ is a value used to represent a certain population characteristic. Because of the impracticality of measuring an entire population to determine this value, parameters are usually estimated.
   a. 15 theorem
   b. Parameter1
   c. Undefined
   d. Undefined

9. In statistics an arrangement of values of a variable showing their observed or theoretical frequency of occurrence is called a _____.
   a. Distribution1
   b. 15 theorem
   c. Undefined
   d. Undefined

Chapter 15. GRADIENTS; EXTREME VALUES; DIFFERENTIALS

10. The most important measure of central tendency, and one of the basic building blocks of all statistical analysis, is the arithmetic _____. It is simply the sum of all the set of values divided by the number of values involved. As a measure of central tendency, it is affected by extreme scores, and it assumes a ratio scale of measurement.
    a. Mean1
    b. 15 theorem
    c. Undefined
    d. Undefined

11. An _____ is an indication of the value of an unknown quantity based on observed data. More formally, an _____ is the particular value of an estimator that is obtained from a particular sample of data and used to indicate the value of a parameter.
    a. ACTRAN
    b. Estimate1
    c. Undefined
    d. Undefined

12. By _____ we mean collecting observations made upon our environment -- observations, which are the results of measurements using clocks, balances, measuring rods, counting operations, or other objectively defined measuring instruments or procedures. _____ may mean simply counting the number of times a particular property occurs.
    a. Data1
    b. 15 theorem
    c. Undefined
    d. Undefined

13. The method of _____ is a criterion for fitting a specified model to observed data.
    a. 15 theorem
    b. Least Squares1
    c. Undefined
    d. Undefined

14. A statistic calculated by multiplying the data values together and taking the N-th root of the result., the _____ is often used as a measure of central tendency for skewed distributions.
    a. Geometric mean1
    b. 15 theorem
    c. Undefined
    d. Undefined

15. _____ is the result of assigning numbers to objects to abstractly represent the objects or characteristics of the objects.
    a. 15 theorem
    b. Measurement1
    c. Undefined
    d. Undefined

16. In a distribution of data or in an interval of data, the _____ is the greatest value.
    a. ACTRAN
    b. Upper limit1
    c. Undefined
    d. Undefined

17. A measure of variability, the _____ is the distance from the lowest to the highest score.
    a. 15 theorem
    b. Range1
    c. Undefined
    d. Undefined

Chapter 16. DOUBLE AND TRIPLE INTEGRALS

1. The most important measure of central tendency, and one of the basic building blocks of all statistical analysis, is the arithmetic _____. It is simply the sum of all the set of values divided by the number of values involved. As a measure of central tendency, it is affected by extreme scores, and it assumes a ratio scale of measurement.
   - a. Mean1
   - b. 15 theorem
   - c. Undefined
   - d. Undefined

2. There are properties of objects that do assume one and only value, and we refer to these characteristics as constants. _____, then, are the invariables that differentiate one class of objects from another.
   - a. 15 theorem
   - b. Constants1
   - c. Undefined
   - d. Undefined

3. Another word for independent variables in the analysis of variance is _____.
   - a. Factors1
   - b. 15 theorem
   - c. Undefined
   - d. Undefined

4. The Greek letter _____ indicates summation.
   - a. 15 theorem
   - b. Sigma1
   - c. Undefined
   - d. Undefined

5. A number that does not change in value in a given situation is a _____.
   - a. Constant1
   - b. 15 theorem
   - c. Undefined
   - d. Undefined

6. In a large distribution of data it is often easier to understand the data if it is grouped into intervals where each _____ can contain more than one data value. Distributions are often reduced to 10 to 20 intervals.
   - a. ACTRAN
   - b. Interval1
   - c. Undefined
   - d. Undefined

7. An _____ is an indication of the value of an unknown quantity based on observed data. More formally, an _____ is the particular value of an estimator that is obtained from a particular sample of data and used to indicate the value of a parameter.
   - a. ACTRAN
   - b. Estimate1
   - c. Undefined
   - d. Undefined

8. _____ is implied when data values are distributed in the same way above and below the middle of the sample.
   - a. Symmetry1
   - b. 15 theorem
   - c. Undefined
   - d. Undefined

9. _____ are characteristics or properties of an object that can take on one or more different values.
   - a. Variables1
   - b. 15 theorem
   - c. Undefined
   - d. Undefined

10. The _____ is often confused with the median. The Median is a statistic for the distribution whereas the _____ provides a statistic for an interval; it is the center of the interval; the arithmetic average of the upper and lower limits.

Chapter 16. DOUBLE AND TRIPLE INTEGRALS

    a. 15 theorem   b. Midpoint1
    c. Undefined   d. Undefined

11. A _____ provides a quantitative description of the likely occurrence of a particular event. _____ is conventionally expressed on a scale from 0 to 1; a rare event has a _____ close to 0, a very common event has a _____ close to 1. _____ is calculated as the ratio of the number of favorable events to the total number of possible events.
    a. 15 theorem   b. Probability1
    c. Undefined   d. Undefined

12. In statistics an arrangement of values of a variable showing their observed or theoretical frequency of occurrence is called a _____.
    a. 15 theorem   b. Distribution1
    c. Undefined   d. Undefined

13. _____, the height of the curve for a given value of X; closely related to the probability of an observation in an interval around X.
    a. Density1   b. 15 theorem
    c. Undefined   d. Undefined

14. _____ refer to any data source, whether individuals, physical or biological things, geographic locations, time periods, or events; that is, anything upon which observations can be made.
    a. Objects1   b. ACTRAN
    c. Undefined   d. Undefined

15. _____ is used synonymously for variable.
    a. 15 theorem   b. Factor1
    c. Undefined   d. Undefined

16. A measure of variability, the _____ is the distance from the lowest to the highest score.
    a. 15 theorem   b. Range1
    c. Undefined   d. Undefined

17. The very fact that we are measuring objects with respect to some characteristic implies that the objects differ in that characteristic; or stated in another way, that the characteristic can take on a number of different values. These properties or characteristics of an object that can assume two or more different values are referred to as a _____.
    a. 15 theorem   b. Variable1
    c. Undefined   d. Undefined

18. The _____ is another name for the horizontal axis of a graph or plot.
    a. Abscissa1   b. ACTRAN
    c. Undefined   d. Undefined

19. The _____ is the vertical axis of a graph.

Chapter 16. DOUBLE AND TRIPLE INTEGRALS

   a. Ordinate1   b. ACTRAN
   c. Undefined   d. Undefined

20. A _____ involves the addition, subtraction, multiplication, or division of one variable by another variable or by a constant.
   a. 15 theorem   b. Linear transformation1
   c. Undefined   d. Undefined

21. The goal of most inferential statistical analyses is to be able to generalize or apply the findings to the entire population and not just to the sample. The concept of _____ requires that the researcher determine some level of probability that the findings were due to chance or that they actually describe the population. The value of the probability that the findings were due to chance is usually reported when the findings of an analysis is reported.
   a. Generalization1   b. 15 theorem
   c. Undefined   d. Undefined

22. By _____ we mean an average calculated by taking into account not only the frequencies of the values of a variable but also some other factor such as their variance. The _____ of observed data is the result of dividing the sum of the products of each observed value, the number of times it occurs, and this other factor by the total number of observations
   a. Weighted average1   b. 15 theorem
   c. Undefined   d. Undefined

Chapter 17. LINE INTEGRALS AND SURFACE INTEGRALS

1. _____, the height of the curve for a given value of X; closely related to the probability of an observation in an interval around X.
   a. Density1
   b. 15 theorem
   c. Undefined
   d. Undefined

2. A number that does not change in value in a given situation is a _____.
   a. Constant1
   b. 15 theorem
   c. Undefined
   d. Undefined

3. A _____ is a value used to represent a certain population characteristic. Because of the impracticality of measuring an entire population to determine this value, parameters are usually estimated.
   a. 15 theorem
   b. Parameter1
   c. Undefined
   d. Undefined

4. In a large distribution of data it is often easier to understand the data if it is grouped into intervals where each _____ can contain more than one data value. Distributions are often reduced to 10 to 20 intervals.
   a. ACTRAN
   b. Interval1
   c. Undefined
   d. Undefined

5. An _____ is an indication of the value of an unknown quantity based on observed data. More formally, an _____ is the particular value of an estimator that is obtained from a particular sample of data and used to indicate the value of a parameter.
   a. Estimate1
   b. ACTRAN
   c. Undefined
   d. Undefined

6. _____ is used synonymously for variable.
   a. 15 theorem
   b. Factor1
   c. Undefined
   d. Undefined

7. The very fact that we are measuring objects with respect to some characteristic implies that the objects differ in that characteristic; or stated in another way, that the characteristic can take on a number of different values. These properties or characteristics of an object that can assume two or more different values are referred to as a _____.
   a. Variable1
   b. 15 theorem
   c. Undefined
   d. Undefined

8. The same statistical principles apply to the evaluation of observed _____ between sets of data. The field of statistics provides the necessary techniques for making statements of our certainty that there are real as opposed to chance differences.
   a. Differences1
   b. 15 theorem
   c. Undefined
   d. Undefined

9. The probability of correctly rejecting a false Ho is referred to as _____.
   a. 15 theorem
   b. Power1
   c. Undefined
   d. Undefined

10. _____ is implied when data values are distributed in the same way above and below the middle of the sample.

Chapter 17. LINE INTEGRALS AND SURFACE INTEGRALS

a. Symmetry1
b. 15 theorem
c. Undefined
d. Undefined

11. A special case of the dichtomous variable is the _____ which is created by converting a level of a qualitative variable into a binary variable.
    a. Dummy variable1
    b. 15 theorem
    c. Undefined
    d. Undefined

12. _____ are characteristics or properties of an object that can take on one or more different values.
    a. 15 theorem
    b. Variables1
    c. Undefined
    d. Undefined

13. A measure of variability, the _____ is the distance from the lowest to the highest score.
    a. Range1
    b. 15 theorem
    c. Undefined
    d. Undefined

14. An _____ is any process or study, which results in the collection of data, the outcome of which is unknown. In statistics, the term is usually restricted to situations in which the researcher has control over some of the conditions under which the _____ takes place.
    a. ACTRAN
    b. Experiment1
    c. Undefined
    d. Undefined

15. In statistics an arrangement of values of a variable showing their observed or theoretical frequency of occurrence is called a _____.
    a. Distribution1
    b. 15 theorem
    c. Undefined
    d. Undefined

16. The most important measure of central tendency, and one of the basic building blocks of all statistical analysis, is the arithmetic _____. It is simply the sum of all the set of values divided by the number of values involved. As a measure of central tendency, it is affected by extreme scores, and it assumes a ratio scale of measurement.
    a. 15 theorem
    b. Mean1
    c. Undefined
    d. Undefined

17. By _____ we mean the cumulative frequency, counting in from the nearer end.
    a. Depth1
    b. 15 theorem
    c. Undefined
    d. Undefined

18. In a factorial design with two or more main effects or grouping effects, there is a possibility of a significant _____ effect, AB. With a significant _____ you have differences in estimates of the population variance in the various combinations, or cells, of one main effect paired with another. Interactions must be explained before main effects in a statistical analysis. The _____ is tested using an F test in an ANOVA that compares the MSab/Mserror.
    a. Interaction1
    b. ACTRAN
    c. Undefined
    d. Undefined

19. By _____ we mean an average calculated by taking into account not only the frequencies of the values of a variable but also some other factor such as their variance. The _____ of observed data is the result of dividing the sum of the products of each observed value, the number of times it occurs, and this other factor by the total number of observations

   a. Weighted average1   b. 15 theorem

   c. Undefined   d. Undefined

Chapter 18. ELEMENTARY DIFFERENTIAL EQUATIONS

1. A number that does not change in value in a given situation is a _____.
   a. 15 theorem
   b. Constant1
   c. Undefined
   d. Undefined

2. There are properties of objects that do assume one and only value, and we refer to these characteristics as constants. _____, then, are the invariables that differentiate one class of objects from another.
   a. Constants1
   b. 15 theorem
   c. Undefined
   d. Undefined

3. _____ are characteristics or properties of an object that can take on one or more different values.
   a. Variables1
   b. 15 theorem
   c. Undefined
   d. Undefined

4. In a large distribution of data it is often easier to understand the data if it is grouped into intervals where each _____ can contain more than one data value. Distributions are often reduced to 10 to 20 intervals.
   a. Interval1
   b. ACTRAN
   c. Undefined
   d. Undefined

5. The very fact that we are measuring objects with respect to some characteristic implies that the objects differ in that characteristic; or stated in another way, that the characteristic can take on a number of different values. These properties or characteristics of an object that can assume two or more different values are referred to as a _____.
   a. 15 theorem
   b. Variable1
   c. Undefined
   d. Undefined

6. An _____ is an indication of the value of an unknown quantity based on observed data. More formally, an _____ is the particular value of an estimator that is obtained from a particular sample of data and used to indicate the value of a parameter.
   a. Estimate1
   b. ACTRAN
   c. Undefined
   d. Undefined

7. The _____ refers to the amount of change in Y for a 1 unit change in X; or in-other-words, the rate of change in the predicted value as a function of a change in the predictor variable.
   a. Slope1
   b. 15 theorem
   c. Undefined
   d. Undefined

8. By _____ we mean an average calculated by taking into account not only the frequencies of the values of a variable but also some other factor such as their variance. The _____ of observed data is the result of dividing the sum of the products of each observed value, the number of times it occurs, and this other factor by the total number of observations
   a. 15 theorem
   b. Weighted average1
   c. Undefined
   d. Undefined

9. An _____ is any process or study, which results in the collection of data, the outcome of which is unknown. In statistics, the term is usually restricted to situations in which the researcher has control over some of the conditions under which the _____ takes place.
   a. Experiment1
   b. ACTRAN
   c. Undefined
   d. Undefined

Chapter 18. ELEMENTARY DIFFERENTIAL EQUATIONS

10. Another word for independent variables in the analysis of variance is _____.
    a. 15 theorem
    b. Factors1
    c. Undefined
    d. Undefined

11. _____ is used synonymously for variable.
    a. Factor1
    b. 15 theorem
    c. Undefined
    d. Undefined

12. The most important measure of central tendency, and one of the basic building blocks of all statistical analysis, is the arithmetic _____. It is simply the sum of all the set of values divided by the number of values involved. As a measure of central tendency, it is affected by extreme scores, and it assumes a ratio scale of measurement.
    a. Mean1
    b. 15 theorem
    c. Undefined
    d. Undefined

13. The defining characteristics of populations are called _____. Observations must be made on every single member of the population in question in order to precisely state the value of _____.
    a. 15 theorem
    b. Parameters1
    c. Undefined
    d. Undefined

14. The number of times a particular score or observation occurs is its _____.
    a. Frequency1
    b. 15 theorem
    c. Undefined
    d. Undefined

15. The outcome of a trial is called the _____.
    a. Event1
    b. ACTRAN
    c. Undefined
    d. Undefined

16. _____, the height of the curve for a given value of X; closely related to the probability of an observation in an interval around X.
    a. 15 theorem
    b. Density1
    c. Undefined
    d. Undefined

ANSWER KEY

Chapter 1

1. a	2. b	3. a	4. b	5. a	6. b	7. a	8. b	9. a	10. a
11. b	12. b	13. b	14. a	15. a	16. a	17. b	18. b	19. a	20. a
21. a	22. b	23. b	24. b	25. a	26. a	27. b	28. a	29. a	30. b
31. b	32. b	33. b	34. b	35. a	36. a	37. b	38. a	39. a	40. b
41. a	42. b	43. b	44. a	45. a	46. b	47. a	48. a	49. b	50. a
51. b	52. b	53. a	54. b	55. a	56. b	57. b	58. a	59. b	60. b
61. b	62. b	63. a	64. a	65. a	66. b	67. b	68. b	69. a	70. b
71. b	72. b	73. b	74. a	75. a	76. b	77. a	78. b	79. b	80. b
81. b	82. a	83. a	84. b	85. b	86. a	87. b	88. a	89. a	90. a
91. b	92. a	93. b	94. b	95. b	96. b	97. b	98. a	99. a	100. a
101. b	102. a	103. b	104. b	105. b	106. b	107. b	108. b	109. b	110. b
111. b	112. b	113. b	114. b	115. a	116. a	117. a	118. a	119. b	120. b
121. a	122. b	123. a	124. b	125. b	126. a	127. b	128. a	129. b	130. a
131. a	132. a	133. a	134. b	135. b	136. b	137. b	138. b	139. a	140. b
141. a	142. a	143. a	144. b	145. b	146. b	147. a	148. b	149. b	150. b
151. a	152. a	153. b	154. b	155. b	156. b	157. a	158. a	159. a	160. a
161. a	162. a	163. a	164. a	165. a	166. a	167. b	168. b	169. b	170. a
171. a	172. a	173. b	174. a	175. b	176. b	177. b	178. b	179. a	180. a
181. a	182. b	183. a	184. b	185. b	186. b	187. a	188. a	189. b	190. a
191. b	192. a	193. b	194. a	195. b	196. a	197. b	198. b	199. a	200. a
201. b	202. a	203. a	204. a	205. a	206. a				

Chapter 2

1. b	2. b	3. a	4. b	5. b	6. a	7. a	8. a	9. a	10. b
11. b	12. a	13. a	14. a	15. a	16. a	17. b	18. a	19. b	20. b
21. b	22. a	23. b	24. a	25. a	26. b	27. a	28. b	29. a	30. a
31. a	32. a	33. a	34. b	35. b	36. a	37. b	38. a	39. b	40. b
41. b	42. a	43. a	44. b	45. b	46. b	47. a	48. b	49. a	50. a
51. a	52. b	53. a	54. b	55. a	56. a	57. a	58. a	59. b	60. b
61. a	62. b	63. b	64. b	65. b	66. a	67. a	68. b	69. b	70. a
71. b	72. a	73. a	74. b	75. a	76. a	77. a	78. a	79. b	80. b
81. b	82. a	83. a	84. a	85. b	86. b	87. b	88. b	89. b	90. b
91. b	92. a	93. a	94. a	95. a	96. b	97. a	98. a		

Chapter 3

1. a	2. b	3. b	4. a	5. b	6. b	7. a	8. a	9. b	10. a
11. a	12. b	13. b	14. a	15. b	16. b	17. b	18. a	19. a	20. a
21. b	22. b	23. a	24. a	25. b	26. b	27. a	28. a	29. a	30. b
31. a	32. b	33. a	34. b	35. a	36. a	37. b	38. b	39. a	40. a
41. a	42. b	43. a	44. a	45. a	46. a	47. a	48. b	49. b	50. a
51. a	52. b	53. a	54. a	55. a	56. b	57. a	58. b	59. a	60. a
61. b	62. b	63. b	64. a	65. b	66. b	67. b	68. a	69. a	70. a
71. b	72. b	73. a	74. b	75. a	76. a	77. a	78. b	79. a	80. a
81. b	82. a	83. a	84. b	85. a	86. b	87. b	88. b	89. a	90. b
91. a	92. b	93. b	94. a	95. b	96. b	97. a	98. a	99. b	100. a
101. a	102. b	103. b	104. a	105. a	106. a	107. b	108. a	109. a	110. b
111. b	112. a	113. b	114. b	115. a	116. a	117. a	118. b	119. b	120. a
121. a	122. b	123. b	124. a	125. a	126. b	127. a	128. a	129. a	130. a
131. b	132. a	133. a	134. b	135. b	136. b	137. b	138. b	139. a	140. b
141. a	142. a	143. a	144. a	145. a	146. a	147. a	148. b	149. b	150. b
151. b	152. b	153. a	154. b	155. b	156. b	157. a	158. b	159. b	160. b
161. a	162. b	163. b	164. a	165. b	166. b	167. a	168. b	169. b	170. b
171. b	172. a	173. a	174. b	175. b	176. a	177. a	178. a	179. a	180. b
181. a	182. b	183. b	184. a	185. a	186. a	187. a	188. b	189. b	

Chapter 4

1. a	2. a	3. a	4. a	5. a	6. b	7. b	8. b	9. a	10. b
11. b	12. b	13. a	14. a	15. a	16. a	17. a	18. b	19. b	20. a
21. a	22. b	23. b	24. a	25. a	26. b	27. b	28. b	29. a	30. a
31. a	32. b	33. b	34. b	35. b	36. a	37. a	38. a	39. a	40. a
41. a	42. a	43. b	44. a	45. a	46. b	47. b	48. b	49. a	50. b
51. b	52. b	53. b	54. a	55. b	56. a	57. a	58. a	59. b	60. b
61. a	62. b	63. a	64. a	65. b	66. a	67. a	68. a	69. b	70. a
71. b	72. b	73. b	74. b	75. a	76. a	77. b	78. a	79. b	80. a
81. b	82. a	83. a	84. b	85. b	86. b	87. b	88. a	89. a	90. a
91. a	92. a	93. b	94. a	95. b	96. b	97. b	98. a	99. b	100. a
101. a	102. a	103. a	104. b	105. b	106. b	107. a	108. a	109. b	110. b
111. b	112. b	113. b	114. b	115. b	116. a	117. b	118. b	119. b	120. a
121. b	122. b	123. b	124. a	125. a	126. a	127. b	128. b	129. a	130. a
131. a	132. a	133. a	134. a	135. a	136. a	137. b	138. a	139. a	140. a
141. b	142. a	143. a	144. a	145. b	146. b	147. b	148. b	149. b	150. b
151. b	152. a	153. a	154. a	155. b	156. a	157. b	158. b	159. a	160. a
161. b	162. b	163. b	164. a	165. a	166. b	167. b	168. a	169. b	170. b
171. b	172. b	173. b	174. a	175. b	176. a	177. b	178. b	179. b	180. b

ANSWER KEY

Chapter 5

1. a	2. a	3. a	4. a	5. a	6. b	7. a	8. b	9. a	10. a
11. a	12. a	13. a	14. a	15. a	16. a	17. a	18. a	19. a	20. a
21. a	22. a	23. b	24. b	25. b	26. b	27. b	28. b	29. a	30. b
31. b	32. b	33. b	34. b	35. a	36. b	37. a	38. b	39. a	40. b
41. b	42. a	43. b	44. a	45. b	46. a	47. b	48. b	49. b	50. a
51. a	52. b	53. a	54. b	55. a	56. b	57. b	58. a	59. a	60. a
61. a	62. b	63. a	64. b	65. b	66. b	67. a	68. b	69. a	70. a
71. a	72. a	73. a	74. a	75. b	76. b	77. a	78. a	79. b	80. b
81. a	82. b	83. b	84. a	85. b	86. b	87. a	88. b	89. a	90. b
91. b	92. b	93. b	94. b	95. a	96. b	97. a	98. a	99. b	100. a
101. a	102. a	103. b	104. b	105. b	106. a	107. b	108. a	109. a	110. b
111. b	112. b	113. b	114. a	115. b					

Chapter 6

1. b	2. b	3. a	4. a	5. b	6. b	7. b	8. b	9. b	10. b
11. b	12. a	13. a	14. a	15. b	16. a	17. b	18. b	19. a	20. a
21. a	22. b	23. b	24. b	25. a	26. a	27. b	28. b	29. b	30. b
31. a	32. b	33. b	34. a	35. b	36. a	37. a	38. b	39. b	40. b
41. a	42. b	43. a	44. a	45. b	46. b	47. b	48. b	49. b	50. b
51. b	52. b	53. a	54. a	55. a	56. a	57. a	58. b	59. b	60. b
61. a	62. a	63. a	64. a	65. a	66. b	67. a	68. a	69. a	70. a
71. a	72. a	73. b	74. b	75. b	76. a	77. a	78. b	79. a	80. b
81. b	82. a	83. b	84. b	85. b	86. b	87. b	88. b	89. b	90. a
91. a	92. a	93. b	94. a	95. b	96. b	97. b	98. a	99. a	100. b
101. a	102. a	103. b	104. a	105. a	106. a	107. b	108. b	109. b	110. b
111. a	112. b	113. b	114. a	115. b	116. a	117. a	118. a	119. b	120. a
121. a	122. a	123. a	124. a	125. b	126. a	127. b	128. b	129. b	130. b
131. a									

Chapter 7

1. a	2. a	3. b	4. b	5. a	6. b	7. a	8. b	9. a	10. b
11. b	12. a	13. b	14. a	15. b	16. a	17. b	18. a	19. a	20. a
21. b	22. a	23. a	24. a	25. b	26. a	27. a	28. a	29. b	30. b
31. b	32. a	33. a	34. a	35. b	36. a	37. a	38. b	39. b	40. a
41. b	42. b	43. a	44. b	45. a	46. a	47. b	48. b	49. a	50. a
51. a	52. b	53. b	54. b	55. a	56. a	57. b	58. b	59. b	60. b
61. a	62. b	63. a	64. b	65. a	66. a	67. b	68. a	69. b	70. a
71. a	72. a	73. b	74. b	75. b	76. b	77. b	78. b	79. b	80. a
81. a	82. a	83. b	84. a	85. b	86. b	87. a	88. a	89. b	90. a
91. a	92. a	93. a	94. b	95. a	96. a	97. b	98. a	99. b	100. a
101. a	102. b	103. a	104. a	105. a	106. a	107. b	108. a	109. b	110. a
111. b	112. b	113. b	114. a	115. b	116. b	117. a	118. b	119. b	120. b
121. b	122. a	123. a	124. b	125. b	126. a	127. b	128. b	129. b	130. a
131. a	132. b	133. a	134. b	135. a	136. a	137. b	138. a	139. b	140. b
141. a	142. b	143. b	144. b	145. b	146. a	147. b	148. a	149. b	150. a
151. b	152. a	153. b	154. a	155. b	156. b	157. b	158. a	159. b	160. b
161. a	162. a	163. a	164. a	165. a	166. a	167. b	168. a	169. a	170. b
171. b	172. b	173. a	174. b	175. a	176. b	177. b	178. b	179. a	180. a
181. a	182. b	183. a	184. b	185. a	186. b	187. a	188. b	189. a	190. a
191. b	192. a	193. a	194. a	195. a					

Chapter 8

1. a	2. a	3. a	4. b	5. b	6. a	7. b	8. b	9. a	10. a
11. b	12. b	13. b	14. a	15. a	16. a	17. b	18. a	19. b	20. a
21. a	22. a	23. a	24. b	25. a	26. a	27. a	28. a	29. b	30. b
31. b	32. a	33. a	34. a	35. b	36. b	37. b	38. a	39. b	40. a
41. b	42. b	43. a	44. b	45. a	46. a	47. b	48. a	49. a	50. a
51. a	52. a	53. a	54. a	55. a	56. a	57. a	58. a	59. b	60. a
61. b	62. a	63. a	64. a	65. b	66. b	67. a	68. b	69. a	70. b
71. b	72. a	73. a	74. b	75. a	76. b	77. a	78. b	79. b	80. a
81. b	82. b	83. a	84. a	85. a	86. b	87. b	88. b	89. a	90. b
91. b	92. b	93. b	94. a	95. b	96. a	97. a	98. a	99. b	100. a
101. b	102. b	103. a	104. a	105. a	106. a	107. b	108. b	109. a	110. a
111. b	112. b	113. a	114. a	115. b	116. b	117. b	118. b	119. a	120. a
121. b	122. b	123. a	124. b	125. a	126. b	127. a	128. a	129. a	130. a
131. b	132. b	133. b	134. b	135. b	136. a	137. b	138. a	139. b	140. b
141. b	142. b	143. b	144. a	145. a	146. a	147. b	148. a	149. b	150. b
151. b	152. b	153. b	154. b	155. a	156. b	157. b	158. b	159. a	160. b
161. a	162. b	163. b	164. b						

ANSWER KEY

Chapter 9

1. a	2. b	3. a	4. b	5. b	6. a	7. b	8. b	9. b	10. a
11. b	12. a	13. b	14. b	15. b	16. b	17. b	18. b	19. b	20. b
21. b	22. b	23. b	24. b	25. b	26. a	27. b	28. a	29. b	30. b
31. b	32. a	33. a	34. b	35. a	36. a	37. a	38. a	39. b	40. a
41. a	42. a	43. a	44. b	45. a	46. a	47. b	48. a	49. a	50. a
51. a	52. a	53. a	54. b	55. b	56. b	57. b	58. b	59. b	60. a
61. b	62. b	63. a	64. b	65. b	66. a	67. b	68. a	69. b	70. a
71. b	72. a	73. b	74. b	75. a	76. a	77. a	78. b	79. b	80. b
81. a	82. b	83. b	84. a	85. b	86. a	87. b	88. b	89. b	90. b
91. b	92. a	93. a	94. a	95. b	96. a	97. a	98. b	99. b	100. a
101. b	102. b	103. b	104. a	105. a	106. b	107. a	108. a	109. a	110. b
111. a	112. a	113. b	114. b	115. a	116. b	117. a	118. a	119. a	120. b
121. b	122. a	123. b	124. a	125. b	126. a	127. a	128. b	129. a	130. b
131. a	132. b	133. b	134. b	135. b	136. a	137. a	138. a	139. b	140. b
141. a	142. a	143. a	144. a	145. a	146. b	147. b	148. b	149. b	150. b
151. b	152. a	153. a	154. a	155. b	156. a	157. b	158. a	159. b	160. b
161. a	162. a	163. a	164. b	165. b	166. a	167. b	168. a	169. b	170. a
171. b	172. b	173. a	174. b	175. b	176. b	177. b	178. a	179. a	180. b
181. a	182. b								

Chapter 10

1. a	2. a	3. b	4. b	5. b	6. b	7. a	8. b	9. b	10. a
11. a	12. b	13. b	14. a	15. b	16. a	17. a	18. b		

Chapter 11

1. b	2. b	3. a	4. a	5. b	6. a	7. b	8. a	9. b	10. a
11. a	12. a	13. b	14. a	15. a					

Chapter 12

1. a	2. a	3. a	4. a	5. b	6. b	7. a	8. b	9. a	10. a
11. b									

Chapter 13

1. b	2. a	3. a	4. b	5. a	6. b	7. a	8. b	9. a	10. a
11. b	12. b								

Chapter 14

1. b	2. a	3. a	4. a	5. a	6. b	7. a	8. a	9. a	10. b
11. a	12. b								

Chapter 15

1. a	2. b	3. a	4. b	5. b	6. a	7. a	8. b	9. a	10. a
11. b	12. a	13. b	14. a	15. b	16. b	17. b			

Chapter 16

1. a	2. b	3. a	4. b	5. a	6. b	7. b	8. a	9. a	10. b
11. b	12. b	13. a	14. a	15. b	16. b	17. b	18. a	19. a	20. b
21. a	22. a								

Chapter 17

| 1. a | 2. a | 3. b | 4. b | 5. a | 6. b | 7. a | 8. a | 9. b | 10. a |
| 11. a | 12. b | 13. a | 14. b | 15. a | 16. b | 17. a | 18. a | 19. a | |

Chapter 18

| 1. b | 2. a | 3. a | 4. a | 5. b | 6. a | 7. a | 8. b | 9. a | 10. b |
| 11. a | 12. a | 13. b | 14. a | 15. a | 16. b | | | | |